The Infographic

History and Foundations of Information Science

Edited by Michael Buckland, Jonathan Furner, and Markus Krajewski

The Infographic

A History of Data Graphics in News and Communications

Murray Dick

The MIT Press
Cambridge, Massachusetts
London, England

This book was set in Stone Serif and Stone Sans by Westchester Publishing Services. Printed and bound in the United States of America.

Library of Congress Cataloging-in-Publication Data

Names: Dick, Murray, author.
Title: The infographic : a history of data graphics in news and communications / Murray Dick.
Description: Cambridge, Massachuetts : The MIT Press, 2020. |
    Series: History and foundations of information science |
    Includes bibliographical references and index.
Identifiers: LCCN 2019029382 | ISBN 9780262043823 (hardcover)
Subjects: LCSH: Journalism--Data processing. | Journalism--Technological
    innovations. | Information visualization. | Visual communication.
Classification: LCC PN4784.E5 D53 2020 | DDC 001.4/226--dc23
LC record available at https://lccn.loc.gov/2019029382

10 9 8 7 6 5 4 3 2 1

For Keir, Tam and Effie.

Contents

Acknowledgments

This book has been a long time in planning and preparation. Throughout this often solitary work, I have been supported and sustained by my wife Jess Cox, without whom this book couldn't have come to be. I owe a debt of gratitude to Brenda Cox, who proofread early versions of this book, and to three anonymous reviewers whose feedback was crucial in shaping (and improving) my thinking. I would also like to offer my thanks (and declare my indebtedness to) the following people and organizations:

- Ciaran Hughes
- John Grimwade
- Nigel Holmes
- Michael Robinson
- Fiona Robertson
- The Department of Typography at Reading University
- The Institute of Education (London)
- The National Archive (London)
- The British Library (Boston Spa)
- Newcastle University (which funded the archive research, the interviews, the color printing, and the permissions in this project).

1   Introduction

This book is a cultural history of the news infographic. It is concerned, like other histories of data visualization before it, with innovation and with pioneers. But it is also concerned with the public, and with the creation and maintenance of shared (and shifting) symbolic, and cultural meanings. It is a history of how the idea of data visualization emerged from fields of knowledge in the late eighteenth-century; through modes of (and shifting attitudes to) formal education, and politics. It is concerned with sites of production, sites of consumption, and sites of resistance; as well as with political, aesthetic, and various other considerations. It is a history of modern, printed, and celluloid popular media, of; pamphlets, reference works, magazines, newspapers, and cinema, up to the interactive, and immersive online media of today. It is a history of how the public came to experience and understand the infographic; but it is also a history of what data visualization can tell us about the past. It is a synthetic history that draws upon histories of ideas (Turner, 2014), including statistical thinking (Porter, 1986; Desrosières, 2002), histories of journalism (Carey, 1974, 2007, 2008; Conboy, 2002, 2004) and histories of communications (Innis, 2007 [1950]; Simonson et al., 2013).

   This book is intended primarily for practitioners, scholars, and critics in communications, digital humanities, information design, and graphic arts. I will offer an interdisciplinary cultural theory of "infographics" (or "data visualization"—I will use these terms interchangeably in this book, though I acknowledge that they represent binary forms among some practitioners). In so doing, I will conceive of infographics as texts; and I will demonstrate that data visualization has as much to tell us about history, as history has to tell us about data visualization. I will argue that to appreciate the role of infographics in today's world, it is necessary to acknowledge that they embrace both explanatory and interpretive approaches to the communication and exchange of knowledge and understanding about the social world. First, though, I will set out the contexts of the object of this study.

The Rise of the Data Visualization Society

Infographics are a constant presence in our modern, mediatized lives, especially in news. They adorn the pages of national and regional newspapers (and websites) around the world; they are popular across quality, mid-market, and tabloid formats and they are routinely found in television news. They are particularly popular online, where freely available software makes it possible for anyone to create slick-looking charts. In interactive form, they involve various specialties, reflected in the wide array of job titles that now exist in the newsroom, such as: interactive news developer, programmer/ data specialist, software developer, data scientist, multimedia producer, and interactive producer. The emergence of these new roles coincides with a working culture at leading media companies that actively authorizes interactive (and hence visual data) journalism. In 2014, *The Guardian* merged its visual journalism, data journalism, and audience development teams, inspired by examples from native digital start-ups, in order to enhance its digital output (Reid, 2014). In the same year, the BBC established its Visual Journalism Unit, a working structure that integrates designers and journalists across broadcast and online mediums.

The increasing visibility of infographics is in turn a manifestation of the increasing presence (and influence) of online audience metrics in newsrooms. It has been suggested that news stories with infographics can generate up to 30 times more page views than stories without (So, 2012)—a fact backed up anecdotally by journalists (based on internal research) (Dick, 2014; Gatto, 2015). But journalists don't just make, repurpose, and critique infographics in the news; they use them routinely to track their online audience. *The Guardian*'s in-house analytics platform, Ophan, allows all of its journalists to quickly see how their stories are performing.

Infographics are today ubiquitous across our modern, networked knowledge economy. In business they are used to convey profit and loss in the narrative sections of corporate annual reports and accounts—sometimes, it has been found, in highly misleading ways (Penrose, 2008). Similarly misleading forms have been identified in political campaigning (Short, 2014). Infographics are a visual rhetoric used to express the key political messages of the day. In classrooms and lecture theatres, from academic critique to sporting analysis, online and offline, infographics are used to communicate statistical truths (and sometimes lies).

The interpretation and analysis of infographics and data visualizations are actively (albeit often invisibly) shaping our lives too. Traders in our financial districts carefully scrutinize the fluctuations in transnational flows of money, in real time. These constantly updated line graphs embody what François Hartog (2015 [2003]) calls the "omnipresent present," or "presentism" that seems to define modern life. In government, our policymakers are increasingly informed by the availability (and visual representation) of Big Data by social scientists and analysts (Gatto, 2015), a situation that is predicted to increase in the future (Mayer-Schönberger & Cukier, 2013). The act of making data visible, "envisioning," presents policymakers with various advantages in the interpretation of complex social structures, toward prediction, and the shaping and reshaping of policy for improving society (Dorling, 2012). They represent a standardized method of communicating information efficiently at a (near-) global level, seemingly unencumbered by the ambiguity of written language. So pervasive are these forms, that, in association with the rise in visual media more generally, they are, it is argued, changing what it means to be literate in the twenty-first century (ACRL, 2011).

Infographic design, it is argued, accommodates both high-level and low-level cognitive processing, making infographics ideally suited to exploiting the particular neurological-visual capability we have evolved with (Spence, 2006). The emergence of infographics, it has been further argued, maps to a collective intuition; or even to universal truths about human cognitive processes (Wainer & Velleman, 2001, 316).

But infographics are not merely representations of data; they coexist with and both influence and are influenced by other visual forms in our modern visual culture. The mediation of contemporary life through television; the ubiquity of video surveillance; and the increasing importance of visual media in modern work and leisure have (among other things) prompted the observation that "modern life takes place on screen" (Mirzoeff, 1999, 1). Our fractured, postmodern lives, it is argued, are best understood through visual media, just as the nineteenth century is best understood through its newspapers and novels (Dikovitskaya, 2012, 78). The rise of the image as commodity and of the intermediation of contemporary life through heavily aestheticized marketing shapes our lived experience, and this in turn requires an alternative to traditional methods of interpreting and analyzing the visual. It is in this context too, I will argue, after the so-called visual turn, that our understanding of the significance of infographics in modern society must be understood.

The Beginnings of This Book

The idea for this book arose after two separate inquiries into UK news infographics (Dick 2014, 2015a), toward the completion of my PhD.

In the first of these, a short-term ethnographic study of interactive graphics and graphic designers working in networked UK newsrooms (the BBC, *The Guardian*, Channel 4 News, and the *Financial Times*), I found a highly professional, albeit professionally mixed, collection of individuals, highly engaged with (and responsive to) their audiences, and dedicated to best practice and excellence in their work. This reality is reflected in the increasing visibility of visual and interactive journalism (such as new awards, and new award categories in existing awards), as well as in growing professional (Cairo, 2012; Wong, 2010) literatures and experimental (McCandless, 2012; 2014) literatures.

My second study concerned the *Daily Express*'s branded *Expressographs*, published during the mid- to late 1950s. Here I found a range of misleading techniques both too frequently and too consistently applied to be accounted for as mistakes, across a span of three years—and upward of 200 infographics.

The infographic in figure 1.1 appeared on page 8, in the June 4, 1959 edition of the *Daily Express*. Compositionally, the *Daily Express* of this era bears the imprimatur of typographic and make-up visionary Arthur Christiansen; and the tabloid style of this graph is clearly informed by the contemporary world of advertising, typified by a variety of bold illustration (Hutt, 1973, 120). A slick, hand-drawn line graph, it shows the rate of infant mortality per 1,000 live births in the UK between 1911 and 1950 for five professional or socio-economic classes: unskilled, semi-skilled, skilled, managerial, and professional. Its labels and legend appear to be Letraset dry transfer letters and numbers (first marketed two years earlier, in 1957). It appears in the

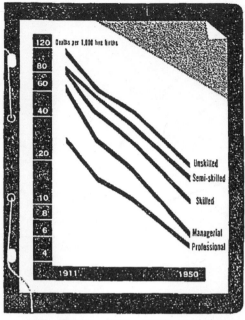

Figure 1.1
Daily Express, June 4, 1959, 8. Reproduced by permission of Reach plc.

middle of the newspaper page; it is approximately 8 cm by 12 cm, and is presented flush left of its accompanying headline: Britain's Babies. It is a visual cliché, of the fever chart, an item commonly found at the foot of hospital beds, but there is uncertainty about its provenance; the caption attributes it to in-house designer Michael Rand, while the accompanying article states that it was "issued by the General Register Office." The focal point of the graph is unmistakably toward the right-hand edge; the eye is drawn down a series of (seemingly) relatively uniform variables. The concluding paragraph of this opinion piece, by celebrated correspondent Chapman Pincher, is a quotation drawn from the report that is used to support the editorial line that, despite the expense, the NHS (National Health Service) has done little to combat the relative differences in mortality between the classes.

This is, of course, factually correct. However it does not allow the viewer to compare the trend in number of deaths by social class. The seemingly random

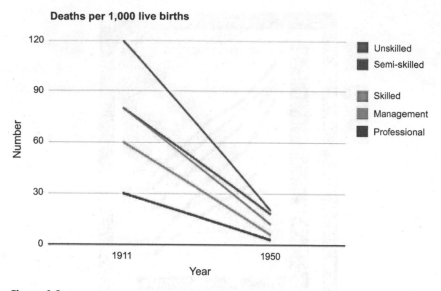

Figure 1.2
When plotted here with even scaling on the vertical axis, the data used in figure 1.1 tell a very different story.

intervals chosen to mark out the vertical axis selectively de-emphasize the rate of decline in mortalities for one group in particular, the nonskilled (down from 120 deaths per thousand in 1911, to 20 in 1950). Using regular intervals on the vertical axis instead, a very different visual narrative emerges.

This visualization expresses with a clarity hard to match in any linguistic turn of phrase, a very different story from the piece that accompanied the original chart. It accurately reflects the scale of improvement in the health of society's poorest and most vulnerable, in the contexts of the discovery of penicillin in 1928 and the establishment of the NHS in 1948.

Both this infographic, and my broader findings in that study, align with a literature on news infographics that stretches back through the twentieth century, which are selective rather than exhaustive, but are scathing in their criticisms of news infographics (Brinton, 1915, 1939; Huff, 1954; Tufte, 1983, 1997; Wainer, 1984; Paulos, 1996). The late 1950s Expresso-graphs seem to bear these criticisms out—they represent a corruption of rudimentary standards in pursuit of raw ideology (in this case, Lord Beaverbrook's idiosyncratic political interests). This in turn begs the question: what does this infographic (in the most popular newspaper of its era) tell us about how the wider public were exposed to and came to understand infographics? A reconsideration of the Expressograph requires us to revisit the legacy of one of its chief authors, Michael Rand, still very much considered a pioneering figure in newspaper design, based on his (later) work as the art director at the *Sunday Times*. More broadly though, it raises a series of further questions that get to the heart of this contemporary, ubiquitous visual phenomenon, namely:

- How (and why) did the infographic emerge in news culture?
- Who were the key influences behind it, and what were the key ideas that informed it?
- Who benefited (who was it aimed at)?
- What were the wider political, economic, social, and technological themes that helped shape it?
- What does it tell us about journalism, society, and the public sphere?
- Was there any resistance to it?

Defining Infographics

Before setting out the theoretical, analytical, and methodological rationale for this book, I will first explore the bounds of what is commonly meant by an infographic. Most rudimentary definitions of the word "infographic" take a formalistic approach, predicated on the compounding of "information" and "graphic." They are: "visual representations of data, information, or concepts" (Chandler & Munday, 2011, 208) or, another example, "a visual representation of information or data, e.g. as a chart or diagram: a good infographic is worth a thousand words" (Lexico, 2019a). Some definitions include an additional purposive dimension; infographics may be "used to represent information or data in an easily understandable form" (Ibid.), or their "primary function is to consolidate and display information graphically in an organized way so a viewer can readily retrieve the information and make specific and/or overall observations from it" (Harris, 1999, 198). It may be said that both in the creation of infographics and in journalism, the process of making information understandable to a mass audience is key to form and function.

In the practitioner literature, which dominates discourses on the origins, application, and practice of infographic production in UK news, definitions have emerged that separate infographics into those serving decorative purposes and those serving informational ones; hence "flavor" or "fact or information," with the use of informational or sign systems seen to be the key distinction between "illustrations" and "graphics" (Evans & Taylor, 1997 [1978], 289). Rather than opt for a label of exclusivity, an early UK pioneer of the form, Peter Sullivan, argued that "anything in a newspaper which is not typographic is in some way an information graphic" (Sullivan, 1987, 39). Others use similar definitions to substantiate different expressions. Graphic artist Nigel Holmes, for example, prefers the term "explanation graphics" (Holmes, 1984). Some infographics are non-statistical; many of Peter Sullivan's infographics for the *Sunday Times* were reconstructions, or process diagrams. The object of study in this inquiry may be defined, in the preceding terms, as primarily concerning "fact or information" infographics, with a clear focus on the communication of data.

Moving away from practitioner-driven definitions from within the news industry, other attempts to define infographics more broadly are manifest in typological and user-defined approaches to the medium. For example, a normative list of graphical forms is presented in *British Standard 7581* (BSI, 1992), comprising:

- Table
- Bar graph
- Line graph
- Area graph
- Pie graph
- Isotope graph
- Scatter graph
- Histogram
- Three-dimensional graph
- Superimposed graph
- Thematic map
- Illustrated graph
- Pictorial graph

This typology is a helpful tool for systematic analysis of the form in so far as British Standards govern data visualization for a mass (nonspecialist) audience, much as newspapers do. It represents a useful way of facilitating analysis and large-scale comparison, albeit at the expense of nonstatistical infographics. Alternatively, Bogost et al. offer a user-centric approach to classifying and theorizing infographics, viewing them as either explanatory, exploratory, or directed (Bogost, Ferrari, & Schweizer, 2010: 42–43), thus shifting the emphasis from production (or creation) to use (or consumption). While this is a useful approach, it does not shed light on the topicality or the veracity of infographics, and how they are presented.

Writing from a mathematical/statistical perspective, Fienberg (1979) builds upon reasoning developed across a series of popular statistical textbooks (Schmid, 1954; Tukey, 1972) to offer a hybrid classification scheme for "graphical methods" by purpose, namely:

1. For illustration (or propaganda—after Tukey, 1972)

2. For analysis

3. For computation

4. For decoration (or aesthetic effect) (Fienberg, 1979, 167)

This approach raises further questions, not least in relation to the common-sense use of the term "propaganda" (Jowett & O'Donnell, 2014 [1986]) here, but it may also be noted that none of these categories speaks to culture or mass consumption; to the emotions, feelings, and ethos of infographics. For example, visual journalists are careful in their use of color, aware of the association of tribal and/or political symbolisms, and they create infographics in the knowledge that some infographic forms seem to be less appealing to their audiences than others (Dick, 2014).

In this book I use the terms "infographic" and "data visualization" interchangeably; and treat them as synonyms or as near-synonyms. The two concepts are clearly related; Alberto Cairo (2012) suggests that they exist on a spectrum, from (respectively) description to explanation; albeit there is some disagreement about the nature of this relationship. Issues of purpose, of methodology, of data volume, and of aesthetics are often cited as essential to understanding these differences. In this work I propose that the epistemic nature of the news infographic/data visualization may be understood by bringing together Cairo's spectrum, and Robert Park's (1940) typology of the knowledge that journalism provides about the social world, distinguishing between "acquaintance with" (infographics that are concerned with news events) and "knowledge about" (data visualizations that are concerned with processes, explanation, and exploration[1]).

Histories of the Infographic

Histories of infographics are broadly aligned on who was responsible for line graphs, bar graphs, and circle (or pie) charts—William Playfair—but they do not all agree exactly how original these innovations were (Costigan-Eaves & Macdonald-Ross, 1990). The majority of the literature on the history of infographics is concerned primarily with pioneers like Playfair, with innovation, and with scientific progress. Across much of this literature, there is little room for the cultural aspects of these communicative phenomena: how they are understood, and what they tell us about the social and intellectual worlds from which they emerged. The current history of infographics can be understood within the following three schools of thought:

- The mathematical-statistical approach
- The neurological-psychological approach
- The cultural–arts historical approach

The Mathematical-Statistical School of Infographics History

Early histories of infographics are unified in so far as they are developmental in nature, and were written by statisticians. Mathematician Howard G. Funkhouser (1937) was responsible for the first major international work, albeit one that draws heavily upon Marey (1876) (which was concerned with the fields of experimental science and medicine). Funkhouser's history focuses upon specific contributions to "the graphical method" and the great figures who made these contributions through the ages, toward the development of a rapidly emerging visual "universal language" (Funkhouser, 1937, 270). Funkhouser identifies in his history different ages; 1860 to 1890 was a "golden age" of graphics, due in part to innovation, but also due to the emergence of a burgeoning bureaucracy that stimulated demand for the form (Ibid., 330).

He is not alone in taking this approach. More recently, psychologist Michael Friendly (2008a,b) is similarly concerned with "milestones" in data visualization. Friendly identifies innovations in data visualization as the basis of history, plotting key events cumulatively in a time series (2008a). Friendly subscribes to Funkhouser's theory of a "golden age" (see also Palsky, 1999), which is defined as "a local maximum in some distribution over history" (2008a, 504), an approach at odds with Thomas Kuhn's qualitative account of the history of scientific revolution (1956).

Both Funkhouser and Friendly are concerned first and foremost with innovation and by extension with the "genius" of the personalities responsible for these innovations, an approach that minimizes historical detail in favor of the dramatization of events (and the personalities involved). The student of history may recognize in this approach the imprimatur of "cyclical teleology," an approach long critiqued (rightly or wrongly—and admittedly, sometimes rather uncritically) (Butterfield, 1931).

Typical questions asked in Friendly's approach include:

• What motivated this development?
• What was the communicative goal?
• How does it relate to other developments—what were the precursors?
• How has this idea been used or reinvented today?

With respect to the fourth of these questions, it is worth revisiting Butterfield's critique of Whig historiography, defined more broadly than a mere bias, to incorporate the historian's pathetic fallacy, the abstraction of events from their contexts, and the construction of a narrative in primary reference to today (Butterfield, 1931, 30–31).

Because in these histories infographics are conceived of as innovations in the field of statistical method, there is no sustained exploration of the sociological or cultural impact of the form. And just as this approach succumbs to the dramatic fallacy of "golden" and "dark" ages, so too is it guilty of intellectual elitism. For just as there are heroes, so too there are villains, particularly those responsible for pictograms: "one of the few graphical innovations...perhaps best forgotten" (Friendly, 2008a, 530).

Friendly's hostility to pictograms represents a problem inherent to approaching infographics in terms primarily of innovation. Some innovations in data visualization, it seems, are worthier than others, but on whose terms? And what is lost should we forget (either through accident, or by design) forms no longer routinely used in the sciences? In failing to engage with the Vienna Method, in conflating cause and effect (clearly Neurath cannot be held to blame for the later misuse of pictograms in newspapers), and in over-exaggerating the nature of the problem (Friendly offers no relative sense of the "large supply" of "bad graphics" as published in the news, implying selectivity), this approach appears to succumb to several of the shortcomings attendant to Whiggish interpretations of history (Butterfield, 1931).

In mitigation of the "modern dark ages" of infographics, a designation covering the first half of the twentieth century, Friendly argues that this was "a time of necessary dormancy, application and popularization rather than one of innovation. In this period statistical graphics became mainstream" (Friendly, 2008b, 37). This process of popularization (and the definition of "mainstream") are rather narrowly defined as encompassing textbooks, curricula, governmental, commercial, and scientific publications (Friendly, 2008b, 37). No mention is made of newspapers, magazines, pamphlets, encyclopedias, television, cinema, or any of the myriad sources of ephemera most commonly associated with popular and mainstream mass media of the contemporary period. What constitutes the "mainstream" it seems, depends upon which tributary is your vantage point.

Fienberg's history (1979) is relatively selective, and is descriptive (rather than normative), comprising a limited series of key landmarks in the history of infographics. Feinberg also sets out a set of qualities and values concerning infographics above and beyond the communicative potential in text and tabular formats, taking after Calvin Schmid's *Handbook of Graphic Presentation* (1954):

1. In comparison with other types of presentation, well-designed charts are more effective in creating interest and appealing to the attention of the reader. (Publicity)

2. Visual relationships, as portrayed by charts and graphs, are more clearly grasped and more easily remembered. (Memorability/clarity)

3. The use of charts and graphs saves time, since the essential meaning of large masses of statistical data can be visualized at a glance. (Brevity)

4. Charts and graphs can provide a comprehensive picture of a problem that makes possible a more complete and better-balanced understanding than could be derived from tabular or textual forms of presentation. (Totality)

5. Charts and graphs can bring out hidden facts and relationships and can stimulate, as well as aid, analytical thinking and investigation. (Analysis/ serendipity) (Fienberg, 1979, 165)

This is a helpful means of understanding the competing forces that have shaped the formation of statistical infographics since their emergence. But as Fienberg's study is concerned with the use of statistical infographics in (professional) statistical journals only, it tells us little about the wider cultural impact of the form.

Building on the research of M. C. Shields (1937), whose expressed concern lay with "physical literature," Tilling's (1975) short history is also very precisely focused, concerning as it does the analytical use of graphical forms found in eighteenth-century scientific journals, textbooks, and treatises on the physical sciences (Tilling, 1975, 211). Though we know that articles on scientific issues were routinely published in nineteenth-century periodicals, magazines, and newspapers, alongside works of fiction, poetry, and literary criticism (Otis, 2002, xvii), as the present study will show, early infographics were (albeit fleetingly) also occasionally published in newspapers of the late eighteenth century and (very sporadically) throughout the nineteenth century. Shifting theoretical focus away from innovation, and toward the problems that infographic methods were designed to solve, Beniger and Robyn (1978) present a four-stage historical process, with each stage corresponding to a particular problem that the leading scientists of each scientific era were primarily concerned with solving. These problems are: data analysis, spatial organization; discrete quantitative comparison; and continuous distribution and multivariate distribution. The authors do not explain the theoretical nature of their methodology, but it is clear that this study is little concerned with the communicative potential in the form. This history argues: "At the turn of this century, statistical graphics had begun to diffuse—through textbooks, college courses, and the mass media—into the popular domain" (Ibid., 6). Yet no publications that may be identifiable as mass media in the conventional sense are mentioned in the appendix (Ibid., 10).

Generally speaking then, the following common factors tend to define the mathematical-statistical approach to the history of infographics:

- These are histories written with respect to infographics in the sciences, with occasional reference to the social sciences.
- They generally privilege the conception of infographics as scientific (or rather scientistic) methodologies; that is, as innovations rather than as communicative forms per se.
- Key figures in the emergence of the form are engaged with, primarily, in the context of scientific culture, while others (especially those whose

contribution to the form comes from outside the mathematical-statistical domain) are often not deemed worthy of detailed inquiry.

- This approach offers little space (but what little there is, is broadly selective and negative) concerning infographics as a popular cultural form; they tell us little about how these forms influence and are in turn influenced by society.

- This approach is bound up (albeit implicitly) with a "transmission" view of communication; these histories tell us little about how people may interpret these forms, and how the wider public's understanding of infographics has developed over time.

The Neurological-Psychological School of Infographic History

Howard Wainer (1990, 2006) a statistician working in the field of behavioral sciences, is responsible, jointly with Velleman (Wainer & Velleman, 2001), and with Spence (Wainer & Spence, 2005), for a series of historical accounts that engage with the psychological, social, and intellectual factors that inform how infographics may be used. This approach is bound up with what are seen as the neurological and psychological truths about human perception that infographic design has the potential to exploit. Where the mathematical-statistical approach tends to conceive of the mass communicative function of infographics as unfortunate but necessary (often corresponding to a "dark ages"), Wainer's approach differs. He acknowledges the value in using infographics as a means of publicizing science to the wider public, and indeed, he recognizes this as serving an essential purpose (2006, 6). Wainer's approach represents a composite history. On the one hand, he seeks to trace the paradigmatic shift (Kuhn, 1956) that led to the regular use of infographics in science, drawing upon the cultural and philosophical milieu of various periods; but on the other hand he paints an engaging, dramatic portrait of key figures, describing William Playfair as a "free-wheeling entrepreneur and confidence man" (Wainer, 2006, 25), a flawed genius and iconoclast. Focusing particularly on the work of Playfair, both Wainer and Spence (2005) and Spence (2006) accommodate the psychological capabilities of the audience in their inquiries into the late Enlightenment culture that informed Playfair's work. Infographics in this approach are discussed in the manner of a technology that may be used to exploit low-level and high-level processing in human perception and cognition.

Here the audience is present in the form of a mechanistic, undifferentiated mass model. Though evidently positivistic, this approach nevertheless engages in some of the (high) culture and ideas of the late eighteenth century. For example, in exploring those "common sense" philosophers of the Scottish Enlightenment, such as Dugald Stewart and Thomas Reid, Spence goes some way toward explaining the intellectual context in which Playfair developed his innovations (2006). This approach, nevertheless, is primarily bound up with elite discourses and histories of science and scientific discourse; there is no engagement with infographic forms in popular culture or popular media, and indeed the issue of audience affect is not covered.

Cultural Histories of Data Visualization

In recent times a range of cultural and arts histories concerning key figures, movements, and related phenomena in infographics have arisen, for example concerning the emergence of network visualizations (Lima, 2011), infographics (Rendgen et al., 2012), and timelines (Rosenberg & Grafton, 2010); including critiques of William Playfair (Dunyach, 2014; Berkowitz, 2018), and Charles Minard's methods (Rendgen, 2018); and concerning Marie and Otto Neurath, Red Vienna, and the origins and influences of Isotype (Burke, Kindel, & Walker, 2013). Chris Anderson's (2018) account of the rise of data journalism in the United States, though it deals with infographics only tangentially, contributes valuable insight into the phenomena, from an interdisciplinary perspective. Anderson considers American sociology and journalism at the turn of the twentieth century, and the subsequent setting out of epistemological boundaries within the former, toward an understanding of the social and historical contexts that made data journalism possible. He finds that, while a number of modern US sociologists, Robert Park chief among them, made use of infographic forms in the early days (in the process of seeking to reach out to the masses), by the 1930s, the discipline had turned away from visualization and toward statistical method and raw numbers. At more or less the same time, infographic forms, influenced by this wave of public sociology, were becoming routinized in some elite American news magazines. It is within this relatively recent body of scholarship (and particularly those works concerned with journalism and communications) that the present inquiry is intended to sit.

A Cultural-Historical Approach to Communications, Journalism, and Data Visualization

The late Enlightenment shift from history conceived of as a series of facts to history as a theory of progress, which led in turn to the rise of "objective," professionalized histories during the nineteenth century, has left us today with a pervasive, and seemingly intractable "knowledge problem," according to Richard Evans (1997). "Objectivity" as a benchmark of validity (or quality), and "progress" as a universal outcome, have both been found to be fundamentally wanting, in the new fragmented landscape. A cultural-historical approach to data visualization must account for this reality—this book therefore requires an ontology, an epistemology, and a methodology, and a clear justification for each.

James Carey was mindful of the overbearing disparity that exists in terms of how communication is (and has been) routinely conceptualized in the academy. He was a keen observer of the limitations of what he termed the "transmission view of communication" that he saw as unduly dominant. In this view, information is imparted, sent, or transmitted from one party to another. Etymologically rooted in the transportation of goods and people, as much as it is in the transfer of information, the transmission approach to communication speaks to the mercantile spirit and the frontier mentality (Carey, 2008, 12). It implies and privileges (even fetishizes) individual agency, at the expense of the wider social and communal connotations of communication. It privileges novelty and originality; again, it does so often at the expense of wider associations, such as sharing, participation, association, and fellowship.

Carey developed an alternative to this: his "ritual theory of communication" informed by a diverse range of past thinkers, from Max Weber to Clifford Geertz. This approach is predicated on the conception of communication as a symbolic process toward the production, maintenance, repair, and transformation of reality. In this view, infographics are a medium whose meaning is created between publisher and audience. This meaning is created anew every day, in a ritual mediated by norms (professional and cultural), that are in turn fostered through shared learning and the construction of wider knowledge throughout society. In this view infographics are much less about the expression of novelty or originality, but are rather about developing and maintaining a common order of things, contributing toward the habituated, lived, and experienced reality of a highly complex social process: modern life (Carey, 2008, 15). This is not to say that the ritual approach either denies or affirms the transmission theory, merely that it offers a different mode of context for the creation of knowledge and the bounds to what we can know about infographics. This book is, accordingly, concerned less with infographics as a scientific method, and more as they represent a means of communication. This is a history of popular info-graphic forms. The emphasis here is not exclusively upon novelty, excellence, and innovation. On the contrary, I seek to shed light on the often ignored reality of ideology in scientific studies, especially as it finds voice in the positivist tradition that informs much history in this field. Carey reminds us that ideology cannot simply be dismissed using "common sense" definitions, because the "political theory of scientists might be just one more ideology: distortion and fantasy in the service of self-interest, passion and prejudice" (Carey, 2008, 36). My intention is to explore how infographics were conceived by those who used them, which audiences were sought out, what forms of resistance were mobilized, and various other contingencies, in the wider context of the formation of public spheres through time. My emphasis is as much on the invisible diffusion of ideas in society, as it is on the limitations about what can be known about a particular individual at a particular point in time.

This history attempts to embrace (rather than to force out) the tensions from which all historical truths emerge—between causation and chance, free will and determinism, the individual and society. My concern is with facts prised from history books and papers, from digitized and nondigitized newspaper archives, and also where elicited during interviews with those individuals involved in modern infographic production. The increasing availability of digitized archives (specifically archives of newspapers) increasingly informs the nature and process of historical inquiry (Bingham, 2010). And just as statistical charts have influenced historical inquiry since the early nineteenth century (Theibault, 2013), it now seems clear that a historical inquiry into the cultural impact of the form seems long overdue, today, in the age of their ubiquity.

The history of journalism and the history of communications are sometimes thought of as moving through a series of phases. In this book I consider the idea of historical phases as an organizing principle, or method—as a series of responses to social and cultural problems, rather than as being universally applicable, sequentially fixed, or even necessary (and certainly not in terms of being "good" or "bad"). The history I set out here is situated within phases identified in past scholarship in the fields of journalism studies and communications (Carey, 2007; Simonson et al., 2013). Within these, I set out six phases in the history of infographics in popular culture that seem to express the collective mood, in terms of approaches to and forms of news infographics, at various times in history. These are:

- the *proto-infographic*
- the *classical*
- the *improving*
- the *commercial*
- the *ideological*
- the *professional*

Defining the News Infographic

In this study I am concerned with the historical emergence of a particular type of infographic: the news infographic. These are infographics that draw upon various graphical traditions and precedents, and that are presented in a unified graphical style and found within mass media (albeit increasingly in other contexts, too). They embody what historian Martin Conboy calls the "attractiveness of orchestrated variety" (2002, 75) that is routinely found in modern news media. That is to say, news infographics are designed to appeal to particular niche audiences within a general mass news audience.

Analyzing News Infographics

In this project I will conceive of news infographics as visual texts. I use the term "text" in a metaphorical rather than a descriptive way, as a means of establishing methodological consistency. This is not the first attempt to theorize infographics from a semiotics perspective. However, unlike logical approaches in this tradition (Bertin, 1983 [1965]), I do not assume that codes necessarily organize signs. Where they carry sufficient information, and where the audience is sufficiently familiar with their forms and conventions, infographics may (clearly) be used to explain phenomena.

However, cultural meanings (both universal and local) that are inherent to infographic forms are also open to interpretation, from the selection of colors to multimodal contexts to the use of metaphor (whether overt or implied); and these factors in turn affect how audiences may understand information in data-visual forms. As signs operate on different levels, texts may therefore contain within them a multilevel discourse (Eco, 1976). The discursive model I offer here represents a four-part (or three-and-a-half-part) multilevel discourse concerning infographics and data visualization.

Throughout this book I use the term "discourse" in a particular sense. The best explanation of this sense I have found, in the context of the present study, is as follows:

> Every newspaper is a structure of meanings in linguistic and visual form. It is a discourse. All newspapers have distinctive rhetorics, ways of organizing the elements into a coherent whole, styles of presentation. These represent so many ways of reducing the formlessness of events to that socially-shaped, historically-contingent product we call "news"—for potentially, every event on any day in the whole world is "news." (Smith, Immirzi, & Blackwell, 1975, 18)

Smith and colleagues go on to suggest that it is only with the arrival of new categories in our media scape (newspaper columns, or sections, for example) that we begin to sense that something more than simple novelty is at play. These new forms imply a shift in appeal, a new audience, or a perceived change in audience attitudes, any or all of which might suggest a shift in "cultural assumptions" (Smith, Immirzi, & Blackwell, 1975, 19) and so a change in how shared cultural meanings and practices are formed in news.

I will now set out four (or three-and-a-half) discourses[2] that may be detected (to varying degrees) among the guides, textbooks and other publications that shape debate about what infographics are and what they should be, namely:

- The functionalist-idealist
- The pragmatist-realist
- The didactic-persuasive
- The expressionist-aesthete

I will outline how each approach conceives of the infographic (as a noun); and I will set out argumentation between these positions that in turn creates space for a deeper and more nuanced understanding of what infographics are. It is important to note that, as these are discursive approaches, they are expressed relativistically, and in particular contexts—they are not absolutely normative, but instead overlap by degrees.[3]

The Functionalist-Idealist Discourse: Infographics as Methodology

In the first of these discourses, the *functionalist-idealist*, the appeal of infographics is based on a conception of the form, first and foremost, as a scientific (or perhaps more accurately scientistic) methodology. This approach is usually articulated in the works of statisticians, mathematicians, and scientists, and in particular Edward Tufte (1983, 1997), though elements may also be found in the works of Willard Cope Brinton (1914, 1915, 1939), Darrell Huff (1954), Jacques Bertin (1983 [1965]), John Allen Paulos (1996), and others. The intellectual roots of this approach may be traced back to John Locke's empiricism, to David Hume's critique of the problem of induction (1878 [1738–1740]), and to the "common-sense" philosophers of the Scottish Enlightenment (such as Dugald Stewart and Thomas Reid), whose approach to empiricism may, in turn, be traced back to the Aristotelian tendency toward implicit and necessary trust in the senses.

For Bertin (1983 [1965]) infographics function according to monosemy, in contrast to figurative representations, that function according to polysemy. In this view, data visualization is a form of visual logic, and the rigorous application of a monosemic system that depends on a priori rules (present in standards, and in conventions, such as the use of grid lines, legends, labels, etc.). These provide a means by which signs may be used to connect propositions in a logical sequence, in order to "construct the rational moment" (Ibid., 3). However, in this approach there is no space for nonlogical elements in infographic design (symbolic, cultural, compositional, etc.). Neither is there scope for audience affect. And yet today's media organizations know—as their internal research shows them—that certain graphical forms generate negative responses among groups within their audience, whom media organizations are bound, and in some cases bound by legal charter, to serve (Dick, 2014).

This positivist-scientific approach to the infographic finds its clearest expression in Tufte's Principles of Graphical Excellence (Tufte, 1983, 51). For Tufte, graphics necessarily deal in complex, multivariate ideas and they must explain clearly and efficiently: "telling the truth about the data"

(Ibid.). The notion that designer and audience may not share a common and irreducible understanding of what "the truth" means is not countenanced. Tufte argues: "If the statistics are boring, then you've got the wrong numbers" (Ibid., 80). Yet some have long questioned the lack of evidence behind Tufte's claims and norms, and not least the suitability of his approach to infographics in news (Prabu, 1992).

Tufte expresses a low opinion of newspaper graphics, staking the (respectable) scientific claim to the form against what he sees as its misuse and abuse in popular mass media. Lies in newspaper graphics, he argues, are "systematic and quite predictable, nearly always exaggerating the rate of recent change" (Tufte, 1983, 76). This criticism dovetails with some political economy critiques of news values more generally, and what is perceived as an undue emphasis placed upon events and "news hooks" in news coverage (McChesney, 2000). In this reading the rise of the modern, popular (news) infographic represents not so much an appeal to universalism as it does a cynical commodification of information.

Tufte (1983, 57) presents a method of verifying the truth of infographics (an approach that some suspect may be tongue-in-cheek):

Lie factor = size of effect shown in graphic/size of effect in data.

However, the (admittedly limited) empirical evidence in the literature does not necessarily support this idea. On the contrary, recent studies indicate that audiences prefer (Inbar, Tractinsky, & Meyer, 2007), find more memorable (Li & Moacdieh, 2014), and are not necessarily hindered from interpreting (Blasio & Bisantz, 2002) data in "chart junk" forms. More broadly, Tufte's approach is not without dispute within the mathematical-statistical field. For example, it has been argued that Tukey's (1990) emphasis on the impact of graphical display poses a direct challenge to Tufte's tendency toward modernist (Bauhaus-inspired) minimalism (Wainer, 1990, 341). Nevertheless, Tufte's graphical fidelity/graphical impact dichotomy represents a useful point of departure to the second discourse, its practitioners and its advocates.

The Pragmatist-Realist Discourse: Infographics as Technology

The second discourse of infographics, the *pragmatist-realist*, finds voice, by degrees, in the work and thoughts of infographics practitioners working in (or informing work in) the mass media, including Peter Sullivan (1987),

Nigel Holmes (1984), Dona Wong (2010), and Alberto Cairo (2012). This approach involves conceiving of infographics as a form of visual journalism. Standards (and best practice) in this field are drawn both from traditional, liberal journalistic ethics and values, as well as from the positivist canon that informs the functionalist-idealist discourse. For Sullivan space is an invitation to experiment and move beyond statistical charts into the realms of imaginative visual form (Sullivan, 1987, 41). Sullivan writes with concern about the audience that is, not the audience that ought to be (practitioners, after all, have a material interest in ensuring the audience understands their work). His work at the *Sunday Times* speaks to the shortcomings he perceived in the UK education system, in terms of instilling graphical literacy in the wider population. This approach emerges out of the contested professional and organizational values found in the newsroom. It accommodates practical realities such as publication schedule, differentiated audience needs, and constraints on materials and resources, as constraints upon design. Best practice is constructed as part of an ongoing debate and not simply a process of empirically informed improvement. Some ways of separating out these two (in some senses overlapping) approaches are set out in table 1.1.

In the pragmatist-realist view the infographic is conceived of, first and foremost, as a communicative technology (Cairo, 2012). This approach finds its philosophical roots in the American Pragmatism movement, and in particular, in the later educational philosophy of John Dewey, which conceived of thought as an instrument of problem-solving, rather than as a

Table 1.1

A comparison of attributes common to the functionalist-idealist and the pragmatist-realist approaches to data design.

Functionalist-idealist	Pragmatist-realist
Rules (standards) are absolute	Some rules are absolute, some rules are open to interpretation subject to context, work flow, and audience
Multivariate	Variables informed by context and audience
Positivist	Pragmatist
Infographics should be self-explanatory	Audience understanding requires testing
Infographics shouldn't patronize	Infographics shouldn't confuse

function of representation. In Dewey's approach, education is conceived of as "a continuous process of growth" (1916, 22). In challenging "formal discipline" and the classical methods of learning by rote, Dewey argued for a more holistic, pragmatic form of education—one less tied to "verbal visual forms," encompassing a more holistic sense of observation.

In conceiving of infographics as a technology, it may also be said that the pragmatist-realist approach owes a philosophical debt to Marshall McLuhan. He argued that the favoring of the visual organization of knowledge in modern societies is a consequence of the increase of information (1964, 128). In McLuhan's approach new technologies are conceived of as an extension of the body; literacy is conceived of as a "visual technology" that equips us to undertake information-gathering, in a highly visual modern culture conceived of as a networked, globalized village. In these terms the infographic is both medium and message. McLuhan's philosophy is bound up with a shift in the "human sensorium" brought about by the rise of the printing press and of the "context of altering the relation of the spoken word to the visual image and the consequence of this shift for tradition, knowledge, culture, and social relations" (Carey, 1986, 35). The infographic in this reading represent a manifestation of what Carey called *visual practice*.[4]

The Didactic-Persuasive Discourse: Infographics as Ideology

The third discourse in infographics, which may be called the *didactic-persuasive* approach, is given clearest expression in the work of Otto and Marie Neurath and their various artistic collaborators during the first half of the twentieth-century. Their pioneering Isotype "picture language" embodies a key organizing design principle in pictograms; namely, that the repeated use of figure icons affords a means of achieving graphic fidelity better than re-sizing icons. Isotype was not conceived of as a universal language per se, but (alternately) as a "universal slang," a "universal jargon" (Burke, 2013b, 89), or a "language-like technique" (Ibid., 91) for expressing statistical truths.

This third discourse has long been criticized among statisticians as being unduly reductive, at the expense of full numerical accuracy (Burke2013c, 197), and while some manifestations of this discourse adhere to methodology, it is distinct from the other discourses in so far as it conceives of infographics as being, fundamentally, ideologically purposive. Born of the conviction that statistics should represent a tool in the proletarian struggle, Isotype was intended to inform a socialist conception of adult education toward realizing a fairer society (Hartmann, 2006, 279–280). The interactive use of Isotype, as found in exhibitions staged at the Gesellschafts- und Wirtschaftsmuseum in Wien (Museum for Social and Economic Affairs in Vienna), between the mid-1920s and mid-1930s, gives voice to the particular interpretation of empiricism and positivism that the logical positivist group, in which Neurath was an active participant, broadly adhered to. This approach valorizes the notion of public verification and confirmation as the basis of knowledge, rather than personal experience (as is found, for example, in the empiricism of Hume and others). But although Isotype's aesthetic may be said to reflect the time in which it was conceived, it would be a mistake to assume that the form is simply a composite of logical empiricism and modern art and design. After all, Neurath, as Burke reminds us, would likely have dismissed much with respect to "functional design" as fundamentally pseudo-intellectual (in Burke, 2013b, 78).

The Expressionist-Aesthete: Infographics as Aesthetic

A fourth discourse (albeit one barely formed, by comparison with the others), the *expressive-aesthetic*, is informed by postmodern thought and finds echoes in fin-de-siècle aesthetic sensibilities (Wilde, 1891). It may be detected in the graphical work (and thinking) of one of today's better-known data visualization artists—David McCandless. For McCandless, the potential in infographics is bound up in expressive experimentalism, with a premium on aesthetics and an emphasis on the importance of play and fun. McCandless's approach represents a challenge both to the positivism of the functionalist-idealist and to the pragmatist-realist liberal ideal of journalism as Fourth Estate. This approach foregrounds aesthetic impact before other considerations. As such, it is subject to criticism within both the first and second discourses. Nonetheless, the pioneering and innovation in this approach make it popular among some in the media industry.

It is amid and between these at times overlapping and competing approaches that a clearer understanding of data visualization may be situated.

Methodological Approach: Archive Research

In setting out the following narrative, my methodological approach to archival materials has been influenced primarily by modern historicism (Evans, 1996, 11–12; 1997, 103–160). My approach to *history* in this project is therefore guided by the following assumptions:

- That documents may accommodate a limited range of different meanings, as they are written and framed for particular audiences.
- That historical research is analogous to a dialogue between historian and document(s).
- That the historian is not omniscient, and that there is no absolute truth in history.
- That language and grammar are not arbitrary.
- That there is a difference between theory and methodology in historical research.
- That historical time is fundamentally linear and sequential.

My approach to primary sources in this project, the majority of which I accessed in digitized form, incorporate the fundamental rules (or at least the spirit of the rules) of verification established by Ranke. In addition, I also used a range of ad hoc heuristics, informed by the field of information retrieval, toward addressing those limitations associated with historical research in modern digitized newspaper archives (Hitchcock, 2013). My approach to these documents may be defined as "source criticism." Key newspapers at key moments within the histories of British journalism, communication, and culture were selected in order to identify wider truths about the culture of the news infographic. This process was guided by practitioner literature, by conversations with contemporary infographic artists, and by means of systematic searching (and browsing) of the following digitized newspaper archives and online sources:

- British Newspapers 1600–1950 (Gale Cengage Learning)
- NewsVault (Gale Cengage Learning)
- 19th Century British Newspapers (Gale Cengage Learning)
- Picture Post Historical Archive
- 17th and 18th Century Burney Newspapers Collection (Gale Cengage Learning)

• The digitized archives of the *Daily Express*, the *Daily Mail*, the *Daily Mirror*, the *Daily Telegraph*, the *Financial Times*, *The Guardian* and *The Observer*, *The Independent*, the *Sunday Times*, and *The Times*

Given the scale of this project, and the fact that the material with which I was concerned was often hard to find, my approach involved non-probabilistic convenience sampling. I undertook several generic keyword searches (and combinations of these) including terms and phrases such as: "an analysis of," "analysis," "axis," "calculated," "calculation," "diagram," "explains," "guide," "map," "number of," "our analysis," "overview," "plan," "show," "shows," "shows that," and "working." The relevant materials I found using these terms were then analysed for more suitable terminology. Bylines of known infographic artists were searched, and used to increase the sample.

Methodological Approach: Interviews

In order to supplement my archive research, I undertook a series of semi-structured, active interviews with five infographics professionals who have experience with working in UK newsrooms (Ciaran Hughes, John Grimwade, Nigel Holmes, Michael Robinson, and Fiona Robertson). Some interviews took place in person, some took place remotely. Through all of them, I held to a small number of main questions, mostly concerned with biographical factors, using probes and follow-up questions where appropriate. My method of sampling was circumscribed by various factors. Those working in the field are comparatively scarce and so I took a purposive-homogeneous approach, targeting particular individuals within particular organizations. By degrees, I also engaged in snowball sampling; conversations and meetings with some collaborators led to names and details for future, prospective interviewees, albeit these were not always taken up (due to time constraints and issues around access). Because the construction of meaning involves collaboration (Garfinkel, 1967), and because all agents involved in the process of interviewing contribute toward these meanings, in practice all interviews are necessarily tempered with "bias" in a narrow, positivist sense. Yet this in itself does not invalidate the information generated, nor does it lessen the value of the findings I draw upon here.

Method of Analysis

My approach to interpreting meanings in this project required a novel, composite interdisciplinary method of analysis, predicated on the pragmatic notion of *paradigm interplay* (Schultz & Hatch, 1996). This approach encompasses both cultural and compositional aspects of data visualization, and draws upon a range of perspectives. First, it entails a visual discourse analysis (Albers, 2013) of select infographics, with an emphasis on semiotics. This approach is concerned with categories such as appropriation, composition, focal point, framing, juxtaposition, media, and medium. Second, I drew upon key texts concerning Conceptual Metaphor Theory (Lakoff & Johnson, 1985 [1980]), with a view to exploring meaning and function, and the broader culture of visual symbolism in news infographics. This follows from the principle that metaphors represent more than mere ways of talking, that they help us to think conceptually about the social world, too. Given that meanings in news infographics are often informed by accompanying texts (in the form of both literal text, and organizational structuring), I derive a third influence in my analysis from Nerone and Barnhurst's (2003) concept of the form of news as *media environment*. Lastly, in keeping with the idea that infographics are bound by a limited range of meanings, and interpretations (and in terms of exploring the issue of standards in news infographics), I drew upon conventional, positivist principles of best practice in infographic design (BSI, 1992).

Overview of Chapters

In the following chapters, I will set out the emergence of infographic forms (and some direct influences on them), within a wider history of journalism, culture, and communications in the UK.

In chapter 2 I consider the influences and first expression of infographics in the context of the print cultures of late eighteenth- and early nineteenth-century Britain. This emergence is best understood as a multilevel discourse, within the wider political, economic, social, and technological contexts that defined this period. They emerged in elite print and consumer media, and were used to communicate useful knowledge to a section of society that had grown increasingly dependent on the world of commerce: what Margaret Hunt (1996) has called the "middling sort." This occurred during the partisan developmental stage in British journalism history, an era defined by party and political patronage of news. Joseph Priestley's wall charts, which were key to the proto-infographic phase, were methodologically aligned with a Newtonian worldview—technologically emblematic of a modern, liberal-arts pedagogy; ideologically laden with a millenarian (and dissenting) radicalism; and aesthetically radical, in their anti-classicism. William Playfair's classical graphical forms broadly conformed to the same Newtonian worldview and methodological principles (though this component was less important in his work). His infographics represent a technology and an aesthetics of political persuasion. Ideologically anti-Jacobin, and strongly supportive of English national imperialism, Playfair's graphical works were more concerned with persuasion than with encouraging critical engagement. Their relative lack of popularity reflects this wider perception. In this chapter I show how the infographic owes its most significant intellectual debts to the Enlightenment ideal of associationism, and to the broad, cosmopolitan ideal of civilization as communication. The first data visualizations were understood within a scientific paradigm of "truth to nature." Difficult and expensive to produce, they embody the idea that commodification is a key driver of visual culture, for a tiny (often) enfranchised, rising urban polity. The chief site of resistance to these forms was traditional classicism.

In chapter 3 I explore how infographics became institutionalized through the print and political cultures of the nineteenth century, in the shift from the partisan to the independent developmental stage of British journalism history that was defined by descriptive, objective reporting. During the improving phase infographics became a key vehicle for reform, aimed at Britain's growing middle classes. The sites of production during this era were the movement for moral improvement and its survey work, journalism and publicity (fields that were not yet formally or professionally distinct from each other [Anderson, 2018]). They were published in a wider context of Victorian news culture, comprising popular (radical and illustrated) and respectable (national and local) newspapers and within a print culture that was available to the public via the emerging library network (I explore this field by means of an exploratory snapshot of public and private library catalogues of the era). Infographics were published too in the contexts of the period's cultures of education and literacy. Resistance to data visualization, whether stated or implied, arose in various forms during this era, the main site being aesthetic elitism, although romantic mysticism was no doubt a factor too. A belief in the centrality of written language in the communication of God's will, what historian J. F. C. Harrison (1971) has called the "whip of the word" (enforced in both evangelism and utilitarianism), and the residue of classicism among powerful, educated editors within the period's respectable press, represent two further, key brakes on the infographic. I set out a critique of two key visualizations from this period (alongside a consideration of related printing and technological factors) situated in reference to two important figures during this era: Joseph Fletcher and Florence Nightingale. These (and other data visualizations of this era) owe clear methodological debts to Adolphe Quetelet's foundational statistical methods, and to principles of cartography (both of which, in turn, owe a debt to the Newtonian worldview). For these individuals, data visualization represented a technology for achieving progressive change; they are ideologically redolent of an increasingly powerful, liberal, "improving sort," who laid the foundations for social reform in nineteenth-century Britain.

In chapter 4 I show how infographics finally reached the masses during the independent stage of UK journalism history in the context of an interpretive shift that only became possible after the rise of the New Journalism, at the turn of the twentieth century. Between the 1880s and the 1930s, during the commercial phase, social-scientific forms and pictograms were both incorporated into an emerging, modern news design. They were employed authoritatively and creatively (if at times misleadingly, and on occasion, with more than a hint of propaganda) as a means of explaining news events. The pictogram found in its naive form (such as in popular almanacs of the Habsburg Empire) had been employed as an ideological means of pulling together different ethnicities within a multilingual empire. Similar forms were presented to modern British news audiences in the context of rising visual and consumer culture; the illustrated press was aimed at the modern middle classes while the New Journalism was aimed at the undifferentiated masses. This generation of infographics spoke to the increasing political significance of nationalism. Sites of resistance to these new forms (and in particular, to pictograms) were several, and included conservative elitism (cultural, political, and pedagogical), localism, and scientism.

In chapter 5 I consider how and why news infographics emerged after World War II in the UK. I explore two phases here: the ideological and the professional. Infographics published in British newspapers since the 1930s represent diverse forms that reflect the growing marketization of newspaper culture. These diverse forms drew discursive inspiration from the traditions already outlined here; and during the professional era, standards specifically concerning news infographics (conceived of as a tool, rather than a method) were first set out. Infographics across these two phases arose both as excessively misleading tabloid propaganda (the *Daily Express* of the late 1950s), and as progressive, upmarket, public-interest visual journalism (the *Sunday Times* of the late 1960s and the 1970s). They were aimed at new, postindustrial, professional audiences. During the 1980s, political upheaval and new technological advances contributed to the increasing independence of the infographic artists in the newsroom. During the 2000s, further technological advances aligned with changes in audience behavior and made it possible for a new generation of standard-bearing infographic designers and data journalists to take their place in contemporary UK newsrooms. The principle sites of resistance to this generation of infographics were intellectual critiques, including tabloidization, and in practical terms, the politics of the newsroom.

Chapter 6 comprises three parts. First, I set out a summary history of news infographics in the UK. Second, I set out a critique of what may constitute best practice in news infographics, drawing upon traditions in standards and ethics from the social sciences and from journalism. Third, I engage with a range of criticisms of infographics and data visualization from cultural and philosophical disciplines, toward presenting a defense of the infographic, and I outline the concept of the *synopticon*, a data visualization that embodies the importance of sound data design as a tool in the functioning of modern life.

2   Confronting the "Chaos of Being": The Politics of Visual Knowledge

No frost can freeze Providence.
—Proverb

In this chapter I consider the historical origins of the data visualization, exploring the range of meanings encoded within pioneering visualizations that speak to the different ways in which they help to make sense of the social world. I situate the emergence of infographics in the print culture of late eighteenth- and early nineteenth-century Britain. I argue that as an intellectual breakthrough, data visualization is best understood as a multi-level discourse, within the wider political, economic, social, and techno-logical contexts that shaped this period. They emerged in elite print and consumer media, and were used to communicate useful knowledge to a growing middling sort, during what may be called the partisan develop-mental stage in British journalism history.

I will set out the first two phases in the emergence of data visualization: the proto-infographic and the classical. The first is primarily concerned with Joseph Priestley, whose chronographic visualizations served as inspi-ration for the emergence of the form proper. The sites of production in Priestley's works were his belles-lettres pedagogy, and the cultures of pub-lishing and journalism of mid-eighteenth-century England. These works were received within those cultures of literacy, learning, and knowledge, particularly prevalent among England's dissenting community, as much as by the wider cultures of reading and leisure of this period. The politics that informed Priestley's innovations were radical millenarian; and the aesthet-ics were associationist. I will conclude this section with a theoretical cri-tique of Priestley's key visualizations.

The second section in this chapter concerns the emergence of data visualization in the works of William Playfair. The sites of production for these visualizations was the Scottish Enlightenment and its reference literature, and the cultures of journalism and publicity of that period. The critical reception of these works was informed by a growing elite reading culture, particularly concerning useful knowledge, and by increasing demand for news and current affairs, after the French Revolution. The politics that gave rise to Playfair's innovations were anti-Jacobin, the aesthetics, touched on briefly, were (as with Priestley) associationist. I include in this section a critique of a selection of Playfair's visualizations.

In concluding this chapter, I set out various sites of resistance that help to explain why Playfair's innovations failed to achieve popularity during his own lifetime.

Radical Pedagogy at the Dissenting Academy

Britain emerged in the eighteenth century as the first industrialized nation, coming to dominate Europe's trading empires, due in large part to its expanding trade with North America and the West Indies. Trade fueled empire, and empire fueled trade, and a booming domestic market was fueled both by population growth and by improved productivity (particularly in agriculture). This period's elites saw their incomes rise across the century, and this new money created a demand for (among other things) cultural commodities, including educational and training materials and programs. Education served as a socializing function that constituted, according to Maura Henry, one of the defining factors of elite culture of this period (2008, 313–315).

Joseph Priestley was both a beneficiary of and a leading contributor to this burgeoning culture, central to which was the creation and circulation of knowledge. Born in Fieldhead near Leeds in 1733 and brought up in the dissenting tradition—his father and aunt were strict Calvinists—Priestley entered the dissenting academy at Daventry in 1752. Paid for by the new money of the dissenting industrial classes, and situated in one of the relatively new towns that were appearing in England at this time, Daventry, in keeping with a small group of progressive dissenting academies, represented a new nexus of power for politically marginalized groups. Baptists, Presbyterians, and Congregationalists (or Independents) would not submit to the rites and articles of the Anglican Church at the time, meaning, in theory at least, that they could not graduate from English universities, join the learned professions or hold civil, military, or crown offices.[1]

At Daventry, Priestley acquired a grounding in mathematics, science, and philosophy informed by the ideas of Newton and Locke (Lawrence, 1987). It was here too that the he encountered the single text that would most inspire his subsequent work, not least his philosophy of education, David Hartley's *Observations on Man* (1749). This optimistic, radical, and fundamentally deterministic text proposed that the age was defined by "the diffusion of knowledge to all ranks and orders of men, to all nations, kindred, tongues, and peoples," a progress that "cannot now be stopped, but proceeds ever with an accelerated velocity" (quoted in Porter, 2002, 246–247). Intellectual historian Clarke Garrett argues that Priestley shared Hartley's desire for an empirical "Christian apologetic" whereby "religious and moral 'facts' were demonstrated to be as tangible and scientific as physical 'facts'" (1973, 54). This approach, Robert Anderson suggests, speaks broadly to the confluence of religious dissent (in the form of Unitarianism) and science in eighteenth-century England that in turn informed a certain progressive faith in useful knowledge, commerce, and industry (Anderson, 1987).

Priestley started work as tutor in languages and belles lettres at another dissenting academy, Warrington, in 1761, where he found himself surrounded by peers of a similar religious background to his own and sympathetic both to his philosophy and to his politics (Schofield, 1997, 94). An engaging teacher, Priestley encouraged free thought, and free expression, eschewing the classical model of education (and the curriculum) then found at Oxford and Cambridge; he made science and empirical investigation central to his teaching, rather than the classics (Kramnick, 1986). Priestley sought to put the dissenting academy at the center of scientific progress and social improvement, toward the betterment of society, with the aim of uncoupling higher learning from classical humanism and from the exclusive grip of the learned professions. A sense of radicalism was reflected both in his curriculum (that controversially included modern history), and in his approach to teaching, which encouraged critical engagement. Science was not seen as inferior to the classics in this syllabus. In the tradition of Milton's *Areopagitica* (1644) Priestley believed in debate and vigorous dispute in the free marketplace of ideas, a state of anyone vying with everyone that may reveal a single, divinely ordained truth (Thomas, 1987).

The dominant classical-humanist mode of British education during this period relied heavily upon oratory and rote learning. The memorization and articulation of ancient speeches, long the mode of classical education in the West, from the sixteenth to the eighteenth century, represented a means of preserving and sustaining ancient Greek and Roman rhetorical and community ideals. For Priestley, however, schooled in the Newtonian worldview, languages were rather an "art" of man that conformed to laws of science. Priestley was less concerned with polite, or classical, knowledge, as articulated in the philosophy of Addison and Steele and found in *The Spectator*, than he was with useful knowledge—knowledge that was authentic, systematic, and scientific (Burns, 1986). For him oratory was a secondary consideration; in Priestley's worldview, the senses were paramount (Townsend, 1993). He privileged the eye over the ear and held a suspicion of fine words, and what he saw as the sophistry of radical skepticism (Bygrave, 2012). His approach must also be considered in the wider scope of educational philosophy of the eighteenth century, which was defined by the principles of transmission and innovation, the former manifesting in an appeal to reason rather than to authority, the latter implying a rejection of the principle of imitation that drove earlier humanist approaches to philosophy (Parry, 2006). Priestley's timelines, in keeping with the histories of Voltaire, Hume, Robertson, and Gibbon (Makkreel, 2012), embody the idea of a universal narrative history as progressive, in science as in culture. It is within these intellectual and social contexts that his contributions to data visualization are situated.

Journalism and Journalists in the Eighteenth Century

Most contemporary histories recognize that the newspaper press (and the journalist) played a significant role in eighteenth-century politics, a period defined by a gradual progression toward political modernity (Brewer, 1997) as much as by a growing commercialization in public life (McKendrick, Brewer, & Plumb, 1982). However, this role, as Conboy reminds us, was "brokered in the interests of a commercial elite" (2004, 69). The Stamp Act of 1712 represented both a means of control and a means of generating tax income toward paying for the infrastructure that underwrote the government's initiatives in trade and empire building. As a consequence, Black (1987) suggests, conservatism tended to define newspapers from 1725 until the end of the century—in terms of coverage, modes of production and distribution, and the audiences addressed as much as by the journalistic techniques employed (typography notwithstanding). Newspapers of this era were "efficient but monologic" (Conboy, 2004, 72), absent of discussion or interpretation. The conservatism that defined this newspaper culture would inform how modern newspaper journalism would be reproduced and received in the following century. But it also created space for a counterdiscourse that would find voice in the era's flourishing political pamphlets and books, against which the press would seek to compete, in order to be seen to discursively represent the public's interests and concerns (Ibid.).

From the seventeenth century, the "journalist" and "journalism" appeared in many guises; though the only common themes among them, Conboy suggests, seem to have been a profit motive and some claim to periodicity (2004). These journalists' output may be said to defy modern categorization (Ward, 2004). Nevertheless, Joseph Priestley's contribution to this period's journalism culture, as much as his contribution to its educational culture, is significant. It comprises two, in some ways oppositional, strands: his theological journalism and his political pamphlets (and in particular those aimed at his fellow dissenters). In terms of the former, in 1768 Priestley established *The Theological Repository*. His editorial policy was open to all, of any denomination, as well as deists and even nonbelievers—a potentially incendiary approach not well disposed to avoid the draconian blasphemy laws of the time (Schofield, 1997). Priestley wanted the journal (in keeping with his pedagogy) to represent a lively and independent space for debate and discussion, albeit one framed in cool, rational, enlightening terms (Braithwaite, 2003). In practice his contributors were of similar convictions, and indeed, much of the material published in the journals he wrote himself (Schofield, 1997). The first number, published on January 2, 1769, contained twenty-four pages and cost one shilling, but the lack of consistency in periodicity (and price) no doubt contributed to its struggling commercially (McLachlan, 1923). In principle (if not in practice) then, this was journalism that sought to nurture a critical public sphere.

Priestley's pamphlets, on the other hand, were radical and incendiary. In them, he moved far beyond the call for legal equality for dissenters, to demanding the formal separation of church and state (Kramnick, 1986). For Priestley and others, the issue of dissent had evolved from being simply a matter of religious observance, to being bound up with normative accounts of how civic society should function (Hampsher-Monk, 2006).

Edmund Burke recognized the social as much as the political ramifications of Priestley's politics (Crosland, 1987); his use of gunpowder as a metaphor in *Reflections on the Present State of Free Inquiry in This Country* (1785) was seized upon by Burke, in *Reflections on the Revolution in France* (1790), as evidence of Priestley's insurrectionist tendencies, and so the moniker "Gunpowder Joe" was born (Crosland, 1987). But more than chemistry, what Burke really feared was the potential for revolutionary ideas to spread through the social order and across borders. The nexus of scientific advance and the "global village" it seemed to support represented an existential threat to Burke's conservatism. Priestley's journalism discursively bridged the scientific and the political, the moderate and the radical.

Eighteenth-Century Print Culture

From the late 1730s, new circulating, subscription, and proprietary libraries fostered print culture, particularly within urban areas (with their growing numbers of print-dependent professional classes). So too did the lending of books via bookshops and coffee houses, street-hawkers, and group subscriptions. Caution must be exercised with regard to any presumption that these factors truly democratized reading and print culture beyond the artisan classes during this period, however. Michael Harris suggests that newspaper reading in London (which cannot be taken as reflective of the wider country) rose significantly, from around a quarter of residents in 1750s to a third during the 1780s (Barker, 2000). Newspaper circulation numbers rose rapidly during mid-century, albeit from a very low starting point, measured often in the hundreds (Ibid.). Modern research suggests that the boom in publishing during this time was merely a reflection of already established audiences reading even more. Eighteenth-century newspapers were published by and for an elite; the lower classes were in turn forced to seek out their news from unofficial (unstamped) and ephemeral publications, pamphlets being chief among them.

Eighteenth-Century Education

Though inspired by radical pedagogy, Priestley's chronographies were not intended for a wide-ranging public. At Warrington he sought to provide a new generation of gentlemen (many of whom were from the same middle-class dissenting stock as himself) with the skills required in order to run the country (Kramnick, 1986). His syllabus was aimed at "gentlemen" of a "liberal education" and offered knowledge "which is peculiarly requisite to gentlemen who intend to travel" (Priestley, 1778, 15). The audience for his synoptic charts were the same hard-working bourgeoisie that surrounded him at Warrington; those who found the religious life most easy to attain; those happiest, in the middle class of the period. Priestley was no ardent supporter of the laboring classes and he had no ideological concern with social inequality; indeed he betrayed a preference for self-help over social leveling (Braithwaite, 2003). He was alive to the privilege of life in his own era. His reading of history, in keeping with his approach to scientific progress, were both teleological and pragmatic (Thomas, 1987). Priestley sought to bring down the barriers between men of learning and the world around them, between theory and practice (Kramnick, 1986). His approach to education was scientific, mechanistic, and materialistic. He saw himself at Warrington as working on an assembly line of young men, readying them to take their places in society, to improve the lot of their fellow men, to increase the wealth of their country, and to do their best according to God's will. Lauded in the press, and recommended by celebrity authors, such as Maria Edgeworth and Erasmus Darwin, Priestley's charts inspired a wider culture of visual education during the late eighteenth and early nineteenth century (Rosenberg & Grafton, 2010). Some of his peers at Warrington and among the wider group that surrounded the publisher of many of his works, Joseph Johnson, shared his enthusiasm for visual education (Watts, 1998).[2] Moreover, later generations of educational reformers shared his belief in the power of visual learning aids. In *Practical Education* (1798), a work collaboratively written by Maria Edgeworth and her father Richard Lovell Edgeworth, a philosophical justification for a scientific, learner-centered approach to education is set out, drawing upon the educational philosophies of Rousseau and Locke. The Edgeworths recommend using the form of Priestley's *A Chart of Biography* (Priestley, 1765a), albeit without the names; students should be tasked with piecing together the names on their own accord (Edgeworth & Edgeworth, 1798, 265). The Edgeworths critically engaged with Priestley's work, suggesting that *A New Chart of History* "though constructed with great ingenuity, does not invite the attention of young people: there is an intricacy in the detail which is not obvious at first" (Ibid., 313). Such a device, they suggest, is best kept for "pupils at a more advanced age" (Ibid.). Critically, they suggest that the chart should be employed toward helping pupils to memorize material (Ibid., 264), in keeping with their more general philosophy that children of age eight or nine should not be exposed to political arguments they would not understand. Chronographs were therefore perceived as the safest way to incorporate history into British primary education, as a form of rote learning. But on what philosophical basis?

The Association of Ideas

In his rules of oratory, Priestley maintains that effective argumentation arises by combining an analytical approach (starting from simple assumptions and leading to commonalities) and synthetically (working "from above" down to fine detail). This reasoning of cause and effect was informed by both John Locke and David Hartley, and by the law of the association of ideas (DeBerg, 2011). Priestley believed that the mind is comprised of sense impressions that come directly from the immediate lived environment—a classic tabula rasa (McEvoy & McGuire, 1974). Were it possible to shape the environment in such a way as to materially affect those sense impressions, so the theory goes, then the individual could be changed for the better (Eagleton, 2016).

Priestley's charts seem to embody the associationist principle of uniformity amid variety, popularized by David Hartley. Priestley conceived of this theory as being psychologically effective, rather than being an innate property of things—it explained, for him, the pleasure things give to us in terms of the moderate exercise of intellectual faculties that they require of us. As such, his charts may be said to embody the spirit of moderation. Priestley was concerned with what he calls "standards of taste" or "aesthetics" in all educational endeavors and, in relation to oratory, he says: "We may expect that, in consequence of the growing intercourse between all the nations of the earth, and all the literati of them, a uniform and perfect standard of taste will at length be established over the whole world" (DeBerg, 2010). Priestley's charts may be considered, in this respect, as representing a cosmopolitan visual language intended to be shared in open, critical discussion, among lettered fellows. Normatively speaking, they represent an early technology that might be seen to support Marshall McLuhan's twentieth-century vision of a "global village."

Like John Locke, his major influence, Priestley showed little interest in the arts. However, this supposed philistinism invites a different way of understanding beauty, as something, for example, that may arise in the reading of his charts. Priestley's approach to aesthetics appears to run contrary to the dominant ways of thinking about art and beauty of his time, which seem to run in a relatively clear theoretical line from Lockean empiricism, through nascent theories of aesthetics, to the notion of the disinterested observer and the expressionistic genius of the artist. Townsend suggests that one reason why the notion of disinterestedness passed Priestley by may be accounted for by a singular political fact—his status as an outsider in society, a dissenter (Townsend, 1993, 570). Priestley's aesthetics disavow any hierarchical notion of beauty, which therefore makes possible an egalitarian principle of seeing all visual "arts" as being equally important, a thoroughly democratic approach to visual culture.

Politics and the Public Sphere

Although the elite dominated politics throughout this period, in the expanding network of towns and urban spaces, the middling sort and even the poor were still capable of influencing political outcomes. Increasing urbanization during this period created new spaces in which to challenge social constraints, and in turn encouraged social mobility. Print culture became more visible in these spaces, and literacy rates became more concentrated within them. A culture of socialization, in the form of volunteerism and mutualism developed, which in turn harnessed a spirit of independence and community participation that was geared around the wider aims of political reform (Dickinson, 2008). Priestley developed his visualizations in this increasingly politicized environment, during a time defined, according to Hampsher-Monk, by a fragmentation and resynthesis of political discourse (Hampsher-Monk, 2006). His politics were reformist not revolutionary; his approach to the idea of government and politics was one of experimentation, simplification, and minimalism in keeping with his rational dissenting philosophy (Seed, 1985).

Priestley's charts reflect the new visual order that emerged during the mid- to late eighteenth century, when power shifted away from the pageantry of court and toward the civic infrastructure of the modern city (Kramnick, 1986). Priestley was clearly attuned to the visual power that

A New Chart of History wielded: "What torrents of human blood has the restless ambition of mortals shed, and in what complicated distress has the discontent of powerful individuals involved a great part of their species!" (1769b, 17).

His charts imply a belief in progress that was emblematic of the time; the achievements of Newton and the thinking of Locke fed in turn into a new trade-empire symbiosis (Porter, 2002, 245). This new culture of applied science emerged in the various literary and philosophical societies that formed across the industrial Midlands and the north of England, including The Lunar Society, of which Priestley was an active member (Ibid.).

In terms of historiography (and epistemology), Priestley's *A Description of a Chart of Biography* (1765b) owes a declared debt to Isaac Newton's chronography. Before this generation of charts, earlier works of chronography were often expressed in tabular form, such as, for example, Francis Tallents' *View of Universal History* (1695), which was popular in the dissenting academies (Rosenberg & Grafton, 2010). Priestley's was not the first attempt to express time in linear graphical form. Jacques Barbeu-Dubourg's *Carte Chronographique* (1753) drew upon cartographic principles and employed a tightly uniform scaling; but given that it is fifty-four feet in length, the chart is neither synoptical nor practical.

Approximately three feet by two feet, Priestley's chart presents the period spanning 1200 BC to 1800 AD, divided into equal fifty-year intervals. Across

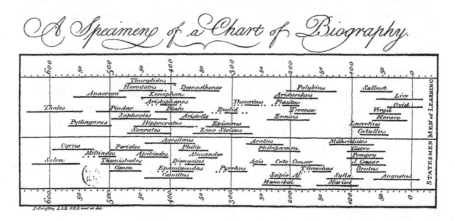

Figure 2.1
A specimen of Priestley's *A Chart of Biography*, in J. Priestley, *A Description of a Chart of Biography* (Warrington: Warrington Academy, 1765b).

this expanse are scattered two thousand celebrated names, each represented by a line, its length relative to the life span of the person named, with dotted lines used to suggest uncertainty. The focal point in this chart is the crowded top right-hand side, which represents an increasing abundance of great names in Priestley's time—a visual representation of predestination.

This pedagogic device, published (along with a pamphlet) to accompany Priestley's lectures at Warrington, invites the reader to juxtapose the lives of great individuals in order to better understand the processes of history by means of critical, constructive deliberation. Economic historian Harold Innis, who attributed the rise of the timeline (or at least the notion that underpins it) to "the dominance of arithmetic and the decimal system" warned against the ahistorical application of this "procrustean device in the appraisal of civilizations in which it did not exist" (Innis, 2007 [1950], 29). It may be said that the timeline has certain consequences for the interpretation of history, not the least that it seems to provide rhetorical support for questionable notions such as "dark ages" and 'golden ages." But more importantly, timelines also serve to offer insights into the acts of powerful bodies and individuals in society; for those who know how to use them, they serve to support open, critical reflexive debate. Designed in order to be scanned, rather than read, this chart serves to simplify (and to demystify) the process of historical time, posing a challenge to the political status quo.

For Priestley, time, as a function of the general state of knowledge, and of the general rate of improvement in wider society, was accelerating (Priestley, 2005 [1817]). His *A Description of a Chart of Biography* (1765b) instrumentalizes this acceleration. Priestley interpreted the meaning of this acceleration as a millenarian; he looked to the fin de siècle to ring in new knowledge, new politics, and a new, increasingly perfect world—all of which was God's ordained plan (Kramnick, 1986). This process (and its manifestation) was for Priestley thrilling and inspiring, a visual manifestation of the sublime (Rosenberg, 2007). Priestley's is therefore a materialist history. It is fun (trivial), but serious (deterministic). It is improving and internationalist in outlook while also being patriotic in nature; he intended that familiarity with great men "inspires the mind with a taste for solid glory" (Priestley, 1788, 15).

The choice of names in this chart reflects Priestley's awareness of his audience, as well as being an astute piece of localized marketing.[3] Priestley was mindful of other aspects of his audience too—captains of industry are

time-poor, and so this chart is marketed as a time-saving tool for impart-
ing useful knowledge. The chart proved commercially successful, passing
through nineteen editions, and it contributed in no small measure to Priestley's rising personal acclaim (Schofield, 1997). The method used in producing this chart is line engraving, an intaglio process that involved the
removal of slivers of metal one at a time, using a burin. It was a difficult
process to execute, and hence time consuming.

Priestley's chart comprises two metaphorical conceits. The first is an orientational metaphor (Lakoff & Johnson, 1985 [1980]) that conceives of time as
a line (or as in an individual life, a series of discrete lines) proceeding forward
(in this case left to right) in an essentially linear manner.[4] This accords with
the Newtonian principles that guided Priestley's scientific inquiries.

The second metaphor represents time as a river.[5] Lakoff and Johnson
suggest that the way in which we understand time and space is essentially
metaphorical, and that in modern, industrialized life, time has come to be
associated with metaphors that express quantitative value (1985 [1980], 8).
Priestley's charts visually embody this modern ideal. Each of the two thousand discrete lines on *A Chart of Biography* represents a life's work, and the
value attributable to that time (measured in achievements and prestige),
relative to the length of the line (and relative to the lengths of lines representing other celebrated individuals) represents both a commodification of
time, and a commodification of history.

Compositionally (and methodologically), Priestley's *A New Chart of History* (1769b) is designed in sympathy with *A Chart of Biography* (1765a); it
adheres to the same dimensions and conventions and they share the same
scaling (Schofield, 1997, 132; Rosenberg, 2007, 62). Empires are juxtaposed
one against the other. The focal point in this chart is the green expanse of the
Roman Empire on the bottom-left of the chart; the most significant empire
across time and space, the Roman Empire regarded itself as having an intrin-
sic duty in spreading civilization (Bell, 2011). The idea of the nation before
1800, according to Breuilly, was exclusively bound up with political elites and
monarchy and by association with elite culture. This gradually (clearly after
Priestley) began to encompass territories and their peoples, often in response
to geopolitical threats, as a function of political longevity and stability, and
the late Enlightenment idea of historical stages (Breuilly, 2011).

The framing of this chart is bound up with utilitarian knowledge—more
specifically, knowledge toward a better understanding of empire, in terms

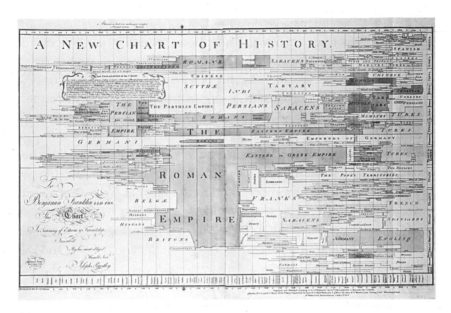

Figure 2.2
J. Priestley, *A New Chart of History* (Warrington: Warrington, 1769b).

of those factors present in its rise and in its decline. This chart may be used interactively.[6] The media and standards employed are all either sympathetic to or essentially the same as those employed in Priestley's *A Chart of Biography*, emphasizing their mutual pedagogical utility. The metaphorical devices in this chart are also essentially the same. They may be used one above the other, positioned on the wall so that time is "represented as flowing laterally, like a river, and not as falling in a perpendicular stream" (Priestley, 1769a, 2). The idea of "truth to nature" in the universal metaphor may be said to represent a regime of knowledge (or a way of knowing) that predates modern objectivity (Daston & Galison, 2007). This chart also accommodates the imperial gaze; it is a technology of colonial "knowledge" that encourages reflection upon the British Empire (Bell, 2011). European thinkers in Priestley's time, according to Bell, tended to view the world as comprising binaries of civilized and uncivilized peoples (Ibid.); this rhetorical approach may accommodate ambivalence on the matter of empire, weighing dignity (and more importantly, as far as Priestley was concerned, providence) against concerns for the human consequences of empire (Welch, 2011).

There is a seeming paradox in this chart. Priestley's methodology conforms to rational, scientific, Newtonian orthodoxy; and yet he fully acknowledges the communicative and emotional power in the form and that this
emotion seems to be constitutive of the process of the knowledge it reveals.
It explores the revolutionary idea of empire from an ambivalent perspective. On the one hand, Priestley expressed horror at the bloodiness of empire
building, but on the other hand, he averred that (like the river flowing) it
is both natural and inevitable: it is God's will. Predicated on the psychological notion of associationism, this visualization speaks to a belief in the
universality of sensory perception, and in turn to what Welch describes as
a conflation with the idea of self-evident natural rights (2011). Priestley's
charts represent, in summary, a deterministic epistemology that combines
methodological rigor with radical (but not revolutionary) political and ideological activism.

The Scottish Enlightenment and Its Culture of Publishing

At the bottom right-hand side of Priestley's *A New Chart of History* (1769b)
the Scots as an empire disappear from view shortly after 1600 (more specifically, after the Union of the Crowns, in 1603); thereafter, the English are
seen to dominate the landmass of Great Britain. Scot William Playfair was,
as he attests, familiar enough with Priestley's visualizations to have made
use of their design and their methodology. What he thought of their con-
tents, we do not know. But the political significance of this reality had been
brought painfully home to the generation before Playfair, in the form of a
major national humiliation. The Darien scheme, a patriotically informed
business venture intended to develop a Scottish empire on the Isthmus of
Panama, in Central America, had raised a remarkable sum of money given
the nation's relative poverty. But by 1700 the scheme's failure had plunged
the country into crisis, and by 1707 Scotland had signed the Acts of Union
with England, forced to relinquish its sovereignty and trade, as well as its
powers to issue coinage and to set taxes. These events did not pass without
heated political debate.

Some, including patriotic Midlothian aristocrat Andrew Fletcher, had
argued against Scotland's incorporation into the union. Fletcher, being for
localism and self-government, was opposed to international trade. He felt
that in the open market, Scotland would lose out to its larger and more

powerful partner. He argued that Scotland should be ruled from a city of a scale that made face-to-face civic engagement possible; a necessary component in classical models of democracy. Against this position, David Hume argued that Scotland's old moral economy was no panacea, and that it was unstable and prone to deliver its own social ills, such as indolence. He argued instead for modernity, for cosmopolitanism, for urban growth, and for the new political economy. He argued in favor of the new communications technologies and systems that would lead to a higher standard of living, which may in turn be reflected in, among other things, a thriving literary culture (Davie, 1981). Influenced by Hume, and Adam Smith, and in the context of the remarkable economic growth Scotland experienced after the Acts of Union, it is possible to conceive of Playfair's visual innovations—the line chart, the bar graph, the pie chart—as status symbols in this new exchange society. They are, after Marshall McLuhan, a very modern extension of man.

Eighteenth-century Scotland's Enlightenment culture was heavily influenced by its oldest universities. William Playfair was well acquainted with this world; his older brother John, who had provided his education from the age of 13, would later become an internationally renowned professor of natural philosophy, at the University of Edinburgh, in 1785. The dominant outlook in Scotland during this era was, according to Jonathan Israel (2011), informed by liberalism, Calvinism, and Newtonian philosophy with a heavy emphasis on "design," on one hand, and by the Francophone Enlightenment of Montesquieu, Voltaire, Rousseau, and the *Encyclopédie*, on the other. Scotland's leading intellectuals forged a distinct path and within the power politics of the still relatively new union, they sought to establish a justification of, and a rationale for what Scotland would bring to its larger, wealthier neighbor. This contribution would be a culture of *usefu' plans and beuks*, on Burns's terms,[7] influenced by the soft diplomacy of *auld* alliance ally France (Davie, 1981). If a single literary work could embody Scotland's Enlightenment it would be *The Encyclopaedia Britannica*. Comprising up-to-date, useful (rather than polite) knowledge, this text represented a new dawn of critical enquiry, equipping (so it was thought) the time-poor businessmen of smaller, "backward" nations to compete with the subjects of their wealthier, larger rivals (Yeo, 2001).

Playfair's Scotland was a hotbed of intellectual dispute among followers of two opposing political and moral philosophies: "Common Sense" and

"Moral Sense." The Common Sense approach was essentially a pragmatic one: philosophy should serve the individual and society, and (essentially) the current order (Israel, 2011). It was with this side that Playfair aligned himself.[8] A range of further cultural associations, principles, and ideals informed Playfair's infographics, some of which drew upon the same intellectual sources as Priestley.[9]

Eighteenth-Century Journalism, Publicity, and Propaganda

Playfair has often been described by historians as a journalist, but the term "journalist" wouldn't appear until the 1830s (Conboy, 2004), after which, the disreputable "writer" of the eighteenth century would be jettisoned in favor of a new, respectable, professional status (Aspinall, 1945). It has been suggested that before news discourse emerged in the mid-nineteenth century, via the confluence of various technological and cultural advances, news media were written by "publicists" rather than by journalists (Chalaby, 1998). However, it is important to remember that newspaper journalism as a concept is also defined by those who call themselves (and whom society recognizes as) journalists (Conboy, 2004), and so we should beware of casting too narrow a definition that may elide significant traditions. It is perhaps more helpful to think of this era as one in which the boundary work of journalism had not yet been clearly established as methodologically distinct from (among other fields) publicity and propaganda. It would therefore be misleading to reduce the infographic to little more than an early form of publicity (in Jurgen Habermas's terms either *critical* or *manipulative*), as this would ignore the historical contribution infographics have made to informing us through late eighteenth- and nineteenth-century political journalism and authorship.

The nature of Playfair's journalism serves as a useful illustration of this point. In 1785, he privately circulated a version of *The Commercial and Political Atlas*, what would become the first known published work containing statistical graphics (Wainer & Spence, 2005).[10] He later moved to Paris, in the light of increasingly benign commercial and trading relations between Britain and France, but returned to London during The Terror in 1793. On returning to England he sought an outlet to condemn the revolutionary violence he'd witnessed for a British audience. In 1794 he was secretly employed by Secretary at War William Windham, to write anti-Jacobin propaganda (Berkowitz, 2018). In a letter addressed to Home Secretary Henry Dundas, dated April 24, 1794, Playfair enclosed a detailed proposal outlining a multimedia propaganda strategy for the campaign. In this strategy, he envisaged a tripartite political class comprising conservatives, reformers, and crucial swing voters, each of which required information written in a discrete discursive style (Berkowitz, 2018, 358). To reach the swing voters, Playfair suggested first identifying the key opinion formers in each town and village (preempting by over 150 years the concept of opinion leadership, an important component of the modern two-step flow of communication theory [Katz, 1957]). Playfair planned a range of publications to this end, including *The Revolutionary Magazine*, for which he sought working capital from Windham for a limited run (Berkowitz, 2018), and a "short history of the crimes & cruelties of the Revolution in France" (quoted in Ibid., 360), taking after the highly popular martyrology genre. Playfair would later draw upon this genre in writing *The History of Jacobinism, Its Crimes, Cruelties and Perfidies* (1796). It is clear then that he was an adept publicist, with a keen sense of the discursive needs of diverse audiences; although he was perhaps not always a commercially successful one.

In 1795 Playfair became joint owner and editor of *The Tomahawk, or, Censor general*, (1795–1796), a two-penny daily supportive of the Pitt government, for which he wrote the leaders (Anonymous, 1823). Later, in 1808, he authored a short-lived weekly paper, *Anticipation* (Ibid., 1823) and then in 1814 became editor of the English-language continental newspaper *Galignani's Messenger*. A short-run, daily royalist newspaper publishing essays, *The Tomahawk* drew upon the same conservatism as John Wilkes's earlier *North Briton* (1762–1763). Through competition and the rising availability of advertising income, bombastic essay journalism of this kind encouraged the daily newspapers of the era to consolidate their position in influencing public opinion (Conboy, 2004). The rhetorical style used was a new trend ushered in after the French Revolution. English newspaper history experienced a wider polarizing effect during this time. Readerships were increasing and newspapers sought to serve a wider (and lower-class) readership with their publicity and propaganda; this in turn led to what Barker describes as a new type of print culture that was both "democratic and demotic" (2000, 176). This would lead to a wider cultural shift, where journalism helped form public opinion, rather than simply serving to sell news (Conboy, 2004). Nevertheless, while it remains unclear whether or not

Playfair received money directly to write government propaganda (Berkowitz, 2018), there can be no doubt that he was a publicist and propagandist, and a beneficiary of the same subsidies that were seen to taint newspaper journalism in the eyes of the public (Aspinall, 1945) during the partisan era.

Late Eighteenth-Century Cultures of Literacy

In 1787, Louise XVI received copies of Playfair's *Commercial and Political Atlas* as a gift from Lord Lansdowne. A keen amateur geographer, he was said (by Playfair) to have been impressed, so much so that he granted Playfair a permit to establish a metals factory in Paris (Wainer & Spence, 2005). As Playfair recalls: "[The King] at once understood the charts and was highly pleased. He said they spoke all languages and were very clear and easily understood" (Ibid., 1).

That infographics appeal because of the universality of the "language" they "speak" is a common trope in the literature. But we should not lose sight of the power dynamics of a "universal language" in the contexts of the Ancien Régime. Just two generations previously, Louis XIV, the Sun King, had presided over a French court whose power structures were seemingly uneclipsable, mediated through a courtly "gaze" of seemingly arbitrary gestures that helped to consolidate his reign. A new spirit of knowledge and industrial progress was gathering momentum by Louis XVI's time— bringing with it a decisive power shift in visual culture, as prophesied by Priestley (Kramnick, 1986). Priestley's scientific equipment, as much as his wall charts, and alongside them Playfair's infographics, were all part of this new visual order—a direct threat to the old, feudal order. They represented an opportunity to cede to the inevitable, and rebalance the power dynamics in society, moving from feudalism to the spirit of moderation and the increasingly empowered industrial classes.

All of Playfair's infographic works were discursively framed for social elites. For example, the *Statistical Breviary* is addressed to "all persons connected with public affairs" (Playfair, 1801b, 4); in particular, it was intended to appeal to the wealthy and (by definition) the busy, because: "Men of high rank, or active business, can only pay attention to general outlines" (Ibid., xiv–xv). His translation of the *Statistical Account of the United States of America* (1805b) is addressed to "commercial men." His *A Letter on Our Agricultural Distresses, Their Causes and Remedies* (1822) is addressed to "My lords and gentlemen." In a message at the beginning of *The Commercial and Political Atlas* (third edition, 1801), he addresses purchasers of a previous edition as "Gentlemen," a term that at the time still conferred privilege based on blood lineage.[11] Playfair thought it likely that anyone familiar with geography or mathematics (fields of study few outside the elite would likely have encountered) would be able to grasp the idea of his charts instinctively, although not everyone agreed.[12]

By contrast, Playfair's newspaper work was aimed at a very different audience. The first issue of *The Tomahawk, or, Censor general* claims to be "a useful, entertaining and instructive work to all ranks [and]...every rational Briton."[13] Though mostly concerned with English-French political relations, this paper exploited popular genres and newspaper conventions of the time in order to appeal to a wide-ranging audience (Berkowitz, 2018). From time to time tabular data were published, but no infographics.[14] Similarly, in *Anticipation* tabular data were published that might lend themselves to representation in graphical form.[15]

We have seen how Playfair was mindful of the discursive needs of different audiences in his propaganda work. Nevertheless, his elite writing was often subject to criticism (some of it ideological) (Berkowitz, 2018). In his obituary, Playfair's literary career was described as *cacoethes scribendi* (Anonymous, 1823, 564), which means having an insatiable desire to write, and which was considered a "bad habit" or even a "disease." Implicit in this is a coded criticism of Playfair's outsider status; the term derives from Juvenalian satire, a manner that was largely the preserve of the dominant, classically educated stratum of society (Clery, 2017). Playfair's charts scarcely merit a mention in this obituary; they are reduced to mere "geometric lines and figures." The *Gentleman's Magazine*, a celebration of polite (and classical) culture, saw little obvious merit in them.

It may be argued, then, on the one hand that a poor audience, lacking formal knowledge of algebra or cartography, may have struggled to understand Playfair's charts. On the other hand, he wrote newspaper copy intended for the pleasure (and amusement) of all. His ostracism from the polite, classical intellectual culture of the day represents a site of resistance to his graphical works. In turn, Playfair's visual forms represent an attempt to move beyond the stultifying field of classicist literary criticism (and polite knowledge) into a new, more democratic, more useful field of political knowledge.

Politics after The Terror

Just as Priestley framed his Chart of Biography in terms of the fast-moving changes under way in the scientific world of his era, so Playfair, in *The Commercial and Political Atlas*, sets out his infographics in the context of "a great change" wrought in part by the French Revolution (Playfair, 1801a [1786], iv), but also by increasing volumes of information.[16]

In 1801 Playfair published the *Statistical Breviary* (Playfair, 1801b). This and a simultaneously republished edition of *The Commercial and Political Atlas* are thought to have cemented his reputation within the political classes, chief among them the Marquis of Lansdown. Scholars have widely lauded Playfair's achievements; his charts are said to show that evidence can be beautiful, embodying the communicative power of visual impact (Wainer, 2006). Moreover, he demonstrates an uncanny understanding of his audiences' psychological needs, which seems both highly prescient (Costigan-Eaves & Macdonald-Ross, 1990), and intuitive (Spence, 2006). However, several scholars have also passed comment upon the erroneous, and in some cases misleading nature of some of Playfair's designs (Funkhouser, 1937; Costigan-Eaves & Macdonald-Ross, 1990; Wainer & Spence, 2005). An aggregate of this opinion would seem to be that visual impact, persuasion, and polemic were of greater concern to Playfair than was the principle of accuracy.

"Exports and Imports of Scotland to and from different parts for one Year from Christmas 1780 to Christmas 1781" (figure 2.3) takes up a full page in a standard, octavo book format. The chart involved both engraving and etching on copperplate in its composition. The focal point in this chart is the £200,000 grid line that draws the eye downward, toward the final two variables, and in particular to Russia and to the yawning trade disparity between the two nations, due perhaps to Scotland's reliance on Russian hemp. The ordering of these variables makes clear the importance of markets to the West (the West Indies, America, Ireland) for Scottish exports, and hence for its continuing economic prosperity. Playfair sets out to explain this chart by means of metaphorical allusion, as a series of piles of guineas.[17] Berkowtiz (2018) suggests that this metaphor may have come to Playfair on account of his experiences during his time in employment at Boulton and Watt's counting house. In accepting this, it may be said that the bar graph is a product of the same modern, materialist culture of commodification as Priestley's charts.

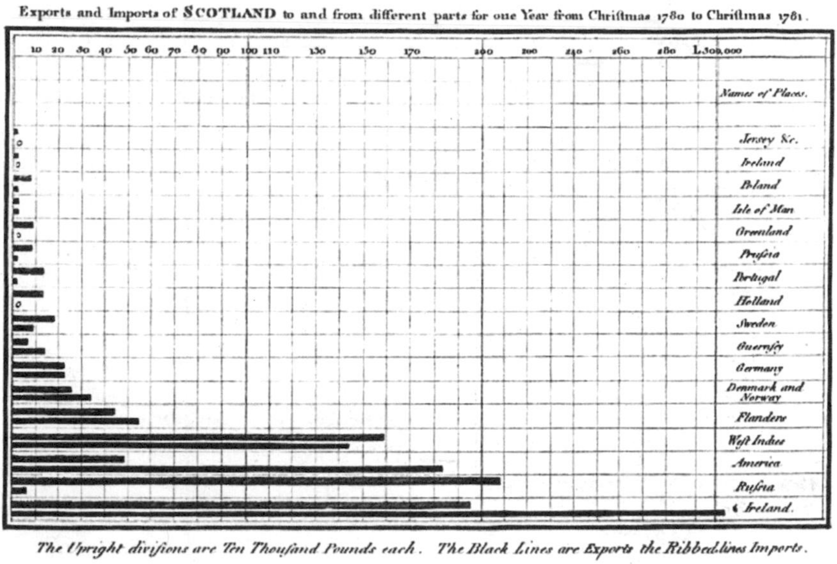

Exports and Imports of SCOTLAND to and from different parts for one Year from Chriftmas 1780 to Chriftmas 1781.

The Upright divifions are Ten Thoufand Pounds each. The Black Lines are Exports the Ribbed lines Imports.

Figure 2.3

"Exports and Imports of Scotland to and from different parts for one Year from Christmas 1780 to Christmas 1781," in W. Playfair, *The Commercial and Political Atlas*, third edition (London: J. Corry, 1801a [1786]).

The graphing of mathematical functions and formulae long predate Playfair's innovations (Funkhouser, 1937), and indeed, as we have already seen, Playfair was candid in his intellectual indebtedness to Priestley. Playfair's line graphs, such as his Chart of the National Debt of England published in *The Commercial and Political Atlas* (1801a [1786]), generally apply the standard of regularity in axis intervals (although, as we see in this chart, in figure 2.4, he occasionally deviates from this principle for rhetorical effect). The use of grid lines, color shading, and a legend (all commonly found in Playfair's charts) represent adherence to a wider range of standards in best practice. In this chart the focal point is the greatest spike, on the right of the chart, beginning at the start of the current war with France. In keeping with the bar chart discussed earlier, this line graph also takes up an entire page in the same octavo-sized book (although it is worth noting that a previous version was available in folio). The scale and the medium both make Playfair's charts much smaller than Priestley's wall charts. Playfair's charts are more personalized and individualistic, and less well suited to interactive

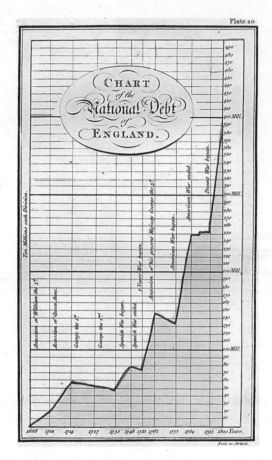

Figure 2.4
"Chart of the National Debt of England," in W. Playfair, *The Commercial and Political Atlas*, third edition (London: J. Corry, 1801a [1786]).

group discussion and deliberation, qualities Priestley's wall charts perfectly embodied.

The key graphical innovation in the *Statistical Breviary*, according to Wainer and Spence (2005), is the circle chart, as seen here in "Statistical Chart Showing the Extent of the Population and Revenues of the Principal Nations of Europe in the order of their Magnitude" (figure 2.5). Playfair did not make clear what the inspiration was behind the circle chart (whether in stand-alone, pie, or concentric format). It is suggested that he thought the form self-evident, requiring no further explanation (Wainer & Spence, 2005). Spence (2005) suggests the likeliest influences are earlier logic

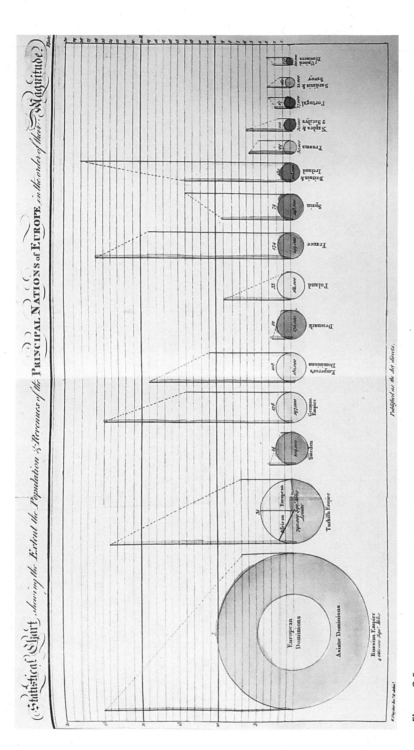

Figure 2.5

"Statistical Chart Showing the Extent of the Population and Revenues of the Principal Nations of Europe in the order of their Magnitude," in W. Playfair, *An Inquiry into the Permanent Causes of the Decline and Fall of Powerful and Wealthy Nations* (London: Greenland & Norris, 1805a).

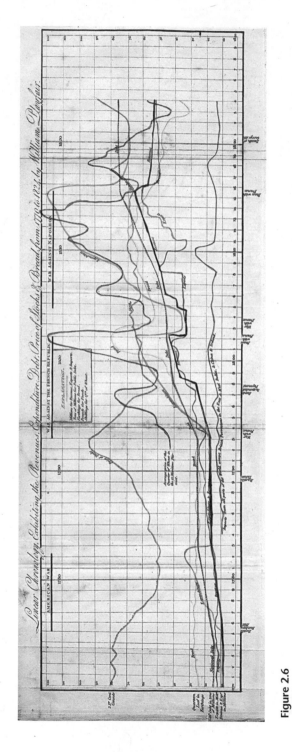

Figure 2.6

A multivariate linear display from Playfair's "experimental" period. "Linear Chronology, Exhibiting the Revenues, Expenditure, Debt, Price of Stocks & Bread, from 1770 to 1824," in W. Playfair, *Chronology of Public Events and Remarkable Occurrences within the Last Fifty Years* (London: G. and W. B. Whittaker, 1824).

diagrams by Leibniz and Euler. In this chart, the world's leading empires (except the United States) are compared in terms of landmass (represented as scaled circles) and in terms of two colored tangent lines attached to each circle; the one on the left of each circle represents population (yellow) and the other on the right of each circle represents revenue (red).

The focal point of this graph are the concentric colored circles that represent Russia's landmass—the eye is drawn up the vertical "revenue" intersection on the right of the outer circle, then leftward along the vertical axis toward a juxtaposition with France—whose revenues are higher, but whose landmass is much smaller. In this view, Russia is unrivaled in terms of landmass; and yet during the eighteenth century the country remained "a poor, backward, overwhelmingly agricultural, and illiterate country" (Riasanovsky, 1984, 284). In *An Inquiry into the Permanent Causes of the Decline and Fall of Powerful and Wealthy Nations,* this chart is mobilized in attempting to persuade the reader that if he wants to preserve his property, then the ongoing wars with France must be paid for. The "justice and expediency" of Pitt the Younger's progressive income tax, introduced in 1799, Playfair argues, is essential to this strategy.[18] The running of the British state, O'Brien (2008) suggests, accounted for increasing volumes of its resources from the Glorious Revolution through to the end of the eighteenth century. O'Brien further suggests that, during this time, royalist and aristocratic propaganda became a cheaper and more effective way of raising revenues than were draconian legal measures pursued against individuals (Ibid.). Playfair's infographic works therefore both discursively support and materially embody these changes in Britain's political economy.

The broad principle of proportionality in this graph (in terms of circumference), speaks to an adherence to geometric consistency. However, given that the eye finds it difficult to comparatively judge differently scaled circles, graphical best practice is perhaps more consistently adhered to in the part-to-whole pie format within this chart. Funkhouser observed that the gradient between the revenue and population lines for each nation is defined by the diameter of the circle, and so its rate tells us nothing meaningful about the tax burden in each empire (1937). Wainer and Spence (2005) suggest in mitigation, however, that Playfair was most likely only concerned with showing either the positive or the negative nature of each gradient.

The visual metaphor employed here (using a circle to represent quantities) spans a range of contingent, mythological meanings. In ancient

Chinese culture, for example, the circle "has a magical value as a protective agent, and symbolizes an impenetrable barrier, warding off demons and keeping them at bay" (Julien, 2012). Similarly, in Jung's research on archetypes, it is suggested that the circle represents "a symbol of the psyche...[and] a symbol of earthbound matter, of the body and reality" (Jung, 1964, 249). The circle is also a receptacle, it is "an archetypal idea...It is the idea of the magic circle which is drawn round something that has to be prevented from escaping or protected against hostile influences" (Jung, 1977, 178). The circles in this chart may therefore be interpreted as discursively framing the spirit of an empire, expressing those anxieties in Britain concerning the French, with whom Britain had been regularly at war throughout the century.

Sites of Resistance

In concluding this section, I will now consider why Playfair's charts failed to inspire imitation among his contemporaries. I start with a consideration of their lack of contemporaneous appeal within the sciences. Several impediments to presenting data in graphical form in the sciences were apparent during Playfair's time. Three in particular have been articulated in the literature (Wainer & Velleman, 2001; Wainer & Spence, 2005); the first two epistemic, with a third technological. First, although graphical forms had been used before Playfair to express numbers, rarely had they been employed in the plotting of empirical data (Wainer & Velleman, 2001).[19] Second, scientific illustration was viewed with suspicion by some; Robert Hooke's *Micrographia* (1665) had been criticized by neo-Platonists on the grounds that images necessarily deceive. The dominant epistemic virtue of truth to nature (Daston & Galison, 2007) in the form of visual metaphors was clearly a contested ideal at the time. Third, the only methods available for illustration in printing at the time were labor intensive, and so were expensive. Copperplate engraving involved an intaglio technique that was very different from the method involved in printing text; this meant that text and image usually had to be printed separately. The range of errors across editions, Wainer and Spence (2005) suggest, implies that Playfair may have engraved the lines himself. For these three reasons then, the emergence of data visualizations within the scientific and social-scientific sphere were necessarily circumscribed. But what of the more general spheres of pamphleteering and book publishing?

The state of print technology would have posed a challenge. Lithography was not invented until 1796 and rotary presses would not usher in "mass journalism" until 1811 (Kittler, 1999, 126). Any images in Playfair's newspaper journalism would therefore most likely have been created as woodcuts, and so would have been relatively expensive. Elsewhere, it has been suggested that Playfair's personal traits and public failings, his "improvidence and brashness" and not least his reputation as a failed extortionist (and bankrupt), contributed to the lack of enthusiasm with which his innovations were subsequently taken up across the sciences (Wainer, 2006). Reputation was undoubtedly important then as it is now. However, Daniel Defoe, like Playfair, was a government spy and a highly partisan polemicist; indeed he was an occasional visitor to debtor's prison. Yet *Robinson Crusoe* (1719–1722) was required reading for generations of scientifically minded evangelicals. It is not so much the reputation of the man, I will suggest, as it is within the discursive nature of the texts that an explanation for the failure of Playfair's ideas to take off more generally must be sought.

According to Habermas (1989), the principle of dialogue was crucial to the culture of critical reflexivity that emerged during the Enlightenment, leading to the separation of opinion from patronage in the coffee houses of the era. This critical-reflexive principle was manifest too in literary devices, such as the *renvois* method of cross-referencing that is used in Diderot's *Encyclopédie* (Sherman, 1976); this tool enabled knowledge to be created in a *rhizomatic* way, "bottom-up," by the reader. Priestley's charts, as we have seen, were created in order to facilitate critical debate among his students and to challenge the attitude toward knowledge that prevailed within the Anglican hegemony; in this respect they may be said to represent the spirit of the bourgeois public sphere in which their author played such an active part. However, while in some limited way Playfair seemed to adhere to this discursive mode[20] the works containing his visualizations seem to speak to a different approach, in three respects.

First, we know from Playfair's private correspondence with the Pitt government in 1794 that he was much less interested in encouraging critical debate that he was in cynically shaping public opinion (Berkowitz, 2018). As we have seen, his early visualizations were didactic in purpose and supportive of the paternalistic voice of the Pitt government. His concerns about government borrowing are overly partisan and are even visually exaggerated in one graph.[21] The charts comparing trade between England

and other nations serve to keep score; Playfair wanted England to "win" (Ibid.). There is no clear separation of facts from opinion in these early works. His narrative text (if not necessarily his charts) does not serve to promote critical debate. On the contrary, it exhibits, in Habermas's terms, aspects of manipulative publicity, seemingly less concerned with creating and presenting new knowledge than with serving the author's ideological and political ends.

Second, we know that Playfair had an ambivalent attitude to the principle of transparency. In 1785 he sent a limited print of *The Commercial and Political Atlas* to James Watt asking for advice—Watt suggested he should include tables "for the charts now seem to rest on your own authority." (Wainer & Spence, 2005, 14). Playfair included them in the first (1786) and second (1787) editions of the atlas, but did not include them in the third edition (1801)—the one published to coincide with the *Statistical Breviary*.

Third, the media Playfair used were suboptimal in terms of encouraging critical (verbal) discourse among groups of participants. On the one hand, Priestley's wall charts could be viewed by groups, and discussed within groups; on the other hand, it is difficult to envisage any more than two or three people crowding around an octavo-format publication. Priestley successfully (and ingeniously) brought a medium designed for the eye into a critical context (his pedagogy at Warrington Academy) that privileged the ear. This was a salient feature that no doubt contributed to their popularity, but it was a different environment from the one in which Playfair's graphical innovations circulated.

Conclusion

Infographics belong to the print cultures of late eighteenth- and early nineteenth-century Britain. They emerged in elite political print media, and were used to communicate useful knowledge to a growing middling sort, during the partisan developmental stage in British journalism history. Priestley's wall charts were methodologically aligned with a Newtonian worldview. They represent a democratizing and a rationalizing technology as well as the cosmopolitan, liberal-arts pedagogy they were created to further. They evince a radical-cosmopolitan ideology; they stand opposed to mysticism and to conservatism. Correspondingly, their aesthetics were non-hierarchical, moderate, and useful rather than polite. Playfair's visualizations conformed broadly (but not exclusively) to the same Newtonian worldview and methodological principles as Priestley's (though this component was less important in his work). Playfair's infographics are discursively situated within anti-Jacobin propaganda and were ideologically supportive of British national expansion and growth. His texts were essentially persuasive, but most of his infographics support critical engagement with the facts.

As outsiders to the classical worldview that dominated the literary and intellectual culture of the period, both Priestley's timelines and Playfair's data visualizations represent attempts to challenge the mechanics of classical knowledge, as driven by orality. These forms are situated within an early-modern communicative turn—after the scientific method of Francis Bacon and Sir Isaac Newton and the philosophy of John Locke, it is an outlook defined (at least in principle, if not always in practice, in Playfair's work) by openness and transparency, in contradistinction with tradition and opacity. These modern forms represent a new visual rhetoric about material and moral progress. They serve a different purpose from the classical method of learning—they encourage individualism, and (again, by degrees) critical thinking. They emerged as a medium of optimistic progress, in contradistinction with the largely pessimistic oratorical-rhetorical tradition. Along the way, by encouraging the engagement of interaction and critical thought, they served to loosen the worldview of classical knowledge, toward a new stage in communications history when print would become established as the dominant, and institutional mode of knowledge production.

All data visualizations are visual metaphors (Wainer, 2006). Priestley's charts flow like rivers, and Playfair's (bar) graphs rise like piles of guineas. These earliest visualizations mobilize abstract forms in order to help their audiences better understand abstract entities. Priestley's charts were concerned with time; Playfair's graphical forms were broadly concerned with the invisible world of individual psychology, as manifested in economic properties (such as money). These earliest data visualizations were discursively nonrevolutionary in nature. They represent a communicative paradigm for the furtherance of a range of ideas collectively bound up with civilization, and with empire. Priestley's charts may be seen to embody a spirit of radical, critical inquiry, and the will to communicate with all, on the one hand, harnessing sociability and embodying ideas such as cosmopolitanism, universalism, and rationalism that were emerging in new urban environments. Playfair's data visualizations, on the other hand, evince a sense of common-sense imperialist-nationalism; and were bound up with ways of thinking that are essentially hostile to Priestley's radicalism, betraying an anti-Jacobin suspicion of internationalism and intellectualism.

The first data in graphical forms did not emerge in the newspapers of the day not just because of the costs and challenges to routines associated with printing them, but also because in their original form, designed to facilitate critical engagement, they were discursively ill suited to the period's newspapers, which were absent of discussion and interpretation. They appear toward the end of the century in Playfair's books and pamphlets and are expressed in a discursive form that was made possible by the political economy of the period's journalism (Conboy, 2004).

In terms of legacy, Priestley's wall charts were popular because as a medium, they were well suited to a particular discursive model—the educational, semi-private sphere of the dissenting academy (one that was not mixed—but the preserve of educated, middle-class men). They offer an innovative solution to a serious problem concerning how historians have traditionally constructed knowledge about the past. Thomas Carlyle articulated this problem in 1830, when he observed that the linearity of prose rendered it an insufficiently flexible medium in which to express and explore the complexity of the "ever-living, ever-working *Chaos of Being*" (1972 [1830], 95). Priestley's timelines encourage a decentralized, rhizomatic way of learning about the past. In using them, we encounter what Staley (2003, 53) calls *translation effects*, which occur when we move from using one medium to another in constructing knowledge about the past; these translation effects free, or on McLuhan's terms, *extend* the mind beyond the imposition and limitations of spoken language. It is little wonder then that Priestley's timelines proved so popular, becoming a great commercial success.

On the other hand, Playfair's infographic pamphlets were less well suited to this critical-discursive environment. Their accompanying text was didactic, and there was little clear separation between facts and opinion; their attitude to transparency was inconsistent and their format was a suboptimal fit in the wider, political-discursive culture. The infographics in Playfair's pamphlets were less discursively scientific than they were persuasive; the preponderance toward technical errors, and the inconsistencies in some of these graphs (across discrete publications), suggests that, while he appealed to the visual language of science, in truth, what was paramount in these graphical forms was the art of persuasion. Infographics were not devised as a mode of mass propaganda although their inventor was active, and innovative, in this field. They were published in the mode of what Habermas (1989) calls manipulative persuasion, presented to an elite public in the late Enlightenment marketplace of ideas. They were inspired by the scientific pillars of Baconian and Newtonian method, and by Scottish common-sense pragmatism.

3 "Arts for Attracting Public Attention": The Improving Infographic

Conscience is your magnetic needle. Reason is your chart.
—Joseph Cook, *Conscience*, 1879

In this chapter, I will set out a third improving phase in the history of data visualization. I will explore how infographics, aimed at Britain's expanding elite, became institutionalized throughout the nineteenth century, and the generations of liberal, moral improvers who were responsible. This period spans the shift from a "partisan" to an "independent" British press. The moral (and medical) visualizations of Joseph Fletcher, John Snow, Henry Mayhew, Charles Booth (figure 3.8) and Joseph Rowntree (figure 3.2) owe a methodological debt to cartography, but also, along with Nightingale and Farr's data innovations, they owe a debt to Adolphe Quetelet's foundational statistics. By turns, all owe an epistemological debt to the same Newtonian worldview that inspired their predecessors.

This chapter is organized into three sections. The first, concerning sites of production, explores the movement for moral improvement, and (separately) the mid-Victorian journalist, and forms of popular journalism. The second section concerns sites of reception including nineteenth-century news cultures (and newspapers), and cultures of literacy and learning (including the role of the useful knowledge press in both). The third section explores sites of resistance to visual journalism during this period, including adherence to the whip of the word (emanating from evangelism and from utilitarianism), and a residue of classicism among editors within the period's respectable press. Through the narrative of this chapter, I set out a critique of two visualizations from this period (alongside a consideration of related printing and technological factors).

Survey Work, Journalism, and Publicity in the Improving Movement

The French Revolution inspired reform of a liberal rather than a radical nature in Britain through the early decades of the nineteenth century, though it may not have seemed that this was inevitable at the time. Sweeping changes in society, in industry, in technology, and in the nation's economy seemed to be exacerbating old social ills and creating new ones. Poverty and mortality became increasingly intractable problems in growing urban spaces. Parliamentary and democratic reform found peaceful expression in the rise of "political unions" across major towns; but also violent expression, including rioting in several towns, following the House of Lords' thwarting of repealing legislation in October 1831. The 1838 People's Charter embodied a coherent and powerful expression of radical reform, given popular voice in a new unstamped press. But radical Chartism ultimately failed to achieve its aims; and the impetus for change during the early nineteenth century would instead be driven by the idea of *improvement*.

In understanding the intellectual basis for this improving movement it is first necessary to revisit the ideas of Joseph Priestley. Welsh suggests that Priestley's later works, which set out a justification for the inclusion of his own class in a proposed new democratic settlement, had conflated social scientific process with natural rights theory. Priestley's radical logic was subsequently reversed by the next wave of utilitarian liberals from the 1830s (including John Mill and Jeremy Bentham) whose ideas, shaped partly by the dominant field of political economy, would seek to uncouple progress from rights, and to depoliticize the response, aligning change with the atomized notion of individual character, and with the broad principle of social utility (Welch, 2012). It is, then, the intellectual and pragmatic vision of those who identified the era's social problems, who formulated solutions, built the political momentum necessary to enable them, and even (occasionally) personally oversaw reform, that is key to the third improving phase of infographic history.

The Rise of the Survey

From 1820 to 1830, a new enthusiasm for statistics began to emerge across the western world (Porter, 1986). The field of political arithmetic, first conceived by William Petty (1623–1687) in the spirit of applying Baconian method to the functions of government, and embodied in the culture of the "blue book" (Englander & O'Day, 1995), was supplanted by a new era of statistics concerned with reform. It was led by individuals who sought to disrupt what they saw as the chaos of politics and replace it with a new apolitical regime of empirical, observed fact. This new approach would come to be seen as a field of action, as an applied science, providing empirical weight to the new, intellectually dominant spirit of political economy. Following the creation of the General Register Office (GRO) (1837), the first wave of statistical enthusiasm was applied to poverty and to the lived environment of the poor; the progressives who undertook these surveys did so in the legal context of the reforming acts of the early 1830s (Porter, 1986). Desrosières argues that these laws in turn informed an approach to statistical thinking bounded by the principles of commercialism and localism, and of the workhouse over direct subsidy (2002, 167).

Separate from (but at the same time, often socially or professionally connected to) the governments of this era, a network of liberal-minded, reforming individuals hailing from business and professional classes busied themselves in statistical pursuits. Within a few years, in the capital and in the major cities of the industrial north, a series of societies was founded, each bearing the imprint of their own members' interests and concerns.

The founders of the Statistical Society of London (1834, renamed the Royal Statistical Society by Royal Charter in 1887) were mostly Whigs with an interest in political economy; they were certainly not rebels, but establishment reformers (Eyler, 1979). So well-embedded in the political circles of the day were these individuals, it is suggested that they represented a "sub-commission of the Liberal cabinet" (Desrosières, 2002, 174). As a class they sought, for a variety of reasons, to avoid radical social upheaval (Porter, 1986, 32). They were collectively bound by middle-class fears (Englander & O'Day, 1995) about the state of the nation, at a critical time in its history. It has been suggested that the aim of the bulk of their early efforts concerning matters of environment and morality was an attempt to shift focus away from and so to protect the ideology of industrial progress that was central to the concerns (and the prevailing ideology) of the established order (Cullen, 1975). Health matters tended to dominate the concerns of the societies in part because health represented "a fundamental component of the well-being of the working classes" (Eyler, 1979, 29–30); but also because data were comparatively easy to produce. The emergence of these new societies coincided, in the 1840s, with a wider publishing revolution; new communications and printing technologies were making possible both increasingly affordable and improved-quality print publications (Koch, 2005).

The early societies expressed a desire to separate fact from analysis in their work (Eyler, 1979) but they also sought to address real-world problems (Desrosières, 2002). In reality, this was a seeming paradox rather than an actual one; far from being objective in aim and in outcome, these early studies were based on unexamined assumptions, and often represent barely disguised propaganda (Abrams, 1968; Cullen, 1975). A rhetorical attachment to objectivity, it has been suggested, may have helped these authors to challenge dissent, raise awareness, or even to influence influential political figures (Eyler, 1979).

Early Sociological Visualizations

Joseph Fletcher was an eminent figure in this burgeoning statistical movement. He converted his statistical enthusiasm into a lucrative career as a civil servant serving various governmental commissions, holding the position of school inspector for the reforming British and Foreign School Society (Cook & Wainer, 2016). Following an earlier disavowal of thematic mapping (Cook & Wainer, 2016, 87), Fletcher went on to make use of the method in subsequent publications, including *Summary of the Moral Statistics of England and Wales* (1849?), at the personal behest, so he wrote elsewhere, of H. R. H. Prince Albert (Fletcher 1849). In his published statistical work, Fletcher addressed a range of social concerns, particularly those he saw as holding back the poor, from crime, to illegitimacy, to pauperism (Spiegelhalter, 2004).

The choropleth map in figure 3.1, "Improvident Marriages in England and Wales, those of Males under 21 being so designated, 1844" (1849?), among the first population density maps of England (Cook & Wainer, 2016, 88), owes a clear debt to Charles Dupin, and his previous innovations in the use of tints and shaded hachures (Funkhouser, 1937). Fletcher's map is framed in terms of middle-class Victorian morality with improvidence defined according to those among the fixed population who were married while under age twenty-one. These data are expressed by county in England and Wales, on a scale of dark tints (degrees above the national average) to lighter tints (degrees below the national average). The focal point in this chart is the dark

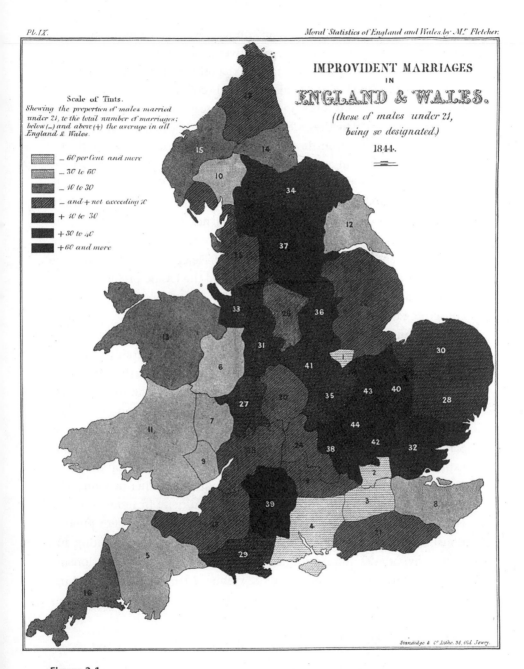

Figure 3.1
"Improvident Marriages in England and Wales, those of Males under 21 being so
designated, 1844," in J. Fletcher, *Summary of the Moral Statistics of England and Wales*
(London: Privately printed, 1849?), plate IX.

stretch down the middle of the map connecting the key sites of industrial England: its coalfields, canals, navigable rivers, and textiles centers.

There is a sense of unambiguous juxtaposition in this map between those areas identified with the new political economy of industrialization (the darkest areas), and those nonindustrial areas around the periphery of the country, defined by the older "moral economy" (such as Cumberland). A well-meaning (if patronizing) progressive, Fletcher identified the fluctuating nature of gainful employment in mining and manufacturing as key drivers of improvidence in these areas. In good times the poor indulged in gambling and travel (*the rail-way mania*); but in bad times, their commitments often proved to be a burden. For Fletcher, the answer to the problems of excessive delinquency and criminality lay in education. Later, as the political and economic outlook stabilized, Fletcher's methods would be applied to what Victorianist Peter Bailey called the leisure problem (Bailey, 1977), an approach that may be seen in Joseph Rowntree's maps (figure 3.2) concerning drunkenness (Kneale 2001, 43).

Maps can be a metaphor for discovery and for dominion. They embody the same principles of logic, order, and discipline that codify empirical scientific processes. Published for an elite, reformist readership, in octavo format, the statistical maps in Fletcher's publication speak to realism, to positivism, and to an implicit faith in man's capacity to reason, and be reasoned with. In journalistic terms, they are a manifestation of what Michael Schudson (1978) calls *naive empiricism*; these maps seem to rhetorically express the facts of Fletcher's wider research and conclusions, on their own terms. That maps do not explicitly reflect reality, but rather may distort it (Monmonier, 2018 [1991]), is not countenanced here. In terms of media environment, the sequence of this map (and others in Fletcher's publications) is no accident; their order implies that the author is generating and testing hypotheses toward informing future policy on the relationship between education and crime (Cook & Wainer, 2016, 88). But his findings didn't necessarily support his conclusions (Ibid.).

Early Public Health Visualizations

Having studied medicine on the continent (and at University College London), William Farr started his career in medical journalism rather than in practice, which in turn helped him cement his reputation as an expert on

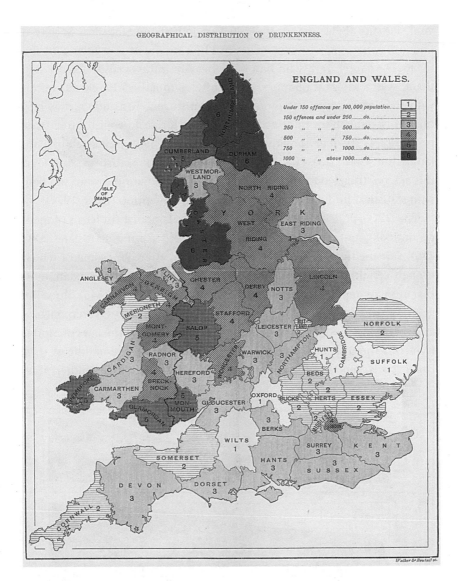

GEOGRAPHICAL DISTRIBUTION OF DRUNKENNESS.

Figure 3.2
"Geographical Distribution of Drunkenness. England and Wales," in J. Rowntree and
A. Sherwell, *The Temperance Problem and Social Reform* (London: Hodder and Stough-
ton, 1899).

vital statistics (Eyler, 1979). In 1839 Farr joined the Statistical Society of London, remaining a core member until his retirement. A regular contributor to *The Lancet*, Farr, who had been heavily influenced by Jeremy Bentham, was a sanitary reformer, combining sympathies for liberal reform with the demeanor of the professional statistician. His outlook was typical of his generation, informed by "high Victorian liberalism: free trade, private property, representative government, self-help, respectability, and family life" (Ibid., 23). Like many of his peers in the statistical societies of this era, he struggled to balance an ideological inclination toward self-help, with statistical findings that mitigated state intervention (Eyler, 1979).

The GRO's policies under Farr were anti-contagionist (in terms of medical outlook), and environmentalist (in terms of reform) (Desrosières 2002, 170). Farr used graphics in his publications for the GRO, some of which, though certainly not innovative, had a striking impact. For example, in his summary report, published in the *Fifth Annual Report* (1843), three line graphs are used to juxtapose mortality rates between Surrey, Liverpool, and an average Metropolis, demonstrating wide variation in the laws of mortality across the distributions (Eyler, 1979) (figure 3.3). The middle of these three charts, representing Liverpool, showed that half the children there

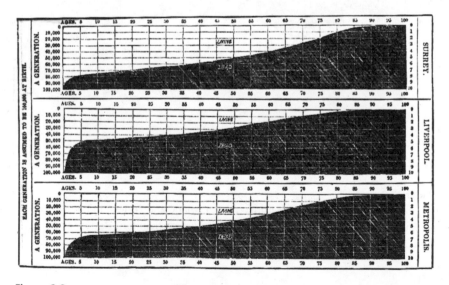

Figure 3.3
W. Farr, *Annual Report of the Registrar-General of Births, Deaths, and Marriages in England and Wales*, fifth report (London: H.M.S.O, 1843), 51.

died before the age of six—challenging previously held convictions of the time that the rapid growth of the city was proof that its environmental climate was healthy (Desrosières, 2002).

Another medical journalist who experimented with data visualization, John Snow, started his trade in London during the mid-1830s, having several papers published in *The Lancet* and the *London Medical Gazette* (Koch, 2005). *On the Mode of Transmission of Cholera* (1849) was published in the same year that Snow published articles about cholera in the *Medical Gazette and Times*. He proposed that the disease was carried in water supplies contaminated with diarrhea and that it passed via human contact and through contact with contaminated matter (Ibid.). In his statistical maps, he used GRO data reports—"Weekly Return of Births and Deaths in London"—to map local incidences of the disease and to compare them with previous outbreaks (Ibid.). The centrality of Snow's findings to medical cartography, geography, and epidemiology are long established in the literature (Vinten-Johansen et al., 2013)—but a question remains as to why he failed to convince his contemporaries of the logical conclusion of his findings. Koch (2005) suggests Snow did not put forward a compelling general theory to substantiate his local findings—he refused to challenge the zymotic theory (the belief that infection was exclusively a consequence of airborne vapors), a theory promoted in the writings, diagrams, and maps of, among others, William Farr.

Through family ties, Florence Nightingale became acquainted with many of the leading medical figures of the day, including Farr (Diamond & Stone, 1981). Nightingale and Farr developed a mutually advantageous relationship based on shared goals, at least initially, in which he provided her with statistical advice, while she provided him with access to her politically influential contacts (Eyler, 1979). When the Crimean War broke out in September 1854, *The Times*'s William Howard Russell sent back a series of damning reports from the front, causing great disquiet among its readers and the wider public (Huxley, 1975), raising awareness of the army's lack of preparedness, and poor medical management of the wounded. War Secretary Sidney Herbert was compelled to act, asking Nightingale to visit the army hospitals, in the Crimea, at government expense (Baly & Matthew, 2004).

Just as Nightingale's presence at Scutari Barracks hospital, Istanbul, had been precipitated by the press, so too her reputation was cultivated, as a consequence of favorable coverage in *The Times* that popularized her

persona as "The Lady with the Lamp" who spent much of her time dot-
ing on convalescing soldiers (Baly & Matthew, 2004). Although taking up
what was primarily an administrative role, Nightingale paid regular vis-
its to the wards, developing a strong affection among the soldiers, leading
to her symbolic association with maternal caring (Ibid.). After the war, in
September 1856 Nightingale was invited to Balmoral to discuss her experiences and thoughts with Queen Victoria and Prince Albert, leading a few
days later to an interview with Lord Panmure, who agreed to the setting
up of a commission to investigate the shortcomings of the army's medical infrastructure. Panmure had not been quite so taken with Nightingale's
arguments as the royal household had been, but nonetheless, in April 1857,
following a combination of influence, royal approval, and threats to go
public with her own findings, the Royal Commission on the Sanitary State
of the Army was established, in circumstances highly favorable to Nightingale's own aims and goals (Ibid.).

Nightingale's *Notes on Matters Affecting the Health, Efficiency, and Hospital
Administration of the British Army* (1858) was damning in its conclusions
about the consequences of the deleterious sanitary conditions in the army
hospitals of the Crimea; deaths from (mostly) preventable disease outnum-
bered deaths on the battlefield (or injuries accrued on the battlefield) by a
factor of seven to one (Huxley, 1975). For Nightingale, disease was a quality
of the human condition, not something that may be isolated and treated in
a particular context. Her discourse represents a composite of medical and
moral terminology typical of the reforming classes of mid-Victorian England, although often framed in rhetorical rather than in instrumental ways,
in appeals to the emotions such as in the tension inherent in dichotomies,
or "morally resonant polarities" (Rosenberg, 1992, 92) of filth and cleanli-
ness, sickness and health.

Nightingale had a natural flair for infographic design, or "statistical aesthetics" (Eyler, 1979, 160), which she sought to popularize in her work.
She was as attuned to the persuasive power of data visualization as she was
in her use of written rhetorical techniques (Brasseur, 2005). She thought
her graphical forms had the power to speak both to the public and to the
Queen (Diamond & Stone, 1981); however, these forms were not discursively addressed to a wide-ranging, reading public—indeed some were only
published, if at all, buried away in the appendixes of several-hundred-page-
long government reports.

In March 1858, Nightingale developed a sophisticated media campaign, in order to maintain the political momentum of the commission's findings and to ensure its recommendations were carried out. She identified a number of editors who could be enlisted in getting her message across, supplying their names to the commissioner (and close personal friend) Sydney Herbert. She focused her efforts on the "heavies"—the quarterlies and reviews (Woodham-Smith, 1950, 310–311), whose editors, according to Aspinall (1945), garnered a higher degree of respect in polite society than any daily newspaper editor of the day could realistically hope for. Nightingale put together individualized "press packs" for each one of these contacts, comprising "outlines, the facts, even the headings for all articles" (Woodham-Smith, 1950, 310); though all were to be published anonymously.

Both Nightingale and Farr were concerned in their statistical investigations with uncovering natural laws about human behavior. If man could discover these laws, he might adapt society accordingly, in an act of progressive improvement (Diamond & Stone, 1981, 75). This deterministic (albeit not fatalistic) principle owes a debt to Adolphe Quetelet (Porter, 1986). In 1831, Quetelet published a map of property crimes in France (Cook & Wainer, 2016), which was used to visually support his argument that, regardless of human agency, crime obeyed natural laws and increased in relation to increasing social inequality (Beirne, 1994). Quetelet's approach was empirical, experiential, and predicated on statistical enquiry. Later, his *Sur l'homme et le développement de ses facultés, ou Essai de physique sociale* (1835), the first work to apply statistical method to social problems, exerted a particularly strong influence over Nightingale (Huxley, 1975). In this book she could perceive the intellectual culmination of a mind she thought keenly attuned, like hers, to the systematic collection of data (Ibid.).

Nightingale was acutely aware of the rhetorical power of infographics, whose impact she framed in associationist terms.[1] She took much the same aesthetic delight in statistics as Priestley took in chronographs; they represented for her a "moral imperative, a religious duty" (Eyler, 1979, 161) toward God's divinely ordained plan. That said, Nightingale's contribution to public health was thoroughly pragmatic (Diamond & Stone, 1981; Gill & Gill, 2005). She was a shrewd publicist and political actor, but her legacy as a popularizer of infographics is not so clearly established. Those texts containing her diagrams were not commonly available in public library catalogues of the day. Passionate statistician though she may have been (Cook,

1913), the Victorian press had, it seems, little to say about Nightingale's innovations. Though read within (and presented to) an esteemed audience, the visualizations of Nightingale, Farr, and Fletcher could hardly be said to have had significant, direct public impact. Nevertheless, they prove that there was an appetite for statistical maps (just) beyond the rarefied circles of early statisticians, reforming politicians, and monarchs.

Nightingale's polar area diagrams (or exploded pie charts) owe a debt to Playfair's innovations, but also, no doubt, to her long-term collaborator William Farr, who experimented with circular charts in his earlier publications. Brasseur (2005) sets out a compelling critique of the visual rhetoric of three of Nightingale's diagrams as they appear in her sixteen-page pamphlet, *A Contribution to the Sanitary History of the British Army* (1859) (a publication that attributes tables and diagrams to Farr). These three lithographic prints, published in a short, highly impactful pamphlet, comprise (according to Brasseur) a coherent (and persuasive) sequential progression in visual rhetoric.[2] The first, titled "Diagrams of the Mortality in the Army in the East" (figure 3.4) sets out monthly mortality rates in the army during the first and second years of the war; the first (larger) diagram concerning mortality rates in the first year draws the viewer's eye to the right, before a dotted line draws attention over to the smaller diagram on the left, concerning the second year's mortality rates. The viewer is invited to juxtapose these mortality rates against a concentric circle in each diagram that expresses the average mortality rate of Manchester, one of the deadliest towns in England at the time.

Inviting the viewer to reflect upon what might be the cause of these discrepancies, the second chart, "Diagram of the Causes of Mortality in the Army in the East" (figure 3.5) demonstrates using color-coordinated polar area diagrams that the majority of fatalities are due to preventable disease (Brasseur, 2005). Having first set out the scale of the problem, and then second, having explored the reasons for the anomaly, Nightingale then sets out in a third diagram (figure 3.6), comprising monthly mortality rates, the outcome of improvements that had been made after March 1855, in Scutari and Kulali army hospitals (Ibid.). Lynn McDonald suggests that this publication was written in response to Andrew Smith's *Medical and Surgical History of the British Army* (1858), which was insufficiently analytical in its conclusions about the scale of the problems faced or about what could be done (2014, 570). Three copies of Nightingale's three charts were framed

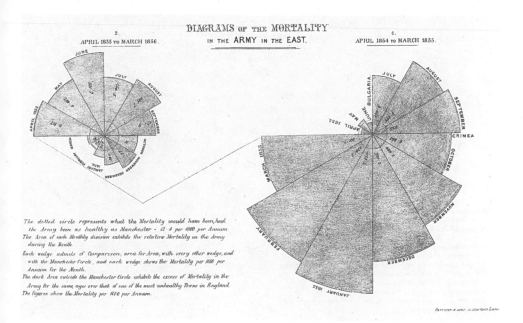

DIAGRAMS OF THE MORTALITY IN THE ARMY IN THE EAST.

2.
APRIL 1855 TO MARCH 1856.

1.
APRIL 1854 TO MARCH 1855.

The dotted circle represents what the Mortality would have been, had the Army been as healthy as Manchester - 12·4 per 1000 per Annum. The Area of each Monthly division exhibits the relative Mortality in the Army during the Month.

Each wedge admits of Comparison, area for Area, with every other wedge, and with the Manchester Circle, and each wedge shews the Mortality per 1000 per Annum for the Month.

The dark Area outside the Manchester Circle exhibits the excess of Mortality in the Army for the same, over that of one of the most unhealthy Towns in England. The figures shew the Mortality per 1000 per Annum.

Figure 3.4

"Diagrams of the Mortality in the Army in the East," in F. Nightingale, *A Contribution to the Sanitary History of the British Army during the Late War with Russia* (London: John W. Parker, 1859). Credit: Wellcome Collection.

into synoptic displays and sent to the War Office, the Horse Guards, and the Army Medical Department, though she never discovered whether or not they had been hung (Woodham-Smith, 1950). Collectively, these three diagrams represent a devastating visual critique of the army's culpability in many needless deaths at the Crimean front.

Nightingale's polar area diagrams play with the metaphorical implications in Playfair's circle diagrams in a highly effective way. These charts challenge the seeming unity, continuity, and coherence of the phenomena they express. The variation in the scaling of each section implies a sense of discontinuity, but also the same spirit of cartographic empiricism that speaks through the wider statistical maps of the nineteenth century. These forms embolden the viewer with a sense of power, authority, and purpose, to cast a scrutinizing lens over the problem of the social ills of the day. But they also represent discontinuity; things clearly cannot simply go on as they are—change is implicit, change is necessary. This pamphlet is a

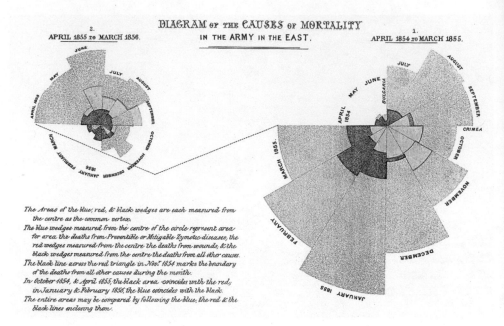

DIAGRAM of the CAUSES of MORTALITY
IN THE ARMY IN THE EAST.

Figure 3.5
"Diagram of the Causes of Mortality in the Army in the East," in F. Nightingale, *A Contribution to the Sanitary History of the British Army during the Late War with Russia* (London: John W. Parker, 1859). Credit: Wellcome Collection.

multimodal medium, combining highly charged interpretive and explanatory discursive elements, into a compelling work of publicity. Nightingale's approach speaks more to technique than to method. She sought to communicate Quetelet's foundational statistics to a nonspecialist, but nonetheless elite audience. Her publications evince an interpretive/explanatory hybridity; her approach (bound up in a media environment that is defined by cool visual forms, and by highly charged language) represents a highly aesthetic multimodal act of publicity.

The Rise of the Modern Journalist

As late as the 1820s, journalism was considered a disreputable trade (Aspinall, 1945). But Henry Mayhew was part of a new generation, who, though involved in "low" forms of journalism, would nevertheless contribute to a shift in the public's view of the craft. Throughout the 1840s, Mayhew

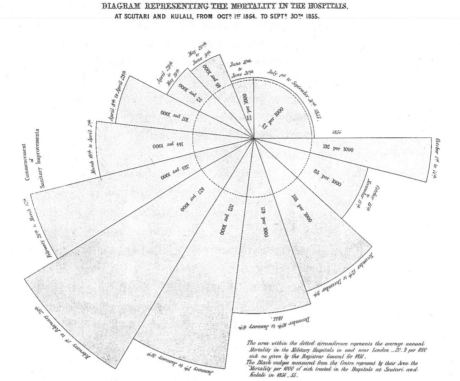

Figure 3.6

"Diagram Representing the Mortality in the Hospitals at Scutari and Kulali, from October 01 1854 to September 30 1855," in F. Nightingale, *A Contribution to the Sanitary History of the British Army during the Late War with Russia* (London: John W. Parker, 1859). Credit: Wellcome Collection.

surveyed London's working class, observing, documenting, and describing their condition. Unlike many of his fellow statistical enthusiasts, Mayhew came to surveys and moral statistics from the position of a popular journalist. His early work included satires and farces, and he was published in some well-known journals, including *Punch*, which it is thought he coedited between 1836 and 1838 (Thompson, 1971). His was a radical journalism inspired by Owenism and Chartism; he was critical of government, aristocracy, and the Church (Ibid., 16).[3] It has been suggested that Mayhew's contribution to the debate on the moral character of the nation was inspired more by the threat of impending personal insolvency, than in any principled stand or objective (Ibid.). Nonetheless, his contribution was significant, and by degrees original; his approach Yeo (1971) suggests, was as much anthropological as it was journalistic. He undertook his research with methodological rigor, and unlike some of his peers, he gave his subjects a means of self-expression.[4]

Mayhew's articles tended to divide opinion; they were considered essential reading among some of his contemporaries (such as William Stanley Jevons, and Reverend Robert Montgomery), but they were dismissed as overly descriptive and insufficiently analytical by others (including Beatrice Webb) (Englander & O'Day, 1995). *The Morning Chronicle* was a middle-class newspaper whose editorial line was chiefly informed by Prime Minister Sir Robert Peel. The newspaper's position was very much in keeping with that of the statisticians of the day, philanthropic and of evangelical spirit. Mayhew's work was idiosyncratically detailed and he was rigorous in his attempts to justify statistical assumptions. But his work also contained a sensationalist component (Thompson, 1971). This created a political tension in the newspaper; which though editorially aligned with the dominant spirit of laissez-faire, had a strong relationship with its Christian Socialist readership (Ibid.).

The subjects of Mayhew's survey were those "according as they will work, they can't work, and they won't work"; and this typology formed the basis of his attempts to define the poor. He wrote eighty-two letters for the *Morning Chronicle*—approximating a million words in total (Englander & O'Day, 1995). However, during the first part of his survey, he parted ways with the newspaper (Maxwell, 1978). *London Labour and the London Poor* (1851) was subsequently published in three volumes; a fourth edition includes a number of statistical maps, published a decade later. These charts seem to represent a simplified reworking of Fletcher's idea (figure 3.7). Mayhew depended on two clerks to collect and analyze the statistics used in producing these choropleths (Englander & O'Day, 1995).

One final reformer, and his visualizations, merit inclusion in this section: Charles Booth, who was born in Liverpool, a city whose comparatively high rate of child mortality had been expressed so compellingly in Farr's early GRO reports. Booth was born to a wealthy, publicly engaged Unitarian family. He was committed to reform—of franchise, of education, and of social and moral conditions (Englander & O'Day, 1995). Booth mapped out poverty in London street by street in his survey, *Life and Labour of the People in*

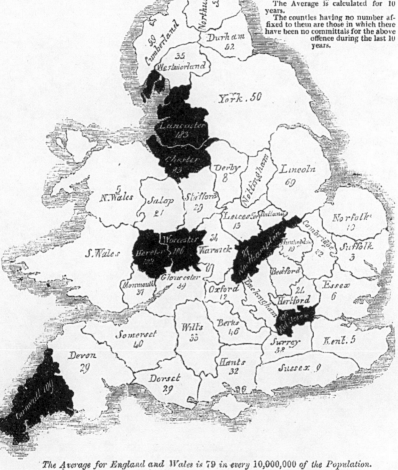

Figure 3.7

"Map Showing the Number of Persons Committed for Keeping Disorderly Houses in Every 10,000,000 of the Population, in the Several Counties of England and Wales," in H. Mayhew, *London Labour and the London Poor*, vol. 4 (London: Woodfall, 1862).

London, between 1886 and 1903 (figure 3.8). An impending sense of social crisis informed his approach, just as disease and social upheaval had inspired the previous generation of social surveyors (Englander & O'Day, 1995). Booth shared with Mayhew a utilitarian duality in outlook, between deserving and undeserving poor. Both were self-taught in statistics and neither were socialist (Ibid.). One significant difference in their work, however, concerned format: Mayhew's was a literary work for a middle-class audience, while Booth's was a highly detailed policy document intended to inform government. At first

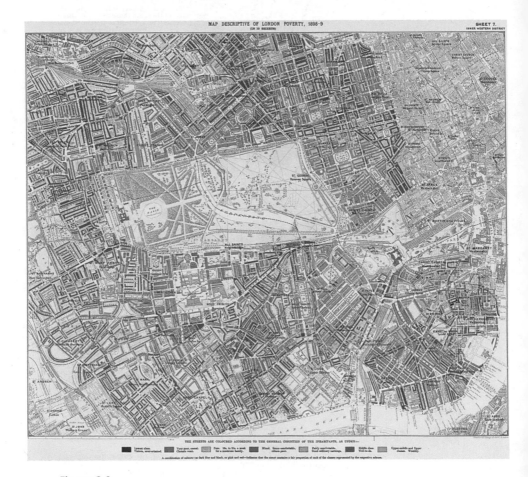

Figure 3.8
C. Booth, "Map Descriptive of London Poverty, 1898–1899," Sheet 7 (Inner Western Central District), in C. Booth, *Life and Labour of the People in London. Final volume, Notes on social influence and conclusion.* (London: Macmillan & Co., 1902).

glance, they may seem to differ, as Raymond Williams observes, in another important way, too, namely: "Booth's deliberate impersonality...belongs to a way of seeing which the new society itself was producing: that *empirical vision of the sociological imagination* [my emphasis]" (1973, 222).

However, while Mayhew's and Booth's work seem to represent very different approaches to the social world, along the traditional interpretive/ explanatory axis, in truth, Mayhew brought both methods together, in the multimodal discourse of *London Labour and the London Poor*.

The defining data visualizations from the 1830s to the 1870s, then, were the work of social reformers. They took the form of thematic maps, other, innovative forms (such as Nightingale's polar area diagrams), and classical charts. They were published in pamphlets, in government reports, and in books, for middle-class audiences. They represent knowledge derived from different fields, from statistical survey work and from politically reforming literary journalism and publicity, contributing by degrees to a new visual print culture. But what was the site of reception for this new literature; and what was the nature of news culture at the time?

Mid-Nineteenth-Century News Culture

Between 1800 and 1850 England's population doubled, from approximately nine million to eighteen million. Industrialism and both commercial and imperial expansion drove employment, and improved prosperity, contributing to a new leisure culture. This growing, increasingly urban population helped to fuel demand for the consumer revolution that had (as we have already seen) emerged during the previous century. A growing middle-class audience spent their new disposable income on new commodities, including newspapers. The abolishment of advertising duty, and of the remaining taxes on knowledge, in 1843 and 1855 respectively, led to a flourishing of respectable daily press (and to the growth of a respectable provincial press too). Mid-century reformers such as James Mill and Thomas Macaulay argued that the liberal "serious" press served an important educational function in wider society (Hampton, 2004).

Between 1817 and 1841, *The Times* established market dominance among its "respectable" peers, under the editorship of Thomas Barnes. *The Times*'s ascent was due to two significant factors: the rising professionalization of its journalism, and the powerful new myth of the Fourth Estate (Conboy,

2004), to which *The Times*'s reporting of the Crimean war had contributed significantly. *The Times*'s audience comprised a powerful elite, and the subject matter it presented to them concerned the public rather than the domestic world. *The Times* published its news in austere, unyielding columns; its copy was written in esoteric language, with little concern about appealing to a wider audience with variegated needs (Bingham, 2004). Little in the way of infographics was published in *The Times* until the 1870s. Respectable and regional newspapers published occasional infographics, though not at sufficient volume during this era to suggest the beginnings of a trend. For example, in 1820, *The Liverpool Mercury* published pie charts outlining the financial state of the British Empire.[5]

Popular Mid-Nineteenth-Century Newspapers

The pamphlets and books carrying this era's infographics were not intended for a mass audience. Can it be meaningfully said, then, that they constitute a form of popular journalism? Hollis, taking an evolutionary approach to the idea of the popular, suggests that the various manifestations of popular journalism may be considered as alternative *species* (1970, vii). Viewed in this way, it is possible to tease out similarities as well as differences in the general evolution of the nineteenth-century newspaper. Conboy (2002) foregrounds the issue of discourse as defining the form of popular journalism, tracing the emergence of news discourse as it speaks to all classes struggling for control of public opinion. He observes a shift from the radical press, to the new commercialism as "a shift from speaking on behalf of the people to building a communal form of address" (Ibid., 68). Taking a discursive approach to understanding the popular requires recognizing the author (and their intentions), the audience (and their requirements), and the forms of address that are used to bridge the communicative gap between the two. The failure of infographics to emerge in early-modern popular newspapers may (of course) be understood with regard to the availability of print technologies. But it must also, as I will now show, be understood within a discursive-historical context.

The Radical Press

In the early nineteenth century, in the aftermath of waves of social unrest caused by the industrialization of the 1780s, and by the Napoleonic wars after the 1790s, a generation of radical, unstamped working-class weekly newspapers emerged, most notable among them being *The Examiner* (1808–1886), *Two-Penny Trash* (1812–1817), and *The Black Dwarf* (1817–1824). Aimed at rousing class consciousness, their publishers had little consideration for commercial concerns (Asquith, 1978). *The Examiner*, prohibitively priced at 6d (half a shilling), was aimed at an intellectual, middle-class radical audience. A range of statistical material is reported on from the earliest years in *The Examiner*, but this was not a newspaper concerned with illustration. William Cobbett's *Two-Penny Trash*, a patriotically radical newspaper written after the manner of a "yeomanly" figure, a mythical dying breed, outfoxed both by an emerging mercantile class, and by the "old corruption" of the aristocracy (Conboy, 2004), published little in the way of statistical material.

Statistics do feature however, in Thomas Wooler's *The Black Dwarf*. A title heavy on satire, if (at times) light on analysis. In the following article, statistics are taken up as a weapon in class struggle:

> In 23 families in England, 4 live without business; 7 by agriculture; and 12 by trade and commerce. Taking the whole of Great Britain, in 25 families, 5 are nobles, gentry, clergy, lawyers, doctors, soldiers, sailors, teachers, schoolmasters, artists, &c.; 4 are handicrafts, trades, smiths, carpenters, masons, tailors, weavers, shoemakers, hatters, shop-keepers, &c.; 7 are employed in manufactures for exporting—total 25. The agricultural population to the commercial, in Middlesex, as 1 to 15; Lancashire as 1 to 5; in Surrey, and the West Riding of Yorkshire, as 1 to 3; in Staffordshire and Warwickshire, as 1 to 2; in Kent they are equal; in Bedfordshire, Cambridgeshire, Essex, Herefordshire, Huntingdonshire and Lincolnshire, Oxfordshire, Rutlandshire, Sussex, Westmoreland and Wales, as 2 to 1; in Caithness, as 4 to 1. The deaths are less in proportion in the agricultural counties, varying from 1 to 72, annually, in Wales; and to 1 in 30 in Middlesex.[6]

This article, in keeping with the radical press more generally, is written in a style that is intended to be read aloud, as "an active, participatory experience" (Barker, 2000, 56), albeit one perhaps not well suited to the infographic. This first wave of radical newspapers then, published before the "era of enthusiasm" for statistics, had little discursive cause to publish statistical diagrams and charts. In addition, the ideological concerns of those middle-class reformers who would go on to make use of them, did not go unnoticed.

The next generation of radical newspapers emerged with a "new rhetoric" of popular journalism, focused on systems, and eschewing the simplistic tropes of the first wave, during the 1830s (Conboy, 2002). The Great Reform Act (1832) had given the middle classes the franchise, but not the working classes; this was an injustice that created demand for a new radical working-class newspaper that was analytical. Typical of this second wave was Hetherington's *Poor Man's Guardian* (1831–1835), which moved away from the airing of individual grievance, toward critical social commentary (Conboy, 2002).

Occasionally, the use of statistics was the subject of comment in the *Poor Man's Guardian*. For example, in 1832, a speech in The Commons delivered by Thomas Spring Rice (who would later serve as President of the Statistical Society of London, between 1845 and 1847), is reduced to farce. Rice, the *Poor Man's Guardian* stated,

> ...made a speech as long as his conscience about Export and Imports, to which the House listened with profound attention....The juggling statistics of Spring Rice were perfectly satisfactory. The honourable House never enquired whether the increase of goods imported into Ireland consisted of luxuries for the rich, or neces-saries for the poor? Oh, no! This would have been a very indiscreet inquiry. What signifies the evidence of a man's five senses compared with the statistics of an econ-omist, who has learned to dispense with every sense, common and un-common? The people are deluded by demagogues and repealers; and all they require to make them know their prosperity is, to renounce the evidence of eyes, ears, back, and belly, and for the future trust only to Whig sincerity and Whig statistics.[7]

Here "Whig statistics" are abstracted, and associated with the idea of the state, going back to the German etymological roots of the term; but the *Poor Man's Guardian* is communicating with an audience that was not involved in running the state. Here statistics represent just another form of "useful knowledge"—propaganda employed by the improving classes, in order to further their own class interests. For commercial as much as for ideological reasons, the Society for the Diffusion of Useful Knowledge (SDUK) (and its popular journals and reference works, and not least the concept of "useful knowledge" that they sought to propagate), were often a subject of satire in the *Poor Man's Guardian*.

The Chartist *Northern Star* (1837–1852), which in keeping with others among the cheap popular press incorporated woodcuts and steel-engraved portraits, featured a number of articles about official statistics, both social and economic (though it does not appear to have published infograph-ics). Joshua Hobson, the newspaper's publisher between 1838 and 1844, also published a radical alternative to the "useful knowledge" found in the *Penny Cyclopedia*, namely the *Poor Man's Companion* (1843). This was a statistical encyclopedia for the working classes, presenting an alternative, radical form of "useful knowledge." It included easy-to-grasp criticisms of free trade and industrialism, as well as a radical calendar, biographies, and information on nutrition (Cordery, 1988). Comparative data in the book were presented in tabular format, rather than in chart form. Some among the improving classes might well have been relieved at this. In 1841, W. R. Wilde, father of Oscar Wilde, was appointed as medical adviser and compiler of the table of deaths for the census report of Ireland. His contribution to the official census report into mortality included a Sanitary Map of Dublin (Robinson, 1982), the publication of which was greeted with profound concern in improving circles. *The Athenaeum* voiced alarm that this color-coordinated map communicated to anyone who laid eyes on it how neatly stratified and separated the classes (arranged by color) had become in the city, and as such, this chart was perceived as representing a threat to social relations.[8] They need not have feared, however, because statistical mapping did not fit within the discursive style of the radical print culture of the period. The *Athenaeum* response speaks more to a moral panic created in middle-class minds, primed by associationism, utilitarianism, and naive empiricism. Later radical titles, such as *Reynold's News* (1850–1967), published many stories on statistics, not least concerning the vital statistics in Booth's surveys. Yet data in visual form do not appear. Radical politics would not find expression in infographic form until the advent of Isotype, almost a hundred years after the *Poor Man's Guardian* was at its peak.

The Illustrated Weeklies

The reduction of the Stamp Act (1836) had paved the way for a new generation of illustrated weeklies during the 1840s. The Conservative-leaning *Illustrated London News* (1842–2003), one of the leading titles in this genre, rarely reported on statistics during the nineteenth century; however, the *Illustrated Weekly News* ran occasional moral panic stories, particularly in relation to crime. One of the most sensational of these illustrated titles, the *Illustrated Police News* scandalized its readership with graphical representations of poverty-fueled violence (Rintoul, 2015). Not all the *Illustrated Police News* reporting, however, was sensational; proceedings of the Statistical Society of London were occasionally reported on—and indeed, in one such example, printed June 1, 1867, the paper urged caution with regard to the idea that the criminal classes were on the increase in England.[9] Fox

(1977) compares the kinds of illustration presented in the *Illustrated London News*, with the illustrations used in contemporaneous government reports on poverty of the time, such as the *Report of the Children's Employment Commission* (1942). By contrast with these official documents, the illustrated press used their illustrations to depict the public lives of the elite; there were no images depicting vulgar poverty. The sense of escapism in these illustrated newspapers, at least before the final quarter of the century, left little discursive space for data visualizations.

The Popular Sundays

The News of the World (1843–2011), *Lloyd's Illustrated London Newspaper* (1842), and *Reynolds' Weekly Newspaper* (1850) were the first commercially successful newspapers in Britain. These Sunday weeklies based their success on a particular discursive style; their content was reader-centered (covering hobbies and letters); their tone mixed elements of sensation, radicalism, and nationalism and they expressed themselves in traditional formats such as narratives (stories) and illustration (Conboy, 2002). For proprietors such as George Reynolds, the new commercial environment represented a conundrum, of how to remain true to the Chartist creed while making money. The answer seemed to be to serve large audiences a miscellany of news, information, and entertainment (Conboy, 2004). Maps were published in this title from time to time, as were the proceedings of statistical society meetings. However, as commercial success made these radical titles increasingly appealing to advertisers, so too the volume and range of political news coverage tended to diminish, step by step, with an increase in human interest material (Conboy, 2004). Ultimately *Reynolds' Weekly Newspaper* and the other working-class popular Sunday weeklies waned as they fell into the same knock-about tropes that dogged the old radical press. While popular as a form of class-conscious satire, these papers failed to build upon their earlier radical political analyses, and so failed to find answers to the ensuing problems that late-modern Britain was experiencing (Berridge, 1978). For a range of reasons, infographics did not represent a good discursive "fit" in the popular press of this period. How, and to what extent, then, might the public have come into contact with the pamphlets and books in which these forms were published?

Literacy

From the publication of the first newspapers, the illiterate were able to participate in literate culture by means of news that was written to be read
aloud, a practice that lasted until the turn of the twentieth century (Lee,
1976). This culture exposed far larger numbers to the news than may be
accounted for in a simple tally of sales (Ibid.). Barker (2000) has argued,
cautiously, that a reading public for newspapers became both more numerous and more diverse between the end of the seventeenth century and the
middle of the nineteenth century. By this time, with the decline of the
radical and Chartist press, the working classes mostly bought cheap Sunday newspapers, while most daily newspapers were bought by the middle
classes (Lee, 1976). This state of affairs would continue until the turn of
the century, a testament, it is argued, to the failings of the Fourth Estate,
before the rise of the New Journalism, which would really engage with its
audience (Ibid.).

Print Culture in the Library Network

Nineteenth-century libraries, including local proprietary libraries, were
important in the cultural life of some towns, but they were not widely open
to the public. (Altick, 1957). Some early nineteenth-century libraries were
(in theory) open to select members of the working classes via trades bodies such as the Mechanical Institutes of the 1820s and 1830s, but in reality
they were dominated by the middle classes (Ibid.). A number of free public
libraries emerged in large towns and cities following the Public Libraries Act
1850, but in some large cities and towns, the levy to establish public libraries was voted down. By the late 1850s, Altick suggests that active borrow-
ers in public libraries comprised between 3 percent and 8 percent of their
local populations (Ibid., 236). Lee suggested that this lack of popularity may
have something to do with residual conflicts, and resentments, in a society
formed and codified around class (Ibid., 36).

Recourse to library holdings of the day may help us discern the likelihood that the reading public (or rather, certain segments of it) had come
into contact with infographics. The following is not presented as a defi-
nitional analysis, nor is it significant regarding holdings within the wider

national public (or private) library network(s). It is offered merely as a simple diagnostic snapshot.

Priestley's *A New Chart of History* (1769b) was held in various private library collections:

- The Liverpool Library at the Lyceum (1814)
- The Liverpool Athenaeum Library (1820)
- The Subscription Library at Kingston upon Hull (1822)
- The Royal Institution (1857)

In addition, his charts and Playfair's *Statistical Breviary* were all held at the private Subscription Library, in Kingston Upon Hull (1822).

Playfair's *The Commercial and Political Atlas* was held by at least two public libraries:

- Rochdale Free Public Library (1873)
- Norwich Public Library (1847)

His *An Inquiry into the Causes* was catalogued in the Liverpool Free Public Library (1872).

Key texts containing infographics by nineteenth-century authors, including Dupin, Guerry, Scrope, Quetelet, Fletcher, Snow, Nightingale, Martineau, Mayhew, and Booth[10] were available in the collections of various private libraries, but none were held in any of the following public library collections:

- Manchester Free library (Reference) (1864)
- Glasgow Public Library (1865)
- Nottingham Free Library (1868)
- Birmingham Free Libraries (Reference) (1869)
- Liverpool free public library (1872)

Lastly, Henry Mayhew's *London Labour and the London Poor* was held in the following public library collections:

- Nottingham Free Library (1868)
- Birmingham Free Libraries (Reference) (1869)
- Stirling's and Glasgow Library (1888)

In summary, those publications that pioneered the use of infographics were available in the collections of private libraries of the nineteenth century, but considerably less so in public libraries, excepting the works of Priestley and Mayhew. A wider and more reliable study may well be possible using items both digitized and in the public domain (one employing historic circulation figures too), but that is beyond the scope of this book. Neither this period's newspapers nor its library network can be considered democratizing sites of reception for the infographic in any meaningful sense. In concluding, I will now consider a third possible field, that of popular education. What likelihood is there that infographics were encountered in the nineteenth-century classroom?

Nineteenth-Century Literacy and Education

Amid the Jacobin panic of the 1790s, the improving classes had sought to propagate literacy (in the form of reading, if not writing) among the poor. It was argued, with more than a hint of hubris, that elementary education would help to quell revolt and sedition, because the working classes, once equipped with a basic education, would see the reasonableness (and utility) of useful knowledge (Altick, 1957). Following in this vein, the mid-nineteenth-century generation of social improvers' approach to education would be similar; their goal would be to establish a means of social control, not education as an end in itself. Education should promote prized qualities, such as self-reliance (Hampton, 2004). Where the academies of Priestley's day had brought "useful knowledge" into the curriculum alongside classical subjects, Jeremy Bentham's ideas, applied through the private school network that emerged during the late eighteenth and early nineteenth centuries, would displace some classical subject matter altogether.

The first infant schools in Britain seem to have originated at Robert Owen's New Lanark, following the establishment of the Institute for the Formation of Character, in 1816 (Hilton & Shefrin, 2009). Owen was involved in the Manchester Literary and Philosophical Society during his time there; and would likely have been aware of the dissenting tradition and its innovation in education. Owen's pedagogy involved discussion and debate, on the same model advocated by Pestalozzi, and lessons involved various visual aids (Donnachie, 2014). His methods were applied to the teaching of poor children and they represent a teaching philosophy as such (Hilton & Shefrin, 2009). Owen's son, Robert Dale Owen, described the process involved in the teaching of history at New Lanark; seven maps, presented along the

"Stream of Time" principle, were used (Donnachie & Hewitt, 1993). One educator at New Lanark, Catherine Whitwell, even developed her own visual teaching aids including history time-charts, and other visual materials (Donnachie, 2014).

As the nineteenth century progressed, a new market in visual teaching paraphernalia emerged, and with it a number of organizations serving to harness the interests of middle-class and elite parents in their children's education. It is clear from a rudimentary scan through Shefrin's (2009a) inventory of the Darton's educational aids that a number of timelines for children were published; however, it is less clear whether infant schools for the poor could afford them, or find teachers with the aptitude and skills necessary to make best use of them (Shefrin, 2009b). In theory, then, and in practice, visual teaching aids became increasingly popular into the nineteenth century.

A robust theorization of the use of visual aids in education emerged in Jeremy Bentham's *Chrestomathia* (1843). This work was influenced, in part, by Priestley's educational philosophy—and we know too, from personal correspondence with his brother Samuel, in 1779, that Bentham was directly aware of Priestley's timelines (Bentham, 2017 [1777–1780], 212). Bentham's own *Panopticon* (Bentham, 1791), theoretical plans for a reforming, as much as a punitive, institution, and the Monitorial system of education, developed by Andrew Bell and Joseph Lancaster, were two other key organizing influences on his educational philosophy. In this work Bentham provides designs for a built environment, an administration, and a pedagogy for the education of middle- and upper-middle class children, with an emphasis on scientific, "useful" knowledge (Taylor, 1982). The use of visual aids in the form of wall charts and diagrams are recommended; and these are included within Bentham's educational legacy (Crimmins, 2017). However, as is in keeping with what may be considered his wider educational philosophy (Itzkin, 1978), *Chrestomathia* was far from radical. On the contrary, Bentham's approach was institutionalizing; it preserved the status quo, despite the disavowal of arbitrary cruelty and hegemonic practices, and the opening up of opportunities to the lower and middle classes (Crimmins, 2017).

The Monitorial system, in keeping with Priestley's approach, focused on the idea of manufacturing useful members of society. Similarly, Bentham sought to maximize efficiency in his educational factory, to which end visual educational aids fulfilled a particular codified purpose. As Itzkin explains: "The 'Tabular Exhibition' principle (which) laid down the rule that the walls of the classroom be covered with instructive materials so that if a child finished his work and had, for a few moments, nothing to do, he still could not fail to learn" (quoted in Itzkin, 1978, 311). This approach offers little more than an application of a classical theory of "drill" learning to a new syllabus. From Priestley's original idea it is therefore possible to trace the historic bifurcation of uses of synoptic charts in British education into two pedagogies: one radical and based on critical-reflexivity (as exemplified at Owen's New Lanark), and the other conservative, and based on rote-learning (as set out in *Chrestomathia*).

Literacy and the Penny Press

As we have seen, from the publication of the first newspapers, the illiterate were able to participate in literate culture by means of news that was written to be read aloud, a practice that lasted until the turn of the twentieth century (Lee, 1976). This culture exposed far larger numbers to the news than may be accounted for in a simple tally of sales (Ibid.). Barker has argued, cautiously, that a reading public for newspapers became both more numerous and more diverse between the end of the seventeenth century and the mid-nineteenth century (2000, 63). By this time, with the decline of the radical and Chartist press, the working classes mostly bought cheap Sunday newspapers while most daily newspapers were bought by the middle classes (Lee, 1976). This state of affairs would continue until the turn of the century, a testament, it is argued, to the failings of the Fourth Estate, before the rise of the New Journalism, which would really engage with its audience (Ibid.).

Asquith (1978) suggests that by 1851 around two-thirds of men and over half of all women were literate. Using writing as a measure of literacy (albeit the use of marks in marriage registers is methodologically fraught with problems), Lee suggests that around 61 percent of the population was literate in 1850, increasing to 76 percent by 1868 and then 87 percent by 1888 (Ibid., 33). Secondary education would only become a free "right" during the middle of the twentieth century; throughout the nineteenth century, education was largely a privilege with length of schooling determined largely by life prospects (Altick, 1957). In this context, an education of sorts, it was often thought, might alternatively be acquired from the Penny Press.

The Society for the Diffusion of Useful Knowledge's illustrated *Penny Magazine* (1832–1845) served, it has been suggested, as a substitute for early schooling for many (Mainardi, 2017). SDUK's "useful knowledge" papers represented sober, serious-minded journalism comprising information and wholesome entertainment. They could generate high sales, though they did not sell well among the working classes (Asquith, 1978). Charles Knight was a key figure in the improving literature movement of the 1830–1850 period (Altick, 1957). A moderate and tolerant improver, he sought "to make the printed page the agent of peace, justice and pleasure" (Ibid., 281). His *Penny Magazine* (1832–1845) and *Penny Cyclopedia* (1828–1843) both contributed significantly to the education of his audiences (Altick, 1957). Knight's publications were lightly illustrated with useful material: diagrams, musical notation, maps, and tables, in keeping with other "improving" titles of the time, such as (the later) Chambers' fortnightly *Information for the People*. The SDUK published many topographical maps too, often in two-volume sets—Knight was central in making these maps affordable (Cain, 1994).[11] Publishing illustrations in the *Penny Cyclopedia,* of which Knight bore the full costs (Altick, 1957) could be very expensive,[12] and indeed, no statistical diagrams appear to have been published in Knight's newspapers. However, this may be due as much to happenstance as to editorial policy. Having attended a conference at the Statistical Section of the British Association for the Advancement of Science at Bristol, in 1836, Charles Dupin presented a choropleth map of crime rates in England relative to the density of its population.[13] Correspondence after the event between Dupin and George Richardson Porter indicates that the former had failed to find time, while in England, to arrange a meeting with Charles Knight about having the map published (Princeton University Library, n.d.).

The Whip of the Word

The society that was emerging during the nineteenth century was based to a great extent on the written word; as historian J. F. C. Harrison argued, "the *whip of the word* was a most powerful agent in shaping the new society" (quoted in Hampton, 2004, 54). This culture was shaped, by extension, by the influences of evangelism and utilitarianism, and by a striking moral ambivalence in both. In evangelism, on the one hand, reading was considered essential for achieving spiritual enlightenment; a general principle

that led to the flourishing of a large market in Biblical and moralizing literature (Altick, 1957). On the other hand, reading was thought to be capable
of delivering men into the hands of the devil: in particular imaginative, or
"light" literature (Ibid.). In utilitarianism, the valorizing of an efficient and
goals-oriented model of acquiring useful knowledge served to stimulate the
culture of reading. However, an interest in trivia, or the pursuit of knowledge on its own terms was frowned upon. Evangelism and utilitarianism,
though they differed by degrees (and were even in some respects, antitheti-
cal to one other) were unified in their sense of the importance of serious-
ness in reading habits (Ibid.).

The Education and Habits of Nineteenth-Century Journalists

As we have seen, the era of enthusiasm for statistics was driven by a collective of self-taught, improvement-motivated enthusiasts; but throughout
the nineteenth century, the nation's elite educational institutions were
not concerned with statistics. In all her dealings with politicians, Florence
Nightingale was mindful that though MPs had access to statistics, very few
of them seemed to make use of this information. The education these individuals had received, largely at Oxford University, didn't involve tuition in
statistical methods. In 1874 Nightingale sought (unsuccessfully) through personal friend Benjamin Jowett (Master of Balliol College) to establish a Department of Applied Statistics at the University (Flood, Rice, & Wilson, 2011).

The second half of the nineteenth century was a period of improving
standards and professionalization in Britain's press. By the 1860s, university
graduates were increasingly going into journalism (Brown, 1985), and by the
1870s, graduates of Oxford University in particular were in key positions at
The Times, the *Daily Telegraph*, and the *Manchester Guardian* (Brown, 1985).
Parliamentary correspondents of this era were predominantly university
educated too (Aspinall, 1945). Of the seven figures who edited *The Times*,
from its founding in 1785 to 1912, all but one (John Walter) were Oxbridge-
educated. Of the five figures who edited the *Daily Telegraph*, from its founding in 1855 to 1964, four were university educated (two at Oxford). Of the
six figures who edited the *Manchester Guardian* from 1821 to 1944, three had
studied at Oxford. One professional training manual at the turn of the century even suggested that Oxford was one of the best "journalism schools"
in the country (Hampton, 2005, 144). All of these factors contributed to

an increasing professional divide between "reporter" and "journalist" in the newspaper industry. The respectable press, particularly those featuring prominent nonconformists in their ranks, such as W. T. Stead at the *Pall Mall Gazette*, or C. P. Scott at the *Manchester Guardian*, seemed ambivalent (at best) about illustrations, an attitude that appears to have left a long-lasting legacy on press culture.[14] Serious nineteenth-century journalism was founded on the centrality of the word. This ideal would later form the basis, in the early twentieth-century newsroom, of a struggle for control, where professional tribes of "word people" and "picture people" would vie to decide what material form news would take (Lowrey, 2002).

The shift from production to consumption during the nineteenth century led to the emergence of the consumer as a transformative and powerful figure in society and to a boom in new consumer goods (Crowley & Heyer, 2013), chief among them the new woodcut illustrated newspapers. But this new commercial visual culture came under attack from a cast of critics. For example, John Stuart Mill's liberal tome of progress "Civilization" (1836) set out a theorization of civilization whereby intelligence was transmitted top-down through Britain's class system; but this process, he observed pessimistically, was being stunted by the new "arts for attracting public attention" (9). Laurel Brake sets out further reactions, both positive and negative, to this new visual journalism in two directions—one concerning illustration, the other concerning journalism. With regard to the former, exponents of these visual forms sought to identify them with the high culture of fine art, in constructing the idea of using cheap prints to transmit culture, in top-down fashion. However, critics such as John Ruskin disparaged the cheap process involved. Moreover, William Wordsworth dismissed the new illustrated papers in 1846 as representing a "dumb Art" for the intellectually challenged (quoted in Brake & Demoor, 2009, 5). The sheer volume of illustrations produced in the popular press from the 1840s onward, and their capacity to lure the reader into altering their consumer behavior, was clearly something approaching what we might recognize today as a moral panic, among the Victorian elite.

Conclusion

Statistical infographics in the publishing culture of the first three quarters of the nineteenth century constitute an improving phase in the history of data visualization. They embody the new methodological spirit of

Quetelet's foundational statistics, and were a tool of progressive reform. Ideologically speaking, they continued in the same abstract and discursively nonrevolutionary vein as the earliest forms of data visualization. They also share the same vibrant, visually impactful aesthetic of the works of Playfair and Priestley. They were the product of a busy, improving class of individuals, and were bound up in a world in which the knowledge bases in social sciences, journalism, and publicity had not yet become professionally separated and distinct, as they are today (Anderson, 2018). These infographics were created in order to better raise awareness about, and so address by means of moderate reforms, the most serious social ills of the era while remaining true to the spirits of individualism, progress, Christian self-help, and personal (class) self-interest.

In form, many of them took after Playfair's charts, but thematic maps and some innovative, highly impactful forms (such as Nightingale's polar area diagrams) also emerged. They were published in pamphlets, specialist journals, official reports, monographs, and reference works, and were largely read by the serious-minded middle classes. They appeared very occasionally in the serious press of the day, but not the popular press. Infographics were not published for the masses, and neither were they widely available via the public library network. There was little discursive space for infographics in the popular presses of this era. Resistance to the idea of data visualization, whether stated or implied, arose in various spheres in nineteenth-century society. Among radicals, they were tarnished by association with the middle-class improvers. Among the popular press they lacked the lure of escapism to find a foothold. Even within the respectable press, a culture of elitism, of classicism (based on a suspicion of the visual and to a residual classicism in the education of senior journalists and editors) contributed to resistance against them. In the one category of nineteenth-century newspaper that seems, ideologically and epistemologically, most clearly suited to the data visualization, the useful knowledge purveying *Penny Press*, they did not appear, albeit this may be due to historical happenstance. Although infographics emerged within the ethos of utilitarianism among the improving class, a counteracting tension existed that sought to halt, and marginalize the visual; the equally powerful (evangelical and utilitarian) predilection toward "the whip of the word" represented a powerful brake upon the full flourishing of visual culture, in the journalism of the day.

In education we can trace the emergence of a contemporary phenomenon in news infographics to this period. Priestley intended his chronograph visualizations to further critical engagement, but also to serve as an aide-mémoire in the process of learning about history. Later, in Bentham's hands, the benefits of educational wall charts would become associated exclusively with a means of rote learning. This represents the beginnings of the affective resentment that media organizations are aware of today, in how their audiences engage with (or either struggle to, or refuse to engage with) particular graphical forms in the news.

4 "Wider Still and Wider, Shall Thy Bounds Be Set": Empire and Anxiety at the Fin de Siècle

In this chapter I will set out the origins of the fourth, commercial phase in the history of news infographics. This period, spanning roughly the last two decades of the nineteenth century and the first three decades of the twentieth, occurred within the independent stage of UK journalism history. It was made possible by those illustrated newspapers of the 1840s that had both been incrementally increasing public exposure to, and reacting to public expectations about, visual culture. During this period the infographic is first published in truly "mass" media formats; albeit not in any consistent way. Occasional infographics, informed by different traditions and epistemologies, assume a varied (and visually inconsistent) discursive form by the end of this period, with the rise of modern news design. This era also saw the rise of an important component of news infographics—the pictogram. This new form made abstract notions and ideas concrete and recognizable (and memorable), serving as a crucial bridge between cultures of popular media and mass media. They appear at a moment of democratization in print culture that in turn speaks to a wider democratization in society. This generation of infographics embodies the increasing discursive weight of the commodity in popular culture.

This chapter is organized into three sections. First, I consider the emergence of the pictogram in British publishing, against the backdrop of rising nationalistic sentiment that was a defining feature of late nineteenth-century Europe. The pictogram emerges at around the same time that a tradition emerged of infographics being used to spread imperial propaganda in the Habsburg Empire. Its sites of production were popular general reference works. The main site of resistance to this new form is a residual scientism emanating from the international statistical community of the day. Second,

I consider the infographic as it developed within the popular newspapers of this era, particularly in the illustrated press and the new national daily press. These infographics draw upon both classical and pictographic traditions. They were produced in the context of the New Journalism with its appeal to the "attractiveness of orchestrated variety" (Conboy, 2002, 75) as much as by new technologies and new ideals in an increasingly professionalized journalism. I trace the principle site of resistance to these infographics to a powerful, modern, conservative cultural elitism, most clearly articulated in the thinking of Matthew Arnold. I present a case study based on local newspapers (situated in Dundee), to trace the emergence of the early news infographic, in the context of a widespread market consolidation driven both by the decline of local newspapers and by the rise of national dailies, which takes me back to the theme I begin this chapter with—nationalism. In the third section of this chapter, I consider those pragmatic sites of reception that informed the era's cultures of reading, literacy, and education—in particular, the Efficiency Movement in the UK, textbook culture, and new theories of education (deriving in part from John Dewey's pragmatism). I set out a theoretical critique of some select visualizations of this period in the contexts in which they arise throughout this chapter.

The Rise of Nationalism

In the aftermath of the French Revolution, a conservative conception of nationalism, defined by monarchy, faith, and a top-down social structure, had been mobilized successfully against more liberal alternatives (Breuilly, 2011); Priestley discovered this to his own personal cost at the hands of a "Church-and-King" mob, in 1791 (Schofield, 1997). Through the nineteenth century, essentialist ideas of the nation and subsequently, the intertwining of nation, race, and biology all became defining features of political discourse, as nationalism shifted from the edge to the center of British politics. This was a consequence, Breuilly suggests, of three factors: global (and imperial) politics; shifting intellectual currents (including the publication of *On the Origin of Species* in 1859); and last but not least, fast-paced industrialization and urbanization (Breuilly, 2011).

A new and commercially popular statistical visualization emerged in the final quarter of the nineteenth century that in many ways embodied the era's rising tide of nationalist sentiment: the pictogram. Prominent among its proponents was Irish journalist Michael George Mulhall. Born in Ireland in 1836, Mulhall spent time at the Irish College in Rome before moving at age twenty-four to join his brother in Buenos Aires, where, in 1861, he published the first English-language South American newspaper—the *Buenos Ayres Standard* (Kimball, 2016). On retiring from journalism, he moved to England but the communicative imperative of his previous profession left a lingering imprint on his approach to statistics. He published a number of statistical works featuring scaled pictograms, the best known of which was *Mulhall's Dictionary of Statistics* (1892 [1886]) (figure 4.1). The first three editions of this title were expensive, but they were also relatively commercially successful (Ibid.). Mulhall employed both conventional, abstract graphical forms, as well as self-designed pictograms. A series of illustrious figures offered simple testimonies for the dictionary: journalists writing for the "serious" press (including *The Times* and the *Economist*) as well as high-profile names from the fields of economics and statistics. Mulhall was no outsider in the world of statistics; he became a Fellow of the Statistical Society of London in 1880 (Ibid.). But he was not without his critics. Alfred de Foville savaged Mulhall's patriotic bias, but also what he perceived to be his crude, visual commodification of statistics. De Foville satirized his choice of book titles, and the consistent "look" of them, on the shelf (1887). Mulhall's pictograms were, de Foville complained, patronizingly reductive; his grasp of statistics was naive at best and grossly misleading at worst. His talents were said to lie in the arrangement of his *mise en scène*, rather than in the serious business of statistics (De Foville, 1887, 707–708). His works were dismissed as representing little more than a victory of form over content—no more than, to borrow Arnold's critique of the New Journalism, *feather-brained* statistics, or further, to apply this logic to the new era of pictograms, a *New Infographics*. Elsewhere, some of Mulhall's works inspired attacks on his character and his judgment. The Conservative *St James's Gazette* suggested that some of his statistics, concerned with Ireland's demographics after the Great Famine, were as much the product of "muddle headed prejudice" as they were of poor statistical method.[1]

In contrast, the *Pall Mall Gazette*, in its review of *Mulhall's Dictionary of Statistics* celebrated both its entertaining and instructive nature.[2] They were, perhaps unsurprisingly, well received among the illustrated press,[3] and were valued among the day's political elite too. Hansard contains six direct references to *Mulhall's Dictionary of Statistics* between 1888 and 1932,

PLATE IX.

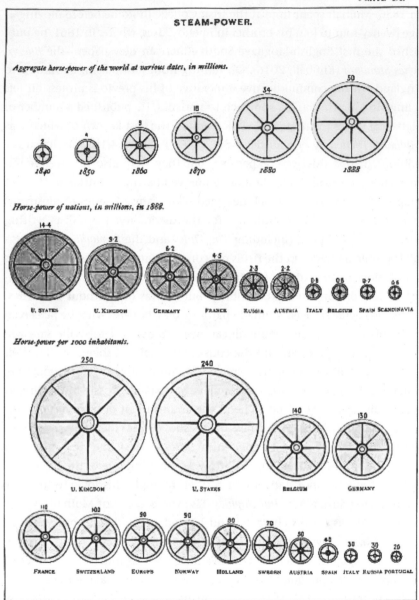

Figure 4.1
M. G. Mulhall, *Mulhall's Dictionary of Statistics,* third edition (London: G. Routledge and Sons, 1892 [1886]), plate IX.

parliamentary contributions made by a combination of free-trade conservatives and socially progressive liberals. Among proponents of the New Journalism, as much as those coming to terms with the acceleration of the pace of news in the serious press, some among Britain's fin de siècle elite found virtue in Mulhall's democratizing statistics. However, he could not shake off (some) legitimate criticisms that his work lacked precision. In his study of these long-forgotten infographics, Kimball (2016) stresses the importance of the theme of global-comparative nationalism, which Turner (2014) argues was among the most important ideas in late nineteenth-century thought. In Mulhall's infographics, Kimball observes an *imperial gaze*, and a particular influence: naturalistic synoptic diagrams that appeared in atlases during the mid-nineteenth century (Kimball, 2016, 143). Clearly, Americans were already exposed to statistical visualizations via the national statistical atlases which, since the first edition in 1870, had included conventional, abstract graphic forms. Soon after Mulhall, a culture of pictographic propaganda began to emerge, in central Europe.

Pictograms in the Struggle for European Nationhood

A generation of late nineteenth-century European intellectuals, Turner (2014) argues, turned their back on Christian universalism and embraced the spirit of nationalism. Hostile to pan-national political arrangements, these nationalists employed a variety of ideological rhetorics (many highly visual) to authenticate the ethnic, as opposed to the dynastic, roots of nationhood and popular identity (Ibid., 156). But just as printing culture and in particular newspapers became essential in shaping a new common nationalist ideology in the late nineteenth century, allowing, in Benedict Anderson's terms, an *imagined community* to speak to and about themselves, in a fixed and more permanent language, so too was the Habsburg Empire developing a highly visual counter-propaganda. A new "universal" language of pictorial statistics was being developed, one that would serve to validate and to sustain the empire and its dynastic basis among its disparate, multilingual peoples. Dalbello and Spoerri (2006) explore the cultural encoding of these pictograms published in almanacs in the late nineteenth- and early twentieth-century Habsburg Empire (figure 4.2). These pictograms represent what, on Habermas's terms, may be described as manipulative

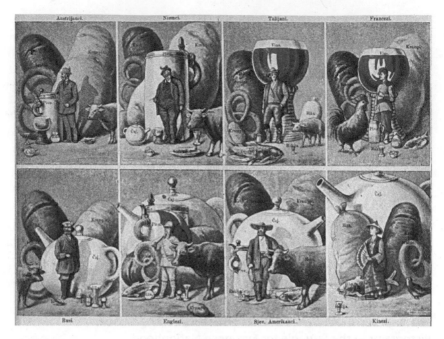

Figure 4.2
"What Different Nations Eat and Drink," *Šareni svjetski koledar* [Colourful world
calander] (Winterberg, Bohemia: J. Steinbrener, 1901), 81–82.

publicity—presented as democratizing statistics, but published at the behest
of an undemocratic imperial order. Naturalistic rather than abstract in
their composition, they represent a form of visual propaganda rhetorically
primed to convince the empire's urban population of the benefits of empire
(Dalbello & Spoerri, 2006, 89). They speak, in turn, to the impending crisis in
identity and in cultural organization that would engulf turn-of-the-century
Europe and culminate in the outbreak of World War I.

The publication of the 1909 *Šareni svjetski koledar* almanac was ordained
by Emperor and King Franz Josef I personally. The publisher, J. Steinbrener,
generally was more involved in Catholic devotional literature (Dalbello,
2002). Given the local peculiarities of high rural illiteracy, and the range
of languages spoken within the empire, sophisticated visual images were
developed to communicate with the masses and were even distributed
among army conscripts (Ibid.). Almanacs like these were published in several European languages and distributed across a global network of Catholic institutions, with warehouses in cities from Milan to Dublin and the

New World, as early as 1874 (Ibid.). The Habsburg almanacs represent an attempt by the fading powers of European monarchy to negotiate a new political settlement with its diverse subjects.

In Louis XVI's purported enthusiasm for Playfair's charts, as in Queen Victoria and Prince Albert's influence upon Florence Nightingale's and Joseph Fletcher's respective works, we see the emergence of abstract visualizations as a means of brokering power between traditional authority and an increasingly powerful middle class. However, the pictograms of the Habsburg almanacs, aimed as they were at a mass, literate reading public (Ibid.), were instead a representational visual form that allowed the powerful (including the commercially powerful) to communicate directly with the masses.

New Commodities, New Technologies, New Journalists, New Journalism

A single material symbol came to define the second half of the nineteenth century better than any other, according to Thomas Richards: the *commodity*, presented within a "system of advertised spectacle" (1991, 8), whether found on display at one of the World's Fairs or advertised in Alfred Harmsworth's *Daily Mail*. A number of changes occurred together toward the end of the nineteenth century concerning the look of, audience expectations about, and the political economy and methods involved in the era's newspapers (Campbell, 2003). There was nothing new in any of these elements in isolation; however; the novelty in this New Journalism resided in their assembly, and in their dressing up to appeal to wide-ranging audiences (Conboy, 2004).

This process of assembly was made possible by innovations in newspaper production. The period between 1800 and 1870 saw rapid advances in the efficiency, and in the capabilities, of newspaper printing. These changes in turn led to the emergence of illustrations during the 1870s, by means of zincography (the mechanical engraving of line blocks), which rendered wood-engraving obsolete (Hutt, 1973). New techniques in paper production led to cheaper and more easily available sources, which in turn led to the emergence of a range of illustrated dailies (Ibid.). Prior to 1890, few daily newspapers used illustrations, but by the 1920s photographic halftones were ubiquitous (London, 1930), prompting debate on their merits. On the one hand, Walter Benjamin (Benjamin & Underwood, 2008 [1935]) was famously critical of this photomechanical reproduction, seeing it as contributing to a wider culture of inauthenticity in art, and by extension, modern life. But on the other hand, the use of line and halftone blocks in 1890s newspaper production led to an increased vitality in the culture of popular news and current affairs. They offered significant time saving in production, and a vastly improved visual character in the era's newspapers (London, 1930), which in turn contributed meaningfully to the press's mythical status as the Fourth Estate (Ibid.).[4]

The old, pre-lithography illustrations had been time consuming to prepare, and relatively labor intensive, but the technology necessary to produce inexpensive and timely news illustrations became increasingly available by the turn of the century, contributing to the emergence of a new visual appeal in the period's newspapers (Monmonier, 1986). A shift toward embracing the visual in UK newsrooms, even among editors of the respectable press, it has been suggested, began to take hold during this time (Anonymous, 1897). Indeed, a number of well-resourced newspapers, including the leading provincial newspapers of the day, had their own photozincography press, as well as in-house arts and engraving professionals to service them (Ibid.).

After World War I, British newspapers started to draw design influence not only from British Sunday weeklies and pictorial newspapers, but also from American tabloids (Hutt, 1973). By the 1920s, the *Daily Mirror* and the *Daily Express* were both seen as having fallen under the spell of the American tabloids, in terms of their use of photography (Baynes, 1971). Twentieth-century modes of transport and communication were helping to speed the process of news production too: car, train, airplane, and not least electrical, wireless transmission helped both to increase the speed of the news cycle, and to extend it to a twenty-four-hour schedule (London, 1930). The 1930s witnessed a key moment of change in typographical culture in Anglo-American newsrooms. Greater freedom over the design of the newspaper emerged, and the idea of "make-up" (i.e., that the presentation of the layout contributes to the way readers understand the news) began to incorporate illustrations. In the culture of the newsroom, journalists began to involve themselves more and more in the production of news (Hutt, 1973). The Victorian news illustrator (or "artist-reporter"), employed in a newspaper art department, had been characterized as a "fireman," dispatched to wherever the action was, in order to send back rough drafts that were polished back in the newsroom (Waterhouse, 1974, 51). But by the end of the century, the newsroom was becoming less anarchic, and more professional, with more specialization and carefully defined and differentiated roles (Brown, 1985). By the 1930s, Bromley suggests, "news processors," that is, people whose knowledge of the news came primarily from producing it, rather than from writing it, had started to rise to the top of the leading newspapers, all based in London's Fleet Street. Key figures in this cultural shift included Harry Guy Bartholomew who had worked at the *Daily Mirror*'s art department during the 1930s, and Arthur Christiansen, long-standing editor of the *Daily Express* (Bromley, 1997). The 1930s was the era in which the journalist wrested control of layout and design of the newspaper from the printer (Collins, 1975).

The Weekly Periodical Press

Chalaby (1998) suggests that central to the New Journalism was a new generation of press barons, including George Newnes, Arthur Pearson, Alfred Harmsworth (Lord Northcliffe), Harold Harmsworth (Lord Rothermere), and William Berry (Lord Camrose), who brought insights concerning the reading habits of popular magazine audiences into popular news publishing. The great commercial success of these ventures led to what Tulloch describes as "a process of magazinization of the press" (2000, 139–140), channeling appeals to different audiences and interests via new sections and inserts and moving toward a personalized end product, on the basis of a proprietor's speculative hunch. This period saw the general absorption of infographics from reference works, almanacs, annuals, weeklies, and other popular miscellaneous tracts, in a process that might be called the *almanacization* of newspapers. For example, some early abstract infographic forms were published in pieces by J. Brand for *Pearson's Magazine* (1896) and by John Holt Schooling for *Windsor Magazine* (1897), and for *Pearson's* (1897–1898). At the turn of the century, *Pearson's Magazine* even engaged in a relatively short-lived experiment, involving photorealistic pictorial statistics (Hedley, 2018).

The Illustrated Weeklies

As we saw in the last chapter, throughout the nineteenth century there was little discursive space for infographics in the *Illustrated London News*. These would start appearing during the early 1900s, in the form of highly polished war pictograms, embodying the same imperial gaze redolent of Mulhall's earlier reference works.[5]

The *Illustrated London News* was a Conservative-leaning newspaper, and its news values reflected middle-class leisure habits and material culture. The paper was unambiguously Royalist in tone and elitist in its (frequent) use of portraiture; the working class were always presented as crowds, while other ethnicities and races were visually *othered*. The infographics in this publication are sympathetic with a far wider scope of process diagrams, on everything from the production of bread, to proposals for the raising of the German battlecruiser SMS *Hindenburg*, which had been scuttled in Scapa Flow. The paper increased in cost to 9d (three-quarters of a shilling) in 1918; the *Daily Mirror* at the time cost a penny. The illustrated weeklies could not compete with dailies on hard news, so they pursued wider-lens stories, without exploring their politics in any significant way. These full-page infographics had to compete with the increasing use of (and scale of) photography and indeed, with full-page display advertisements (starting in 1911).

W. B. Robinson, responsible for a number of *Illustrated London News* infographics from the 1910s to the early 1920s, specialized in complex, synoptic dashboards incorporating a range of infographic styles. For example, dashboards of bar graphs and circle diagrams are used to explore the postwar increase in wages among various trades, as they are perceived to fuel inflation (figure 4.3); national expenditure, borrowing, and revenues, in wartime (figure 4.4); postwar reparations;[6] and cuts in national expenditure, following the *Geddes Report*.[7] Some of Robinson's dashboards employ a combination of abstract and pictographic chart forms; for example, concerning the naval spending by the world's leading powers (figure 4.5). His synoptic diagrams employ a mix of classical and commercial graphical forms; providing a lively discursive space within which the reader is encouraged to compare and contrast a range of data.

The focal point in figure 4.5 is the gold sovereign in the center-right-hand side of the page, representing Britain's naval spending for 1913. This infographic scape takes up a full page (10″ x 14″). It represents a self-contained story, on its own terms, with some brief explanatory text at the bottom. This particular infographic, though visually lavish, has rather limited interpretive potential. The news topic is framed (and metaphorically expressed) in terms of a familiar, "common sense" economic conceit: the government's budget as household budget. Though seemingly intuitive, this is not a metaphor that bears much scrutiny, not least as governments may borrow at much lower rates than households, and in addition, they may print their

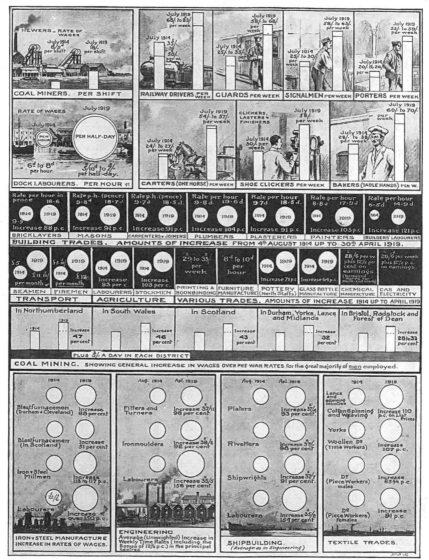

Figure 4.3

"A Prime Cause of High Prices: Huge Increases in Wages," in the *Illustrated London News*, August 16, 1919, 5.

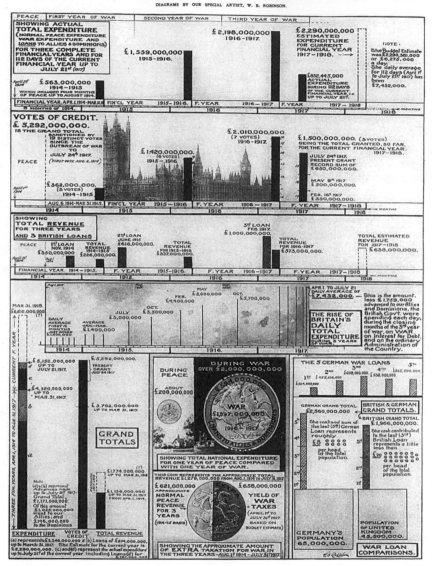

Figure 4.4

"'It will not be want of money…': Britain's Huge Effort," in the *Illustrated London News*, August 11, 1917, 16.

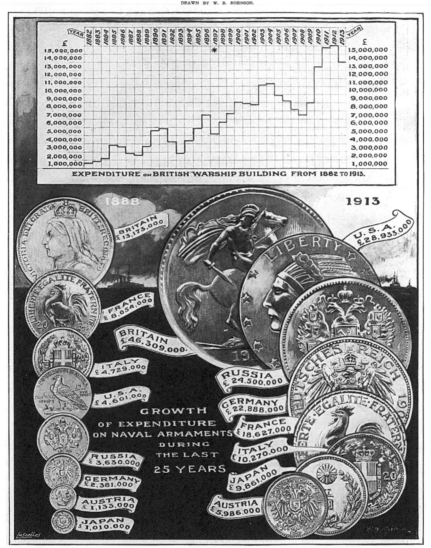

Figure 4.5

"The Navel expenditure of the Powers: Ever-Growing Figures," in the *Illustrated London News*, February 7, 1914, 5.

own money. Alternatively, this visualization may be interpreted within the "nation as family" political metaphor that, according to Lakoff, unites both right-leaning and left-leaning political worldviews as constitutive of, on one hand, the *strict father*, and on the other, the *nurturing parent* (Lakoff, 2002).

In 1924 a number of statistical illustrations were published without byline, exploring that year's general election; an election map[8] and separately, an extraordinary river diagram, showing the fluctuations in British voting patterns since 1832 (figure 4.6). This chart employs a very literal interpretation of Priestley's river metaphor, "The Winding Stream of Party Politics: Elections Since 1832." Framed in a politically partisan manner (Labour and Liberal electoral victories are overcast, while the sun shines on Conservative victories), the river of parliamentary government wends its way, leftward and rightward, back into the hills of history, in the distance, to its source, the Great Reform Act of 1832. Though it may be argued that Charles Minard's ribbon chart method could have been employed to portray the volume of voters more accurately here, any true attempt at accuracy (in terms, for example, of the "turn" in the "river" relative to parliamentary representation over time), would necessarily be confounded by the uneven nature of events; no newspaper-scale metaphor of this kind could sustain the sharp turn from Gladstone's majority of 86 in 1885, to Lord Salisbury' majority of 114 a year later. Nevertheless, it is an ingenious (and highly impactful) form for exploring the complexities of British politics. The focal point is the present day, and the significant (and triumphant) rightward meander instantiated by the 1924 Conservative Party landslide. Methodologically speaking, interpretation beyond the bare numbers is not really possible here; and there is neither sense of "why" nor "how" about the data expressed in the chart. The defining feature of this era of the *Illustrated London News'* infographics is that a wide range of abstract and referential graphical forms were used, sometimes misleadingly, and sometimes in a highly impactful way, in synoptic displays that present data as a commodity.

The Sphere's (1900–1964) early infographics came more in the form of direct marketing than as news stories; for example, unscaled picture-adorned bars were used to promote an offer to readers of a *Daily Mail* reprint of *The Britannica*.[9] This combination of infographics and reader subscription offers, which took many different forms during this time, from insurance to pianos (Conboy, 2004), is indicative of how the New Journalism incorporated other popular media into its message and of how newspapers became a mediating

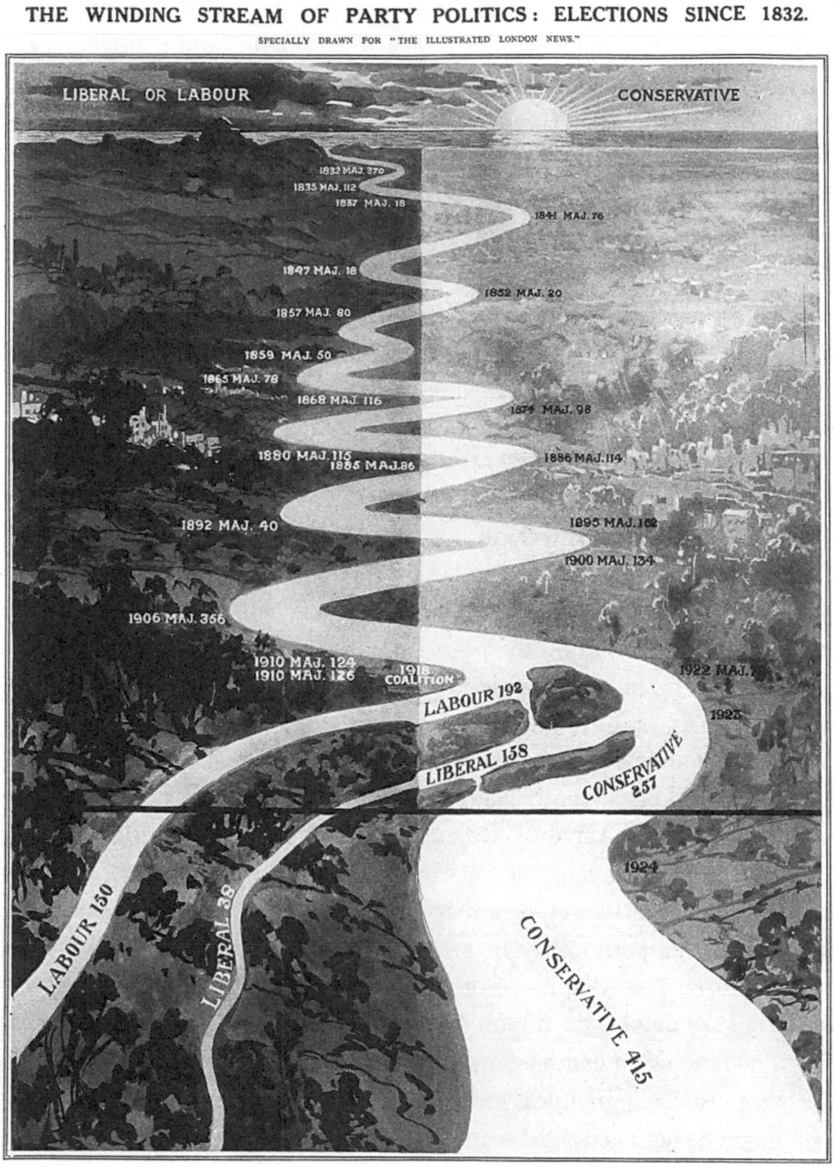

Figure 4.6

"The Winding Stream of Party Politics: Elections Since 1832," in the *Illustrated London News*, November 8, 1924, 12.

commodity while serving, at the same time, to drive commercial culture (Conboy, 2002). The *imperial gaze* is again in evidence and pictograms are used to compare nations and their industries: from a pictogram showing the relative size of British and German naval fleets, at five discrete points in time, since 1867;[10] to one that depicts the relative size of various elite countries' armies[11] drawn by Gordon Ross, a Scottish illustrator who worked in the art department of the *San Francisco Chronicle*. Classical and scientific graphical forms were generally reserved for more sensitive, or serious topics. Standard bar charts are used to show current mortality rates by age range[12] and shipping losses relative to Allied shipbuilding efforts.[13] Line graphs were used to plot the decreasing number of submarines sunk during the war;[14] and comparative mortality rates for 1921–1922 and 1922–1923.[15] A scatter plot is used to show the average rainfall over thirty years; the chart is "decorated" with a frame (figure 4.7). In figure 4.8, a multipanel chart is used to plot the hours of sunshine, heat, rainfall and cloud cover for "The Awesome Summer of 1911."

"The Loss of the 'Titanic.' The Results Analysed and Shown in a Special 'Sphere" Diagram'" (figure 4.9) is a hand-drawn bar chart with variables stacked at arbitrary points to fit on the page. It is used to represent the numbers of those who survived and those who perished. The eye is drawn to the large block at the foot of the display, representing the total number of dead among passengers of all classes and crew. The living and the dead are juxtaposed in binary terms: in black (symbolizing death) and white. This display, like those in the *Illustrated London News*, is both euphemistic and sanitizing. The lack of scaling adds to the sense of collective fate. Everyone is visually organized into two existential classes, regardless of which class they came from. There is no sense of proportionality, no sense of significance, no sense of risk—just bald numbers. The wide range of graphical forms published in *The Sphere* would tend to support the notion that this newspaper was designed to appeal to a wide-ranging audience, comprising those readers comfortable with relatively sophisticated graphical forms (such as scatter plots), as well as those who might be better engaged with data-rich abstract forms, and pictograms.

The *Daily Mail*

Jingoism was key to the Daily Mail's early editorial strategy and it proved to be a highly successful one, leading the title to its first million sales by 1900 (Wiener, 1988). Marketed as *The Busy Man's Daily Journal* and presented

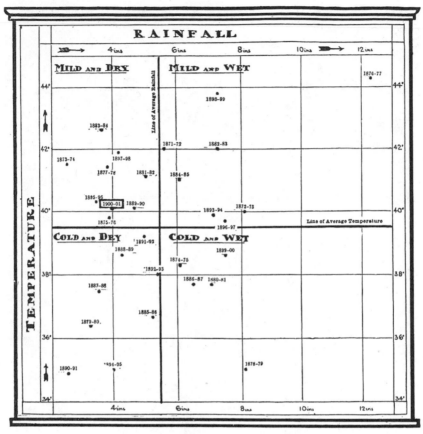

THE DRYNESS OF LAST WINTER COMPARED WITH THE PAST THIRTY WINTERS

It will be noticed that the general tendency of the stream of dots is from the left-hand bottom corner towards the right-hand top corner. That is, with a rising temperature on the scale shown at the side the general tendency is towards a rise in the rainfall gauge shown at the head of the diagra

Figure 4.7

"The Dryness of Last Winter Compared With the Past Thirty Winters," *The Sphere*, July 20, 1901, 18.

as a cut-price bargain, its discursive tone was respectful, but lighter than the quality press (Conboy, 2004). In an act of cross-promotion, imperial gaze-style pictograms were republished as a taster for the *Daily Mail Yearbook* (1901) in the lead-up to Christmas.[16] Others in this style appeared during this time concerning, for example, the relative tax rates of different countries.[17] A particularly impactful manifestation of this style, in the form of war propaganda, was offered by the *Daily Mail* to its readers as the *World Map of War and Commerce* wall poster (circa 1917) (figure 4.10). This

THE AWESOME SUMMER OF 1911 ANALYSED

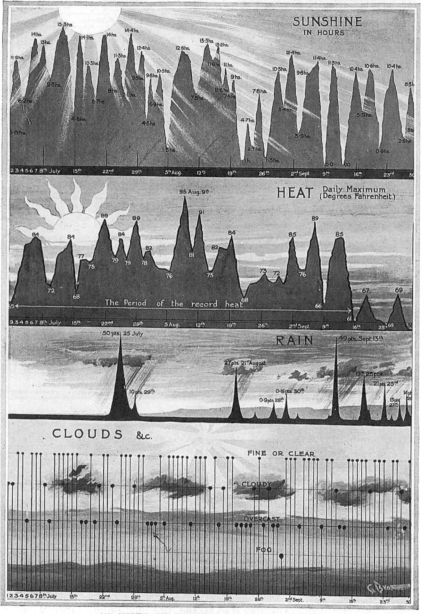

660 HOURS OF SUNSHINE IN THREE MONTHS

Figure 4.8
"The Awesome Summer of 1911 Analysed," *The Sphere*, November 4, 1911, 16.

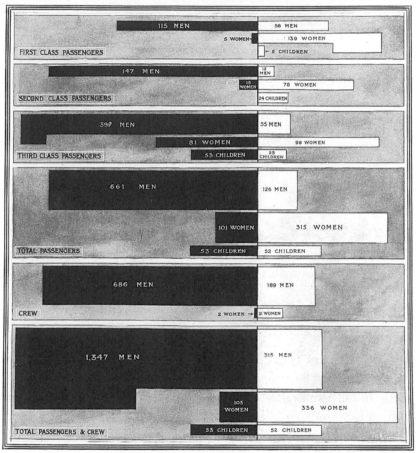

Figure 4.9

"The Loss of the 'Titanic.' The Results Analysed and Shown in a Special 'Sphere' Diagram," *The Sphere*, May 4, 1912, 19.

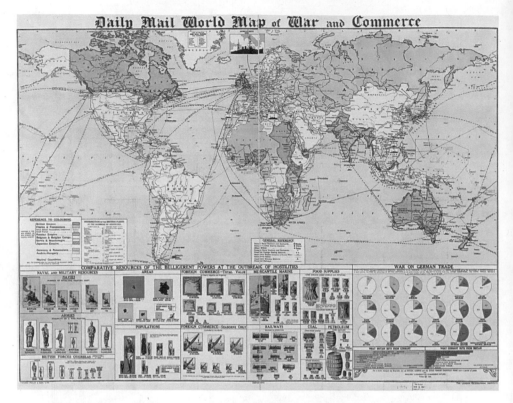

Figure 4.10
Daily Mail, World Map of War and Commerce (London: London Geographical Institute, ca. 1917).

synoptic wall chart, 48 cm x 97 cm, published by the London Geographical Institute, employs a range of conventional statistical diagrams and pictograms, in order to explore the United Kingdom's geopolitical and naval position in wartime. Interactive election charts[18] began to appear, and a decade later, psephological "swing" charts, carrying by-election results, were published. Weather infographics started to emerge during the interwar period.[19]

Further factors in Northcliffe's commercial success with the *Daily Mail* were his insistence on the extension of coverage into new areas of human interest and, not least, his attempts to woo female readers (Bingham, 2004). Indeed, the discursive form of those charts published in sections of the newspaper that were predominantly aimed at female readers seems to reflect different expectations of their readers than do charts published in sections aimed more at men (such as financial and business news). For example, following what is reported as a spate of suicides, and headlined simply "Worry," one feature piece explores the association of depression with various stressful professions. A series of male portraits carry the emotional impact of the story and two charts are used to help narrate it. Both appropriate the serious visual rhetoric of the classical infographic. The first is a hand-drawn line graph, comprising grid lines (albeit irregular ones) and legend, which is used to communicate pseudo-scientific claims (figure 4.11). The eye is drawn along the "line of equanimity" grid line; the trend line rises above this point at key meal times. This graph draws upon two conceptual metaphors. In its display, it expresses the orientational metaphor "Up is good, down is bad," while in its interpretation, it employs the journey metaphor: the (best) way to a man's heart is through his stomach. The media environment within which this graph, and its related feature appear is the *Daily Magazine*; a highly gendered segment within the newspaper, featuring a summary of a recent Royal Agricultural Society show and an article about a portrait painter who paints in the dark.[20] Alternatively, some classical graphs were published on financial matters during the 1930s in a manner that seems to assume both that the (presumed male) reader would understand them, and that the contemporary reader has a grasp of basic standards in the form. For example, a stand-alone chart is used to show the comparative benefits of protectionist trade policies internationally, country by country; underneath it says simply "The above diagram speaks for

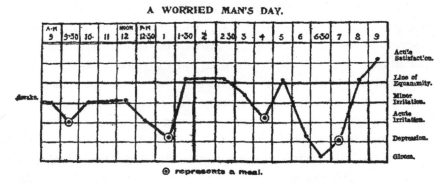

Figure 4.11
"A Worried Man's Day" in *Daily Mail*, June 27, 1905, 9.

itself."[21] Similarly, a complicated synoptic chart is used to compare the rates of manufacture of motor cars in the United Kingdom and the United States, and the associated rise in consumption of oil and rubber.[22]

The *Daily Mirror*

Alfred Harmsworth launched the *Daily Mirror* under the editorship of Mary Howarth in 1903, as a "high class" paper for "ladies," featuring an all-female production staff. Less than six months later, deemed a financial disaster, (he lost £100,000), its staff were promptly jettisoned and the newspaper was turned into an illustrated daily (Bingham, 2004). The *Daily Mirror* made use of the new rotary printing that had enabled the launch of the *Daily Graphic* just over a decade earlier. A newspaper aimed at both sexes, it made pioneering use of photography, although it was routinely condescended to as "low brow" by contemporaries (Bingham & Conboy, 2015). The earliest infographics featuring in the *Daily Mirror* were less concerned with news stories and with lifestyle, and had more to do with advertising and promotions. The first front-page graph supported a page-length mea culpa authored by Harmsworth, where he publicly washed his hands of the old title *Daily Mirror* (while faithfully flattering its audience) before heralding the arrival of its vastly improved replacement: the *Daily Illustrated Mirror*. A pair of circulation graphs were published, perhaps similar to the ones Harmsworth had used to convince a skeptical John Alfred Spender about the success of his anti-Boer editorial in the *Daily Mail* (Engel, 1996). The scaling on the second graph is skewed (starting at 70,000) in such a way that it rhetorically supports a rise that is (visually) equivalent to the preceding, much greater decline (figure 4.12). The mode of these early charts is discursively "serious" albeit conventions were eschewed in a context where not all readers might recognize them, in order to inject a touch of drama. This kind of aggressive self-promotion was an early American influence on the New Journalism (Bingham & Conboy, 2015); and the same method was employed again in subsequent years, to cement (and authorize) the newspaper's later financial success.[23]

From the 1910s onward, infographics in the *Daily Mirror* occasionally appeared in advertisements used to sell food, nutrition and health, and lifestyle products. The earliest seem to have been aimed at the newspaper's housewife readership such as those for Glaxo baby formula;[24] the Glaxo

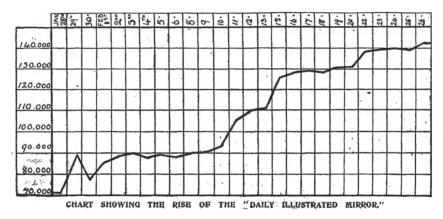

CHART SHOWING THE RISE OF THE "DAILY ILLUSTRATED MIRROR."

Figure 4.12
Circulation chart, *Daily Illustrated Mirror*, February 27, 1904, 1. Reproduced by permission of Mary Evans Picture Library Ltd.

brand more broadly;[25] Allenbury's baby formula;[26] and Brito Margarine.[27] Some were highly misleading. By the mid-1920s these graphs were increasingly published either for their outward visual rhetoric, such as for Sanatogen's food supplement;[28] or to promote "junk science," such as for Cadbury's chocolate or for Ovaltine.[29]

At the start of the 1930s, the *Daily Mirror* was struggling, its circulation down to 700,000 (Williams, 2009). This changed under the editorial direction of former production journalist Guy Bartholomew. Bartholomew borrowed the visual style of the New York tabloids and started pursuing a working-class readership. It was an effective strategy; the *Daily Mirror's* circulation rose to 1.5 million by 1939 (Jeffery & McClelland, 1987). National dailies all changed their layout and typography during this period, reflecting the rise of other visual media, in particular cinema and display advertising. Despite the *Daily Mirror's* early travails, the 1930s saw significant growth in national newspaper sales, a culmination, Conboy (2002) argues, of the spirit of the New Journalism—and of the appeal of a popular visual miscellany. A new working-class audience had survived the Great Depression, and was experiencing a subsequent (modest) rise in incomes (Brown, 1985). As newspaper prices were lowered in an increasingly competitive market, and as audiences increased, new marketing strategies were put to work to maximize circulations (O'Malley, 1997). Advertising became increasingly data driven, rather than hunch driven during this decade and also increasingly measurable, with the establishment of the Bureau of Circulations in 1931. Newspapers had to become more competitive and more efficient in their use of resources in pursuit of these new returns (LeMahieu, 1988). In turn Fleet Street had to reinvent itself for a more visually literate audience (Ibid.).

That advertisers should be prominent in exploiting the earliest uses of infographics in newspapers should come as no great surprise given how important the psychological power of the visual was in the thinking (and writing) of leading publicists and advertisers of the era.[30] A decline in hard news coverage during the interwar period (Seaton & Curran, 2003 [1981]), coincided with advertisers beginning to seriously court the working classes. Display advertising, largely aimed at women, contributed significantly to the increasingly visual nature of the new news culture (Bingham, 2004). During this period, infographics also begin to emerge in the *Daily Mirror* in lifestyle features, concerned with seasonal colds, the tourist economy, and accidents.[31] These charts combined abstract and pictorial elements, and gave the appearance of having been produced in-house. On the one hand, the serious business of calling readers' attention to commodities for sale was usually expressed in the visual rhetoric of scientific forms (albeit, they often failed to conform to best practice). On the other hand, graphs that were used to "tell" stories tended to contain "fun" additions (such as pictorial or illustrated elements).

Bartholomew's changes led to a significant boost in the *Daily Mirror*'s sales. He had perfected a formula that combined working-class discourse with anti-establishment rebellion, as exemplified in William Connor's "Cassandra" column, and in the accompanying work of "people's cartoonist" Phillip Zec (Williams, 2009, 182). In February 1941, the *Daily Mirror* ran an editorial on a common theme at the time; it was critical of the then-chancellor's lack of control over the war budget, anticipating what this might mean for readers in the event of Keynesian "inflation expectations." Zec's line graph serves to illustrate the editorial point in humorous terms; the ever-upward line forms the shape of a hand holding a sword that is seen to be "putting paid to Adolf!" (figure 4.13).

With the New Journalism we see the commodification of infographics in the press. Whereas in the past they served the purpose of furthering an economic argument, or of supporting social reform, the visual display of data was now being used in order to sell newspapers and other commodities. The approach was indiscriminate; sometimes charts were accurate,

Figure 4.13
Phillip Zec, "Putting Paid to Adolf!," *Daily Mirror*, February 6, 1941, 5. Reproduced by permission of Reach plc.

sometimes they were not, sometimes they misled in a way that stoked the narrative, sometimes all that was communicated was the discursive "feel" of the graphical form without any content at all. That it is possible for a newspaper to contain all of these features, which seem to contradict each other, speaks to the diversity of its mass audience. These, for all their faults, were the first truly popular infographics.

The Crisis of Classicism

A new generation of public intellectuals, Matthew Arnold chief among them, soon became concerned, and then increasingly disillusioned with the modern, popular press. The New Journalism and its blend of tried and trusted populist methods and formats was threatening to supplant the *golden age* of public discourse; moral, political, and intellectual life stood, it was feared, on the precipice. W. T. Stead's *The Maiden Tribute of Modern Babylon* is said to have inspired Matthew Arnold's famous denunciation of the sensational New Journalism as "feather-brained."[32] Campbell (2003) suggests that the rise of a popular liberalism under Gladstone and the project of Irish Home Rule, both entwined with the "symbolic power" of the newly enfranchised masses, led to a form of populism that was denounced by Arnold, as it was celebrated by Stead. In addition, a resurgent popular liberalism, Alan Lee (1976) suggests, contributed to the reduction in political reporting during the 1870s and 1880s albeit the New Journalism, in its pursuit of wide-ranging audiences, had been a significant factor too. Lee suggests that this period experienced a gradual shift away from the serious scrutiny of politics and toward the trivial display of interesting things (Ibid.). In this new environment, the sign and publicity became increasingly important. Visual phenomena were increasingly used to mediate public opinion in a process defined as "the power of symbolic production" (Campbell, 2003, 22). In this new environment, power attached itself to "the symbolic form of language itself" (Ibid., 35). It would take the rise of the New Journalism, and the perceived decline of the liberal Fourth Estate, discursively formed by James Mill, Jeremy Bentham, and others around the idea of providing the masses with informal education, to (finally) bring infographics to the masses.

Conboy observes that Arnold's critique of the New Journalism as "feather-brained" was not just culturally elitist, but also gendered, given the influence of the "feminized" illustrated periodicals on its form. The "feminization" of the press was perceived to have started at the *Daily Illustrated Mirror*, according to later critics such as Holbrook Jackson (whose criticisms were contemporaneous with Bartholomew's newly imported tabloid designs). Graphics and layout were seen as having finally trumped text, leading, so critics thought, to the shortening of audiences' already dwindling attention spans—a direct consequence of the increasing influence of women readers and women's concerns (LeMahieu, 1988). While the expression of the New Journalism in the *Daily Mail* had been characterized as more concerned with the manufacture (i.e., reporting, angling, and staging) of news events, rather than with its presentation on the page (Bingham & Conboy, 2015), we have already seen (particularly in relation to the *Daily*

Mail) that some illustrative elements were considered a useful visual rhetoric to communicate with audiences. Moreover, the use of misleading methods in infographic advertisements aimed primarily at women supports the notion that Northcliffe sought to exploit them as a reading market, rather than empower them with useful (in this case accurate, or even meaningful) information (Conboy, 2004).

The Serious Press

As we saw in chapter 3, *The Times* started publishing weather maps in 1875 (Monmonier, 1986), an accomplishment made possible by the still relatively new process of photoengraving; which in turn enabled several daily newspapers to do the same and (after a fashion) to accompany them with barometric and weather charts. By 1900, *The Times* was publishing non-weather maps with relative frequency (although not daily), and it was publishing occasional line graphs concerning commodity prices.[33] That said, Monmonier has suggested that infographics were resisted at *The Times* and other respectable newspapers due to the long-standing tradition of verbalizing news events (Ibid., 56). More recently Wilson Lowrey (2002) investigated this phenomenon in a study of the contemporary newsroom, drawing similar conclusions.

The Financial Press

Classical infographics were being published in the serious press in the final quarter of the century, at around the time that modern financial news emerged (Brake & Demoor, 2009). Early in the new century, they also began appearing in the financial press. One of the earliest statistical charts to appear in the *Financial Times*[34] is based on data from weekly returns of associated banks in the United States, providing a monthly, comparative overview of their loans and deposits from 1901 to June 1903. An accompanying article includes an explanation (with echoes of Playfair) that speaks to the relatively novel use of the form, in terms of expressing financial matters to British news audiences: "Very few persons follow the figures closely week by week, and even if they do so it is only by comparison that they are able to appreciate their importance. A mass of figures will not tell the tale half so graphically as a chart, which enables anyone to see at a glance important features that could not otherwise be grasped" (Anonymous, 1903). Such infographics, used to show financial data, appeared intermittently throughout the first few decades of the twentieth century. During the early 1900s, most infographics were concerned with the performance of American stocks.

Very occasionally, the use of charts moved from the financial to the political, and from reporting, to editorial. In 1921, during a period of heavy losses in the coal industry, the government (under pressure from pit owners) set out plans to decontrol the country's mines and railways. The miners' sought the solidarity of the railway and transport workers' unions in the form of a sympathy strike, but were rebuffed on "Black Friday," April 15, 1921, undermining the "Triple Alliance" among the unions. In August 1921, cost accounting pioneer Alfred John Liversedge authored a piece in the *Financial Times* that took a comparative look at the state of the coal industry (figure 4.14). He claimed that he wished to engage all sides in the debate, toward seeking a harmonious solution to the problem, albeit one on relatively narrowly defined terms. Eight graphs explored the discrepancies between the UK and United States in their respective outputs; among all the variables involved, the authors isolated the following: "the chief factor in the complete explanation is to be sought in the restrictive policy deliberately adopted by the British miners, in keeping with the general policy of the trade unions of this country, during the period covered by our chart" (Liversedge, 1921). None of these charts offers a comparison of wages (which was central to the strike), although the narrative does acknowledge that American wages are "high."

By 1924, the *Financial Times* had started publishing synoptic charts for readers, such as a page-sized chart, headlined "100 Years Chart of the Bank Rate."[35] By the late 1930s, infographics are beginning to appear alongside pictures, in order to substantiate financial stories;[36] and by late 1937, they are beginning to appear (with one or two months' exception) at a rate of around one per month. By the 1950s, the *Financial Times* is employing some of the graphical techniques its Fleet Street competitors have pioneered;[37] and by the 1960s, the stylistic components in its charts give the paper a consistency of style, and a feel that is clearly analogous with its Fleet Street competitors, and concomitant with the rise of the news infographic, which I will introduce in chapter 5.[38]

However, it was the plain, methodologically consistent, discursively "objective" (and often hand-drawn) time-series charts that were the preferred

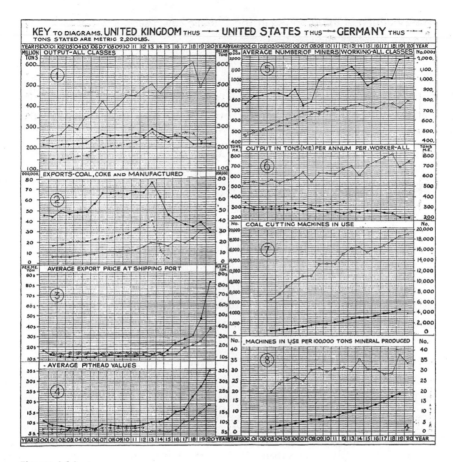

Figure 4.14
In A. J. Liversedge, "Twenty-one years of coal in the United Kingdom, the United States, and Germany Shown at a Glance in Eight Graphs," *Financial Times*, August 10, 1921, 3.

form for infographics in the UK's early financial press (and particularly those in the interwar period). These were discursively influenced by utilitarianism, as they were by the scientism of the early twentieth-century social sciences (and in particular the new field of economics). But these graphs could, on occasion, be employed in a persuasive capacity, too. As the decades wore on, the financial press began to move with the rest of Fleet Street, and "serious" elements were drawn into the new, visually impactful news infographics.

The Evolution of Infographics in the *Dundee Advertiser* and the *Dundee Courier & Argus*

The *Dundee Advertiser* became a penny daily in 1861, under the then-editorship of John Leng, a pro-home rule liberal who improved the news-paper and increased its circulation. Founded in 1816, also as a weekly, the *Dundee Courier & Argus* had followed suit, becoming a daily by the late 1870s—albeit a halfpenny newspaper. A new generation of halfpenny news-papers emerged across the country during this time, starting in London and then spreading to the provinces (Hewitt, 2014). In 1926 the *Dundee Courier & Argus* was amalgamated with the *Dundee Advertiser*.

The first charts that appear in the penny *Dundee Advertiser* were weather related; a series of bar graphs and line charts depicting past annual (monthly) meteorological and weather and water statistics, for 1886 (figure 4.15). Weather charts appear very occasionally in the *Dundee Advertiser* from this period onward; these normally employ a grid, with an explanation as to the intervals of measurement in fine detail, in accompanying text.[39] A num-ber of barometric and meteorological line graphs showing monthly, local trends in atmospheric pressure were published in subsequent years.[40] All of these charts were local in nature, and all appear (based on subject matter and design) to have come from the same source: the Dundee Harbour engi-neers' office, albeit attribution is not made in all of these examples. None of these charts were published in the halfpenny *Dundee Courier & Argus*, whose reporting of weather issues from the late 1870s was largely textual.

Infographics start appearing slightly later, at the turn of the century, in the *Dundee Courier & Argus*. Pictograms feature among the earliest examples: see figure 4.16.[41] These infographics were either republished, or redrafted versions of pictograms found in other popular almanacs, such as the *Daily Mail Year Book* (December 1900), the *Scientific American Reference Book* (1900), and *Mutual Life Insurance Volume* (1905) (figure 4.17). The *Dundee Courier & Argus* had its own photoengraving staff at the time (Anonymous, 1897). These pictograms broadly echo the national-comparative imperial-ism of Mulhall's work.

Some bar graphs also feature among the earliest of the *Dundee Courier & Argus*'s infographics. These, again, are of a national-comparative nature concerning the lengths of merchant ships and battleships[42] and the wages of workers in the UK, United States, and Germany.[43] Axes and scales were

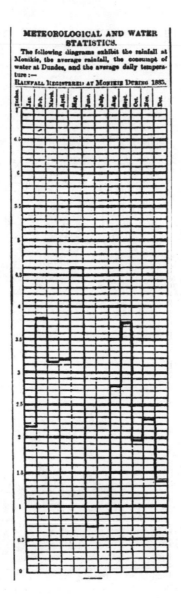

Figure 4.15
From the *Dundee Advertiser*, January 4, 1886, 3.

a)

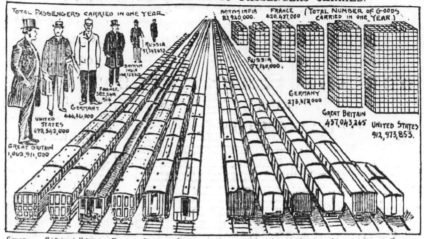

b)

Figure 4.16

From the *Dundee Courier & Argus*, January 12, 1900, 7.

a)

b)

Figure 4.17
From Albert A. Hopkins & R. A. Bond, *Scientific American Reference Book* (New York: Munn & Company Publishers, 1899), 117–136.

not employed in these infographics. In 1905 a bar graph concerning the birth rate in London is published[44] that accords with standard, "good" practice in graphs—around the time that two key texts on graph design were published, W. M. Baker and A. A. Bourne's *Elementary Graphs* (1903), and W. Jamieson's *Graphs for Beginners* (1905). All of these charts were, in terms of subject matter, international rather than locally relevant, and trivial rather than useful.

In accounting for the difference in infographic styles between these titles, cover price would appear to be key—*Dundee Courier & Argus* being a halfpenny daily, and the *Dundee Advertiser* being a penny daily. Lee suggests, tentatively, that the lower-middle and working classes tended to read the halfpenny press, while the penny dailies were largely the preserve of the middle classes. The discursive tendencies of these (at first) different editorial approaches is apparent; they were aimed at two different audiences. The *Dundee Advertiser* furnished its (predominantly) middle-class readers with scientific "news you can use" that was locally useful and reflected their hobbies and pastimes, helping them to accumulate "bridging social capital" (Putnam, 2000). In contrast, the *Dundee Courier & Argus* provided its (predominantly) lower-middle-class and working-class readers with visually alluring (and hence memorable) popular trivia that might prove entertaining to share in social contexts, helping them to accumulate "bonding social capital" (Ibid.). By 1926, the commercial imperatives imposed by advertising, in the context of increased competition, and a local newspaper industry that was consolidating owing to decline, just as national dailies were rapidly increasing (Sutcliffe, 2008) led to the merger of these titles. In turn, both abstract and material forms would be incorporated into a style redolent of the "attractiveness of orchestrated variety" (Conboy, 2002, 75), and one suitable for a wide-ranging local audience.[45]

National Efficiency and Education

In the decades that followed Britain's imperial and commercial boom, culminating in the glitter and grandeur of the Great Exhibition of 1851, a rather less triumphant mood arose. A series of colonial uprisings and calamities from the 1860s onward, and not least the series of humiliating defeats during the Boer War of 1899 to 1902, seemed to portend national decline. As early as the 1880s concerns about Britain's place in the world, and its ability to manage its imperial affairs, had been rising, inspired not least by the increasing influence of America, and of Germany, on the world stage. The solutions to the nation's ills were to be sought in the perceived strengths of these immediate competitors (Searle, 2008). The movement for National Efficiency represented a coming together of various ideas, collectively bound by a sense of patriotic duty that sought to improve the running of government by drawing upon methods and processes from successful technocratic (scientific) and business institutions (Ibid.). A new generation of experts and a new era of expertise were willed into existence in an attempt to manage the chaos of "the vertigo years" (Blom, 2008).

The importance of education to the National Efficiency cause was expressed in the ideas and policies of the Fabians, and in particular in the thinking of Sidney Webb, whose proposals for curricular reform in elementary education were intended to establish quality and consistency and to challenge idiosyncrasies in pedagogy and the ineffectiveness of rote learning (Lowe, 2008). The new industries, particularly petrochemical, car manufacture, and electrical, required a new generation of skilled and semi-skilled workers. These new workers required access to universal secondary education; and many of them required further education that would be provided by a new generation of technical colleges (Ibid.).

In 1914 the Board of Education published a circular on the teaching of geometry in secondary schools (*The Place and Use of Graphs in Mathematical Teaching*), drawing on observations from a 1909 circular on the same theme that suggested that the use of graphs in algebra was "widely misunderstood" (Board of Education, 1914, 14), a consequence of the way they were taught in the period's textbooks as much as the lack of specialized knowledge among the nation's teachers. Yet graphs were seen as being increasingly important. The circular advocates teaching graphs in connection with statistics: "As children nowadays were commonly familiar with temperature charts and the like, often indeed being required to construct them from their own observations, this presents the less difficulty" (Ibid., 19). Nine years later, another circular, revised Circular 884, was published: *Board of Education Memoranda on Teaching and Organisation in Secondary Schools: The Place and Use of Graphs in Mathematical Teaching*. It found that "graphic work in the teaching of elementary mathematics is now general in schools, and has in fact shown much improvement in recent years," but nevertheless "its true aim and purpose were still not always fully appreciated" (Board of Education, 1925, 3).

This circular sets out to establish the qualitative use of graphs in the classroom, which speaks to a pragmatic rather than a strictly theoretical approach to the form: "It is not uncommon to hear the criticism, 'some candidates drew their graphs without scales; the work was therefore valueless.' The criticism is just, but the implication that graphs can only be viewed through their scales is false. What may perhaps be called the qualitative use of graphs has its legitimate and even necessary place.... Only later can the rough terms, 'decrease slowly, increase rapidly' and the like, be replaced by exact quantitative expressions. But the very habit of using these rough terms will itself develop the sense of the need for an exact measure of rate of growth." (Board of Education, 1925, 7). In a further reference to pragmatism, examples for the purposes of plotting on a graph, it is suggested, should be chosen "which lie within the natural interests and knowledge of the class" (Ibid.).

Popular Textbooks

Extant histories suggest that at the start of the twentieth century, infographics became "popularised" (Friendly, 2008a; Funkhouser, 1937). But where were they being published, and for whom? In the United States, as early as the 1860s, large-type illustrated books on arithmetic were commonly available, and by the 1870s, graphs started appearing in textbooks.[46] During this period, British mathematical textbooks were mostly textual (although some made use of diagrams). By the turn of the century, however, textbooks such as W. M. Baker and A. A. Bourne's *Elementary Geometry* (1902) emerge, dealing explicitly with graphs.[47] Statistical maps aimed at slightly older readers were also being published in geographical texts around this time.[48] Meanwhile, the British scientific gazetteers of the period, aimed at amateur geographers, also included abstract graphical forms.[49] During the 1920s, infographics become more visible in mathematical textbooks.[50] The popularization of abstract graphical forms spread slowly through the first quarter of the twentieth century; in textbooks and gazetteers, as much as (as we have already seen) in the illustrated weeklies and popular national daily press, the serious and financial press, and in the "respectable" provincial press.

A New Educational Philosophy

John Dewey's thoughts and works coincided with the rise of progressivism in American life and politics (Dewey & Skilbeck, 1970); and like those
nineteenth-century British progressives before him, he too had a bearing
on the rise of infographics in the mass media. Dewey's theory of education, set out in *Democracy and Education* (1916), stands in opposition to
classical theories of learning, in so far as it acknowledges the importance
of the senses to pedagogy and process. Teaching aids and media that harness these capacities were prized, and their situation within pedagogy he
considered central, rather than peripheral. Later, in *Experience and Education*, Dewey addressed the problem of boredom in traditional education as
being a consequence of a failure to address "internal factors' that contribute toward experiences, as much as any method of teaching does (Dewey,
1997 [1938], 42). In his approach the quality of experience is all, both in
terms of basic, immediate agreeableness and in terms of the legacy of this
memory on future experiences—to this end, the old ways of teaching by
rote were responsible for turning students away from learning (Ibid.). Dewey's approach was not particularly new; it was handed down from Rousseau, Pestalozzi, and others. However, his arguments were, even at the time,
hotly contested (Hickman, 1990).

Darling and Nisbet (2000) suggest that Dewey's ideas took longer to
become established in Britain than in other countries; indeed, not until the
1960s and 1970s do they discern his influence in primary education.[51] In
accounting for this delay, they suggest that his pedagogy only made head-
way as a principle or aspiration among academics and reformers, rather
than with teachers. Indeed, Dewey's influence on British education was
downplayed in the *Plowden Report* (Central Advisory Council for Education, 1967, 189). Nevertheless, Darling and Nisbet insist that he had been
an undisputed (if implied) influence on its predecessor, the *Hadow Report*
(Board of Education, 1931).[52] This report represented the culmination of a
generation of government-appointed consultative committees whose aim
was to look into every aspect of the British education system. It embodies
a spirit of modern progressivism, Breakell (2002) suggests, which defined
British education during the interwar period, particularly in centers of
teacher training where the idea of curriculum was developed upon the principles of "activity and experience" rather than on rote learning. Though the

report makes no reference to the uses of graphs in the classroom, it does recommend that teachers use pictures and pictorial time charts in the early stages of teaching history, before using charts with a more textual form, at the secondary stage (Board of Education, 1931). The promise of pictorial statistics in UK education was first explored over a decade later in the work of Patrick Meredith, who set up and ran a Visual Education Centre at University College, Exeter (Burke, 2011). A contemporaneous review of Meredith's *Visual Education and the New Teacher* (1946) suggests that the successful use of visual aids during wartime training had led to a renewal of interest in their application in the school room, postwar (Hankin, 1948). A generation later, progressivism in modern British education peaked with the 1967 publication of the *Plowden Report*, which introduced a number of recommendations at odds with classical pedagogy, including child-centered education (Breakell, 2002).[53] A few years earlier, in 1962, SMP Books published a new mathematics syllabus with guidance on bad practice to avoid, owing, Breakell suggests, to the increasing presence of poor design in the media of the day (Ibid., 118). By the early 1960s, the critical study of graphs had become incorporated into this syllabus (Ibid.). There are echoes of this time frame in the school exam papers of the era. The Junior Examination, administered by Cambridge University Local Examiners, for children under fifteen, for example, included a variety of diagrams and maps as early as the 1920s; however graphs were a rarity until the 1950s.[54]

Conclusion

Infographics had been commonly used in the natural sciences since the 1830s, but they only emerged in the social sciences after the 1880s, inspired by the educational and statistical works of economists including Stanley Jevons and Arthur Bowley. The charts in Bowley's *Elements of Statistics* (1901) (figure 4.18), a book that contains an outline chapter on some examples of best practice in graphic design, typify the clear, methodically rigorous, spartan graphical style that would subsequently find expression in the "serious" press (and the regional and the financial presses) at the turn of the twentieth century. This 330-page octavo volume (first edition), a text based on various lectures Bowley delivered at the London School of Economics and Political Science between 1895 and 1900, embodies all of the best practice but little of the visual impact of Playfair's graphical innovations.

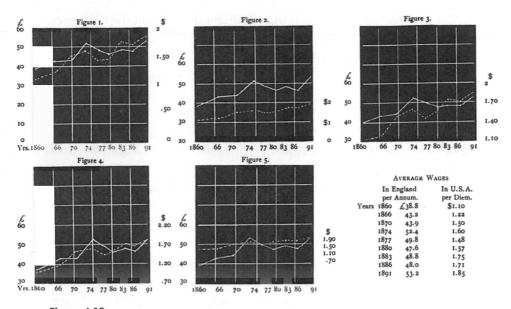

Figure 4.18

J. Bowley, *Elements of Statistics*, sixth edition (New York: Staples Press, 1901), 135.

At the same time, a new graphical form, the pictogram, was also emerging, aimed at a more heterogeneous audience. The pictogram represents a decisive shift away from the abstract, performative metaphors typical of late eighteenth-century graphical forms, such as Priestley's synoptical "river" and Playfair's piles of guineas, to a new commodity-as-symbol materialism, used to articulate the popular ideals of the times, including the mood of nationalism that permeated Britain's popular and political culture, at the fin de siècle (Hughes, 1986, 187).

The commercial phase in news infographics, spanning roughly the 1880s to 1930s, is defined by this historical bifurcation. Two discourses, one scientistic, the other commercial, emerge during this period. The scientistic data visualization draws on the classical abstract forms, deals (often) in abstract phenomena, and is stripped of any visual allure. In these forms, the discursive emphasis is on methodology, while pragmatic, ideological, and aesthetic aspects of data display are collectively de-emphasized. These forms emerged within the modern social sciences, following the long-delayed acceptance of their utility here. They are, communicatively, ideologically, and aesthetically speaking, bound up with the modern ideal of "objectivity" in keeping with the dominant discourse in the fields they emerged from. These forms were subsequently popularized, as Friendly suggests, in textbooks, but also in the serious press (albeit they were not routinized). By the 1910s, they were being discussed in the context of the nation's school curriculum.

At the same time, a new commercial infographic emerged, comprised of representational forms. The discursive emphasis in these forms is on communication, ideology, and aesthetics, while methodological aspects are deemphasized. These commodified forms first appear in popular almanacs and in other reference works. They are employed to communicate with nonspecialist audiences, and the masses. They are communicatively, ideologically, and aesthetically redolent of contemporaneous popular visual (and commodity) culture. They emerged within a popular visual print culture whose origins may be traced to the illustrated press of the 1840s. These forms were criticized for being communicatively down-market (and patronizing), for being overtly ideological, and for lacking methodological rigor. Following the publication of Mulhall's imperial pictograms (and a number of popular almanacs) from the early 1880s, both materialist (pictographic) and abstract (classical) forms began to appear together in the illustrated and periodical presses of the 1890s. Richards observes a discursive shift in advertising during this period from "the macro-politics of monarchy and Empire [to] ... the micro-politics of the body and gender" (Richards, 1991, 7). This shift may be observed too in the move from Mulhall's imperial pictograms (addressed to middle-class audiences) to the pictorial statistics used in early human interest features (and display advertising) of the illustrated weeklies, and then the popular national dailies at the turn of the century—all aimed at a wider public. From these origins, across the first three decades of the twentieth century, the discursive form of news infographics would slowly emerge, incorporating both abstract (classical) and concrete (pictographic) visual components and styles, and employing (or eliding) formal graphical (and journalistic) standards and conventions along the way. These disparate graphical forms were inspired at first by editorial hunch and then later by market research, and mobilized toward broadening the definition of news. All of this was very much in keeping with the New Journalism's "attractiveness of the orchestrated variety" (Conboy, 2002, 75), an approach that was necessary in order to meet the diverse needs of a mass audience. They appeared during an era when the British Empire was thought to be in decline, and where new industries, requiring new workforces with new skills (including familiarity with forms of data representation), it was hoped, would help to arrest this decline. These changes were informed by the spirit of National Efficiency, by a growing culture of textbooks in the sciences and social sciences, and by new, progressive educational philosophies, drawing by degrees on the ideas of John Dewey. The infographic had become a commodity. It served to democratize knowledge, albeit it was also discursively employed toward pulling British society together around a unifying notion of the nation (and the empire) in peril—an increasingly pressing preoccupation during this period.

5 Propagandist, Professional, Processor: The Rise of the Visual Journalist

In this penultimate chapter I will set out two further phases in the history of infographics: the ideological and the professional. The ideological phase, running roughly from the 1930s to the early 1960s, drew aesthetic inspiration from the preceding commercial phase. It took shape in and among the new generation of "news processors" who dominated the 1930s newsroom; a new generation of journalists (such as Guy Bartholomew, at the *Daily Mirror*) who established the primacy of modern design in news. This phase is defined by the pictograph. Some were methodologically consistent and rigorous, particularly those adhering to the principles of Isotype, a method borne of the political turmoil of early twentieth-century Europe, which was intellectually informed by logical positivism and by Einsteinian relativism. Other manifestations (such as the *Daily Express*'s Expressograph—the first regular, branded newspaper infographic in the UK) employed pictograms alongside other graphical forms; their organizing characteristics were a consistent, graphic-art aesthetic and the subservience of method to editorial propaganda. The professional phase, running roughly from the 1960s to the present day, is defined by the emergence of the visual journalist as an active figure in the newsroom contributing to, and by degrees shaping, our modern, visual news culture. These phases occurred during a time when popular culture became less local and more global, and when news audiences became increasingly fragmented, in the context of new, postindustrial educational and commercial realities.

The Expressograph runs from the ideological phase into the professional phase. Given this overlap, I have chosen to structure the following chapter into two sections comprising a series of alternatively discrete and overlapping sites of production, consumption, and resistance. In the first section, I will be concerned with Isotype as state propaganda, as it arose in the

Red Vienna of the 1930s, before finding application in Britain, early during World War II. Resistance to Isotype was mobilized around similar scientistic criticisms that had plagued Mulhall's pictograms. In the second section, I will explore five sequential themes that help to explain the evolution of the UK's newspaper industry from the mid-twentieth century through to the present day. The first theme is competition: from the late 1950s, Britain's national newspapers, though relatively well resourced, found themselves increasingly competing for fewer and fewer readers. The second theme is professionalization: during the early 1960s a new generation of (sometimes) unionized graphic designers, fresh from a newly reformed educational system, started populating British newsrooms, aided by new methods, tools, and technologies. Third, politics, and in particular, Margaret Thatcher's interference in British industrial relations, as played out during the Wapping dispute of the early 1980s. Fourth, computerization: the rise of the computerized and then the networked newsroom during the 1980s and 1990s, respectively. And the fifth theme is convergence: the bringing together of hitherto discrete media forms, practitioners, and practices online during the 2000s.

These forms were received by a public whose cultural tastes were becoming increasingly global (and less local), in the shift to post-industrialism. There were two general sites of resistance to infographics in news and popular culture from the late 1950s onward. First, the struggle for control of the modern newsroom that would eventually, with technological convergence, settle the position of the visual journalist as a key, autonomous contributor, and not merely a service professional for "word people." Second, the academic critique of tabloidization that arose during the 1990s, which arguably owes debts to post-Freudian pessimism about sensory manipulation techniques in early twentieth century mass media and advertising; as well as to the earlier elitist Victorian organizing principle of the "whip of the word." Throughout this chapter are a series of theoretical critiques of select visualizations, situated in the contexts in which they arise.

Isotype: An Iconic Revolution

Around the time that news infographics as a discursive form were taking shape, and increasingly being used to sell products (not least newspapers) to a consumerist British middle class, an infographic counter-revolution was emerging in continental Europe. Beginning in 1925, Otto Neurath, along with Marie Reidemeister (later Neurath), Gerd Arntz, and an interdisciplinary team of experts developed the *Vienna Method of Pictorial Statistics* (Wiener Methode der Bildstatistik), which became known as the *International System of Typographic Picture Education* (Isotype) from around 1935 onward (Hartmann, 2008). Isotype was developed within a radical worldview in order to provide (one-way) communicative means toward political, educational, and ultimately, ideological ends. It was conceived of within a positivist, experimental epistemology that sought to advance and improve knowledge, albeit in practice it has been suggested that the methods employed in its testing were often more arbitrary than rigorous (Cat, 2004).

Isotype is a system of seemingly universally recognizable pictograms that was intended to educate Red Vienna's urban poor about how their society functioned (Hartmann, 2008). Methodologically consistent, its organizing principle is the repetition and combination, not the rescaling, of a range of uniform, formally neutral pictorial symbols. Neurath was aware of scalable pictograms, but found them unacceptable. Their methodology he dismissed as "systematically false" (Burke, 2013a, 12), just as Brinton had critiqued Mulhall's pictograms (Jansen, 2009). Neurath thought of Isotype as a simplified language; a "universal slang" or "universal jargon" (Burke 2013b, 90), not as a language per se (Hartmann, 2008); Isotype was a pragmatic tool rather than a (fully) theorized concept, and could only be fully understood in action (Burke, 2011, 37).

A central assumption in Isotype is that audiences glance (or scan) rather than read modern visual media (Hartmann, 2008; Jansen, 2009). This assumption found similar voice a few years later in John E. Allen's *The Modern Newspaper* (1940); a text that set out the consequences of this widespread media habit for the modern newspaper (Hutt, 1973). Isotype, like modern newspaper design, emerged from (and so reflected) an era visually dominated by cinema, illustration, and mass advertising (Leonard, 1999).

Neurath sought to present numbers visually in order to communicate with as wide an audience as possible, democratizing knowledge for literate and illiterate individuals alike. Indeed, Isotype emerged from a dissatisfaction with the classic phase of infographic design. Neurath was unimpressed by abstract graphical forms, thinking of them as austere and inadequate— and lacking the crucial rhetorical association of form and content that encourages audience engagement in the cognitive process. He wrote that "symbols of men and trees are friendlier to look at. If you saw a row of black coffins and a row of dead babies, you would be able to remember, even after a long time, that this chart was about deaths and births. But the red curve and the black curve could have meant births and deaths as well as the production of wine and shoe polish" (unpublished letter, quoted in Jansen, 1996, 152). Writing later in *Public Opinion Quarterly,* one of Neurath's earliest acolytes Rupert Modley outlined further shortcomings of classical graphical techniques, that they are monotonous and as such are resented by the wider public; they are insufficiently self-explanatory and lack persuasive appeal (Modley, 1938). Isotype was designed to be emotionally affective. These pictograms were intended to evoke what Neurath believed was "a feeling of security, as one has no fear of the little figures as one does of curves and numbers" (quoted in Burke2013b, 86).

Neurath was aware of the limitations inherent to print media in truly democratizing knowledge (Ibid., 32), and so he focused on developing knowledge to be displayed within the lived, everyday environment. Isotype was originally presented to the public in the same format that the Progressive Era social survey movement made effective use of, the *social exhibit* (Anderson, 2018, 45). A range of Isotype multimedia, including signs, table-top displays, posters, and objects, were developed and displayed at the Gesellschafts- und Wirtschaftsmuseum (Museum for Social and Economic Affairs) in Vienna between 1925 and 1934 (Hartmann, 2008; Burke, 2013b). These media were designed and presented in order to encourage and to support critical discussion about the lived environment, and about the statistical state of the world more broadly, among the wider Viennese public.

Words Divide, Pictures Unite

Neurath's philosophy was essentially pragmatic and materialistic; he thought of statistical data as essential to planning the radical socialist economy and society he wanted. For him, thinking was a "tool"; an instrument. He sought a means of communicating thoughts uncorrupted by the inconstancies he saw as being inherent to words; visual education would engender social transformation (Leonard, 1999). Isotype was not intended, nor was it capable of being, rhetorically neutral; on the contrary, it was inherently political and ideological, comprising a series of meaningful, "visual arguments" (Burke2013b, 84–85).

Isotype engenders a radically different philosophical outlook from the one that informed Playfair's classical infographics. Passmore suggests that Neurath perceived there to be no commonality of experience (and therefore no commonality of language) when it came to expressing noumenal abstractions—things that cannot be observed, like behavioral laws (such as rates of interest or currency). Such concepts were therefore essentially meaningless (Passmore, 1967). But they were also, according to Scott, considered impediments to the radical social progress that Neurath sought (1987, 702). Isotype was conceived of as a means of instrumentalizing Marxist philosophy that might empower working people with the confidence to challenge the abstractions of capitalism.

To read the professionally drawn "number-fact pictures" in *International Picture Language* (1936) (figures 5.1 and 5.2), it is first necessary to turn this 117-page octavo book 90 degrees to the right. The eye is drawn away from the abstract bars down to a series of repeated, uniformly-scaled pictograms. Abstract and concrete visualizations are juxtaposed. These pictograms embody the principle of Quetelet's *l'homme moyen* (average man).

Figure 5.1
O. Neurath, *International Picture Language* (London: Kegan Paul, 1936), 77.

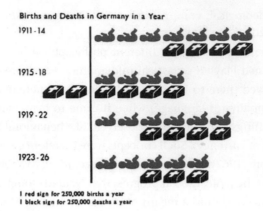

Figure 5.2
O. Neurath, *International Picture Language* (London: Kegan Paul, 1936), 87.

Influences on Isotype

Johann Amos Comenius's *Orbis sensualium pictus* (1653) was an acknowledged influence on Neurath, and on Isotype (Hartmann, 2008); but more broadly, Vossoughian outlines a range of direct influences, both classical and contemporaneous, from cartography, to hieroglyphs, to advertising (Vossoughian & Neurath, 2011, 61). Isotype has been described as Gestalt-like, embodying a similar essential typology to that of Bauhaus (Cat, 2004), which was also a stated influence upon the Vienna Circle of which Neurath was an active member. Neurath's social exhibits are said to owe a debt to, among other things, the World Exhibitions of the mid- to late nineteenth century. In terms of more diffuse influences, Hartmann (2006) observes that internationalization essentially gave rise to Isotype; that it became possible via the nexus of major communicative and transportational advances of the era, not least the railways, shipping, and telegraphy. Separately, the Austro-Marxism of the 1860s (and in particular the ideas of Max Adler and Otto Bauer) and the ideal of creating political change by means of cultural education may also be seen to have been significant in the emergence of Isotype (Vossoughian & Neurath, 2011).

Influence of Isotype in the UK

Isotype charts were first put on display around 1933, in the United Kingdom at the Mundaneum, an international institution dedicated to collecting and classifying the world's knowledge, whose London office Neurath helped to establish (Burke, 2013b, 99). A couple of years later, *International Picture Language* was published in Basic English (a controlled language with a restricted vocabulary, intended to improve readability for an audience with variable levels of literacy) in the UK. Having fled Nazi Germany in 1940, Otto and Marie Neurath were initially interned as "enemy aliens," but on their release in 1941, they moved to Oxford, setting up the Isotype Institute. Thereafter they took up a series of commissions from the British Ministry of Information and other government agencies, producing a range of war propaganda and publicity (Purdon, 2016, 144).

Paul Rotha contacted Otto and Marie Neurath soon after they were released from internment in 1941, during planning work on a film for a campaign for the British Ministry of Information. This film was commissioned in late July 1940 following a nationwide campaign to increase wartime salvage collection that had seen no significant improvement in outcomes (Irving, 2016). A survey by Mass-Observation (a social research institute) had sought proposals from the public for ways to improve the campaign; suggestions included the publication of relevant statistics (Ibid.). Lord Beaverbrook, who was appointed minister of supply in late June 1941, required that the campaign be placed under his own personal management; and in July, a number of textual advertisements were published to coincide with screenings of *A Few Ounces a Day* (1941) (Ibid.).

Isotype infographics are woven into the narrative of this film, to convey the importance of salvage, toward mitigating the loss of ships in transatlantic crossings. A black-and-white cinema bulletin (with sound), lasting six minutes and 40 seconds, this linear (or "cool," on McLuhan's terms) medium makes use of strong narrative structure and recapitulation of key points, toward getting the message across clearly and memorably. Dynamic Isotype figures are accompanied by a single voice narration, which employs even meter and rhyme at key structural points in the film in order to reinforce the message. Narration (by Henry Hallatt) aside, words are also presented as bullet points on the screen. Production effects in the form of explosions and dramatic drumming are mobilized in order to intensify the narrative and to convey the sense of danger that ships are exposed to in wartime.

The film and the wider strategy were considered a success. Mass-Observation found in a study of 550 cinema goers that among a majority of those who had watched the film, Isotype had roused the audience's interest and had contributed to raising awareness (Irving, 2016). Isotype was employed in seventeen more Rotha-directed films, including *World of Plenty* (1943) and *Land of Promise* (1945) and in a range of publications from the mid-1940s onward. It also featured in government public information booklets, such as the *Social Security* (1943) and *Social Insurance* (1944) brochures, as well as in privately published books, such as *The New Democracy* series (1944–1948).

Use of Isotype was relatively rare in newspapers of the 1930s and 1940s.[1] However, the propaganda value of Isotype-style pictograms was recognized, and lauded among radical groups. *The Socialist Publicity Service*, chaired by Patrick Gordon Walker, MP, published a pamphlet, *Putting it Over* (undated) after World War II, calling for a concerted effort to ensure that the postwar settlement for which working-class people had fought was achieved, through a massive, grassroots publicity effort. Though a local newspaper proprietor may be conservative, it was argued, their journalists have more pressing concerns in finding copy: "easy access to news" that is "accurate." The pamphlet called for activists and members to make use of "formalized symbols" in their press releases; these appear as Isotype-influenced pictograms.[2] During the postwar period, the Labour Party and the Trade Union movement returned to a theme first set out in an official Labour Party pamphlet, *The Power of the Press* (1936), namely, that the nation's press were naturally hostile to Labor's cause, and served only to further the interests of their owners and their invisible network of friends (O'Malley, 1997), a perspective that would in turn inform the Labour government's setting up of the Royal Commission on the Press of 1947.

Late in life, Neurath would acknowledge the limitations and the potential to distort reality inherent in Isotype (Burke, 2013b). As Hartmann (2008) observes, its simplistic iconicity, as much as its deterministic nature provide no space for the cultural contexts that contribute to social meanings. As the 1930s progressed the Vienna Method became increasingly associated with marketing, and with propaganda in the United States (Loic & Giraud, 2013); the same may be true with regard to the wider legacy of the Isotype Institute in the UK. This in turn may go some way toward explaining the limited effect of Isotype (and pictograms that employ similar methods), beyond sporadic use in wartime propaganda. Nevertheless, like other infographic forms before them, Isotype has gradually become incorporated into the "attractiveness of orchestrated variety" (Conboy, 2002, 75) of modern, visual news

The rape of justice

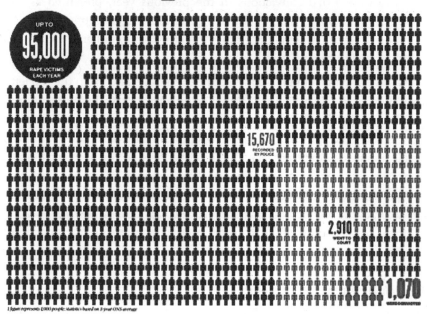

Figure 5.3

The Independent, January 11, 2013, 1. Reproduced by permission of Independent Digital News & Media Ltd.

design. They are published, from time to time, in newspapers in the present day, a testament to the communicative power and impact of the form.[3]

For example, Isotype-style figures were employed on the front page of *The Independent*, on January 11, 2013 (figure 5.3), in order to explore the issue of justice with regard to incidences of rape in the UK. Drawing upon data published by the Ministry of Justice, the Home Office, and the Office for National Statistics, this visualization mobilizes an orderly display of icons, each representing 100 victims of rape. Each stage in (and crucially, those outside of) the criminal justice process, is organized as follows:

- There are on average around 95,000 rape victims each year, which are presented as black icons—symbolizing absence.
- There were 15,670 allegations of rape recorded by police in the previous year, which are presented as grey icons.

- There were 2,910 allegations of rape that went to court in the previous year, which are presented as grey-red hybrid icons.
- There were 1,070 convictions in the previous year, presented as red icons—symbolizing danger, or more specifically the perception of risk of rape among the wider public, rather than the total number of victims, as uncovered in this research.

The eye moves through a downward horizontal plane, from the top left-hand side of the display, down through the allegations, the prosecutions, and finally the convictions for rape, at the bottom right-hand corner of the display. In keeping with Isotype's graphical principles these icons lack detail and specificity; they relay quantitative facts, as much as qualitative ones. The design is undeniably impactful owing to the properties of scaling and proportionality. Just as Neurath's critics bemoaned the lack of numerical accuracy in his pictorial statistics, so too this design may be open to criticism because only whole icons are used, which means 70 convictions for rape are excluded from the display.

Postwar Newspaper Infographics

In the conventional, liberal reading of newspaper history, Lord Thomson's acquisitions of the *Sunday Times* in 1959, and then *The Times* in 1967 represented an important watershed. An older generation of press barons, it is argued, declined after World War II, allowing the old party ties to be thrown off and a genuine moment of editorial independence (and freedom) to settle across Fleet Street (Koss, 1983). Where Beaverbrook had avowed his propagandistic intentions with the *Daily Express* in 1947, Thomson, by contrast, was keen to emphasize his essentially profit-seeking (and hence apolitical) approach (Williams, 2009). It has been suggested that, in practice, only *The Guardian* and the *Sunday Times* under Harold Evans could be said to be truly editorially free during this period (Seaton & Curran, 2003 [1981]). But what is not open to dispute is that this period began in an abundance of advertising revenue, then as circulations started to slow, an increasingly high-stakes spirit of competition set in, due to various factors not least that immediately after World War II, newspapers had to compete with news on the radio (Williams, 2009). The Independent Television Network (ITV) was launched in 1955, in order to challenge the BBC's monopoly in television broadcasting, just as the lifting of paper rationing encouraged newspapers to increase their page numbers (and their cover prices). The new broadcasters began to chip away at newspapers' advertising revenue (Ibid.). Finding it impossible to compete with television news in terms of immediacy, a shift from hard to soft news ensued in the newspaper industry. These changes occurred in the contexts of new skilled and semi-skilled clerical and white collar jobs, and near full employment; a new Britain was being forged, as Harold Wilson observed at the 1963 Labour Party Conference, in the "white heat of technology."

The *Daily Express*

The emergence of the infographic as a regular feature in British news culture can be traced back to the Expressograph, which first appeared in the *Daily Express* during the mid-1950s (Dick, 2015a). This was a lavishly financed and comparatively visually alluring newspaper (Greenslade, 2004), due in large part to its innovative editor, Arthur Christiansen, but also due to Lord Beaverbrook, who had shown, as wartime minister for information (and as we have already seen), a keen sense for visual propaganda methods, some of which were considered innovative at the time (Taylor, 1972). Too consistently misleading to be accounted for by accident, the Expressograph of the late 1950s was a propaganda vehicle for Beaverbrook's peculiar political interests and foibles (Dick, 2015a), contributing to the broad, popular, visual appeal of the title.

The visual appeal of much of the early Expressographs relies on popular illustrated forms of the era: the 1950s saucy postcard and popular newspaper cartoons. Re-scaled pictograms appear, alongside line graphs and bar charts, accompanying "hard" and "soft" news stories alike, and even featured on editorial pages. From 1959, these infographics start to acquire a more polished, crafted, and consistent feel; a house style (whether formal or informal) seems to be emerging. Presentation becomes more impactful. Trend lines are expressed in thick, alluring displays, defying the narrow lines conventionally used in amateur, scientific graphic forms.

Under Arthur Christiansen, Raymond Hawkey had been made design director at the *Daily Express* in 1959, putting together a graphics department (with Michael Rand loosely involved) in order to produce in-house news graphics and features illustrations (Collins, 1975). Though Hawkey and Rand were not involved in the newspaper's overall layout, they were nonetheless recognized in the newsroom—both were accepted as members of

the National Union of Journalists, the first graphic designers, it has been suggested, to have achieved this recognition (Ibid.). Hawkey, perhaps mindful of
his own legacy within this new field, set out a justification for graphic design
in the newsroom: "Its function: to introduce a feeling of modernity into the
paper while retaining the robustness of traditional methods of presentation"
(Hawkey, 1975, 116). The discursive approach Hawkey takes in describing the
contribution graphics make to newspapers carries the same inflections as may
be found in justifications for the New Journalism. Infographics call forth a
multiplicity of new voices, allowing the journalist to speak in "an almost endless variety of accents and intonations, he was suddenly able, when he wished,
to sing! And to sing anything from grand opera to the blues" (Ibid., 119).

The *Daily Mirror*

Throughout the 1960s, by contrast with the *Daily Express*, infographics
rarely appeared in the *Daily Mirror*.[4] Data were as likely to appear in table
form as graphical form. However, one area of the newspaper where infographics continued to appear was among display advertisements.

It is a striking feature of this era that infographics are so prevalent in the
visual appeal of news and comment in one popular title, the *Daily Express*,
but virtually absent from a direct competitor, the *Daily Mirror*. An explanation lies in the nature of audience segmentation. Conboy suggests that,
after World War II, the *Daily Mirror* shifted its discursive appeal decisively
toward a "plebian-popular identity" (2002, 126) expressing itself in a very
different popular demotic to that used in the *Daily Express* (Smith, Immirzi,
& Blackwell, 1975). The *Daily Mirror's* visual appeal lay in its illustrations
and photography; the collectible, and indeed, the decorative nature of its
prints continued to be important to its working-class audience (Conboy,
2002). Under Lord Beaverbrook, however, the *Daily Express* addressed itself
to a young, aspirational, go-getting generation, one increasingly exposed
to infographic forms in education, in (new skilled and semi-skilled, often
clerical) work, and in consumerist leisure.

The *Observer*

In the late 1950s upmarket broadsheet *The Observer* faced serious financial
problems. The sale of the *Sunday Times* to Roy Thomson in 1959 led from

a relatively comfortable existence to all-out competition (Cockett, 1991). Thomson appointed Harold Evans with the intention of developing "a more aggressive, intrusive style of journalism" (Ibid., 238), an approach that reflected the social mores of the time. With the emergence of the *Sunday Telegraph* in 1961, and the arrival of color magazines at these two competitors in 1961 and 1964 respectively, advertisers were increasingly drawn away from *The Observer* (Ibid.). The newspaper's problems in fact preexisted these events, to which end Bill Smart from the *Daily Telegraph* had been appointed in 1958, in order to develop a business strategy. He found that the newspaper's politics were considered too radical and its readership too young for some advertisers' tastes (Ibid.). Politics and foreign affairs were seen as the paper's strengths and market research had shown that its most successful job advertisements were for scientists; so an editorial shift was made in a more science-oriented direction (Ibid.).

Efforts to lighten the tone were set out; chief among them, a new review section, The Week, was started by William Clarke in February 1958. Infographics appeared in this column from the outset although they were inconsistent in form and amateur in look and design. From 1958 to 1960, these infographics were often (though not exclusively) conventional, "serious" chart formats. Some were relatively complex,[5] and many were small, fitting within a single column, across a page of seven.[6] There was very little sense of consistency, or style, and the discursive connection between text and graph in these early examples could be tenuous.[7] Little thought seems to have gone into how these crude hand drawings helped to tell the stories they referred to. They are largely concerned with political polling and economic and financial data. Initially they were unattributed, but eventually John Davy and Richard Leadbetter were bylined. In general, these charts are methodologically sensible and sound, and they often state their source, unlike some Expressographs.

In 1960, relatively bold charts started to appear, taking after the style developed at the *Daily Express* during the late 1950s.[8] From around 1961, infographics across *The Observer* start to acquire a more consistent appearance.[9] From the mid-1960s until 1975, Raymond Hawkey served as presentation director of *The Observer* and the *Observer Magazine* (Milward-Oliver, 2010). During this time the paper's infographics became increasingly impactful, and visually arresting.[10] These changes caused some dismay among the paper's journalists; and despite an upturn following the launch of its magazine, they did little to shore up *The Observer*'s dwindling circulation (Cockett, 1991). This may also help to explain the association of infographics with the "lightening" of serious political reporting, found among newspaper audiences on the left.

The Emergence of the Visual Journalist

Mike Randall was an influential figure in the process of design modernization that slowly filtered through Fleet Street during the 1960s, and into the 1970s. Randall had risen through the ranks at illustrated newspapers including the *Daily Sketch*, and then the *Sunday Graphic* during the 1940s and 1950s, before becoming editor of the *Daily Mail* in 1963, where he liberalized the tone of the newspaper, in order to appeal to younger readers. He eventually moved to become managing editor at the *Sunday Times* in 1966 (Leapman, 1999).

During the 1960s qualified designers (often coming from book and/or magazine publishing) were increasingly brought into newsrooms expressly to improve overall design, or to provide a makeover for specific news features areas (Collins, 1975). During this decade, the field of art and design attained its modern educational status following the publication of *The National Advisory Council on Art Education* report (1960), which proposed a new qualification—the Diploma in Art and Design including four specialties (one of which was graphic design).[11] Also during this era, Letraset had developed a dry transferable lettering, comprising classic and contemporary fonts that were used extensively by the period's graphic designers. Letraset and the Rotring technical pen were the tools that defined this first wave of visual journalists. Affordable for amateurs as well as professionals, they were used in design studios and in advertising agencies. They would also contribute significantly to the development of infographics in British newspapers,[12] until they were superseded by desktop publishing, during the late 1980s.

The *Sunday Times*

Harold Evans edited the *Sunday Times* from 1967 to 1981 cementing the paper's reputation as a voice for liberal reform through campaigning, and particularly through innovative and well-resourced investigative journalism.

The Sunday Times had featured occasional infographics during the 1950s and early 1960s.[13] During the Evans era, a clearly identifiable (albeit unbranded) infographic style began to emerge complementing (and situated within) the newspaper's wider journalistic style. Coauthor of the industry design "bible" *Editing and Design* (1978, with the *Sunday Times* art director Edwin Taylor), Evans served as an advocate for good news design, and his enthusiasm for the visual in news would find peak expression in the pioneering work of Peter Sullivan.

Sullivan wrote a history of infographics (1987), albeit one that draws a little too much on his own work and work from the archives of his employers, and too little on his predecessors and contemporaries. Nevertheless, it is an important work, because for the first time, it situated the craft of infographic design within the practices of the newsroom. Sullivan elaborates on those factors that shape infographic design in news, where audience affect (and feedback) inform future work and where creativity serves as a function of white space, in a busy, and fast-changing schedule. Sullivan's approach is fundamentally pragmatic.

Innovation in infographic design at the *Sunday Times* during the Evans era had as much to do with style as journalistic substance. While infographics continued to be used in business and political reporting (as they had been through the preceding decade), under Evans, they start appearing in news features as well. A wide range of pressing social concerns were covered graphically: from the rising cost of social security[14] to the problem of screening for cervical cancer;[15] from the increasing rate of murder in the capital;[16] to redundancy;[17] and from the abolition of hanging[18] to crime in general.[19] The results of the *Sunday Times* polling, on both political[20] and social attitudes, also started appearing in graphical forms.[21] By the end of the era, a discursively impactful model of news infographic had emerged, mixing conventional forms along with integrated, metaphorical pictorial elements; an approach pioneered by Peter Sullivan that would later find a distinctive voice in the work of Nigel Holmes, during the 1980s and 1990s.

In design terms, Sullivan's work is perhaps more clearly defined by nonstatistical than by statistical forms; by his highly innovative, synoptical process diagram such as the one that concerned the unfolding of the Notting Hill riots.[22] Sullivan was, it is claimed, the first designer-as-reporter in modern news, employing modern reportorial rather than classical narrative methods in his work. He reported back to the newsroom with synoptic diagrams of the Aberfan disaster in 1966; the eruption of Mount Etna in 1971; hostage taking at the Munich Olympics in 1972; and the Herald of Free Enterprise disaster at Zeebrugge in 1987 (Evans & Taylor, 1997 [1978]). Sullivan drew upon the same pool of ideas and language long used to perpetuate the liberal Fourth Estate mythology, in defining the modern designer-journalist, as he conceived his profession. Designer-journalists, he said, "develop a sixth sense about potential stories" (Sullivan, 1987, 31). They are bold, resourceful, self-confident (and by definition, independent) in news-gathering situations; and they are attuned to the facts of the story, rather than its "visual dressing up" (Ibid., 42).

There is a clear echo of Neurath's appeal to the audiences' glance, in Evans's functional description of what makes a "good" graph: "The drawing has to appear interesting; it has, in this, not to distort the facts. But a good analytical chart does something more: it *explains itself at once*" [my emphasis] (Evans & Taylor, 1997 [1978], 309). Some of the graphs Evans uses as exemplars in *Pictures on a Page* (Evans & Taylor, 1997 [1978]) toy with conventional standards in infographic design. Some do not have labelled axes. Some are what Darrell Huff (1952) called "gee-whizz graphs": line graphs that do not use a zero base on their axes, and, in so doing, tend to exaggerate the rate of change. This approach has been roundly denounced by Tufte (1983, 76) although other scholars are rather more even-handed on the matter (Wainer, 2006, 34). Sullivan was well-aware of the "esoteric rules" that guide scientific graph making but mindful too that some of his readers brought specialized knowledge to graphs that appeared in some sections of his newspaper (Sullivan, 1987, 46). Absent from the blanket denunciation of the gee-whizz graph in newspapers (and in news more broadly), is any awareness of differentiation among (and within) distinct groups in mass audiences, to which newspapers are designed to appeal. Readers whose jobs or pastimes require a concern with marginal change, and who are schooled in the exploitation of such conventions, will not be misled. A truncated axis in a financial or economic infographic aimed at a readership familiar with such conventions is entirely in keeping with, and is in fact symptomatic of, the "attractiveness of orchestrated variety" (Conboy, 2002, 75) of the modern newspaper.

Harold Evans saw the relationship between "word people" and "picture people" in the newsroom as a partnership of equals (Evans & Taylor, 1997 [1978], 290), but it would be misleading to consider this as typical of Fleet

Street during this era. Peter Sullivan was mindful of the lowly status of the infographic artist in some contemporaneous newsrooms and he ascribed the failure of infographics to become truly popular in UK newsrooms to a general hostility to, and snobbery about, visual material in education (Sullivan, 1987, 17)—which had, he suggested, seeped into the training of the modern journalist (Ibid., 51). During the 1960s, the teaching (or more accurately, the training) of journalists in the UK began to assume an inherent contradiction: professional components were conflated with the history of a craft (Bromley, 1997) and skills were taught within a codified (and hierarchical) division of labor in the modern newsroom. Here, the journalist dealt in originally crafted words, not in pictures (Ibid., 335), an approach that served to entrench the cultural divide that existed within many newsrooms.

Tabloidization in the Upmarket Press

The term "tabloid" is rooted in the form as much as it is in the content of newspapers. It speaks to the shift, in the early to mid-1970s, to tabloid formats across Fleet Street, but it is also associated with a rise in sensationalism and in personality-driven news content. There were pockets of resistance to this trend; Tulloch (2000) observes that this was an era defined by a stand-off between "quality" tabloid journalism (such as the *Daily Mirror's Mirrorscope* section, launched in 1969) and down-market tabloid journalism. A new generation of interfering proprietors emerged, although, unlike Beaverbrook, they seemed to be inspired by pecuniary ends first and foremost (Williams, 2009). This battle for attention was played out before a society in which living standards were improving steadily and where disposable income was increasing; a more complex range of marketing methods emerged to cope with (and exploit) this new-found leisure, and the money that people increasingly had to spend on it.

Certain types of "soft" features material were increasing in column inches, at the expense of "hard" political news coverage, a shift predicated on improving newspapers' "saleability" in an increasingly competitive market (Wiener, 1988). Later, the serious press would be accused of being implicated in this process too, in a downward spiral of *tabloidization*. Some have decried the "dumbing down" effect of modern tabloid journalism (Franklin, 1997), while others argue that these new forms may bring a wider public into political debate who might otherwise choose to stay away (Gripsrud,

2000). A third position is that tabloidization became so imprecise as to be virtually useless to anything but journalism: "a miscellany of symptoms for a cultural malaise" (Turner, 1999, 68). My own belief is that the concept can help to perpetuate an unjustified sense of media elitism, and that in some applications it represents a modern, secularized "whip of the word." For example, one approach to measuring the effect of tabloidization takes the ratio of visual material (including diagrams) in newspapers, relative to the amount of text, a higher ratio serving as indicator of over-simplification, and hence of distraction (McChesney, 2007). But as we have seen, the *Sunday Times* under Harold Evans's leadership challenges this idea. Widely accepted as representing an apex in British investigative journalism, this newspaper was awash with visualizations that typify the spirit of serious public interest journalism. Under Evans, the *Sunday Times* was both a commercial and a journalistic success (Williams, 2009); and in the work of Peter Sullivan and others, it set a high benchmark in data visualization in British news.

Infographics during the Wapping Years

The major economic themes of the newspaper industry in the late 1970s and early 1980s were consolidation and concentration of ownership, while the major technological innovations saw the combination of "computerised typesetting, photo-composition and web-offset printing" (Hutt, 1973, 159). Together these changes, economic and technological, revolutionized the industry, putting labor relations under enormous strain in the process. The stranglehold of the old press barons on newspaper editorials was beginning to loosen and an era of increasingly powerful print unions was emerging (Williams, 2009). Publication of the *Sunday Times* was suspended between November 1978 and 1979, as a consequence of strike action over the proposed introduction of new print technologies (Ibid.). Thompson's titles were put up for sale following journalists' decision to strike for more pay, in the aftermath of the lockout. Rupert Murdoch eventually bought *The Times* and the *Sunday Times* in 1981.

The proliferation of new, computerized print technologies that could be used by unskilled workers (at a lower rate, and on reduced benefits), posed a significant threat to the working rights that print unions had negotiated over decades. These unions had two significant sources of power during this period: the apprenticeship system (which allowed them to control access to the profession) and the "closed shop" requiring that anyone providing illustrated copy to be published in newspapers had to be a union member. The new printing technologies made it possible for illustrated work to be produced off site, away from the unions' control. In 1979, the *Leggatt Report* found that the Society of Lithographic Artists, Designers and Engravers (SLADE) were forcing studio workers and advertising agencies unwillingly into a closed shop—recruiting an estimated eight thousand people in the process—a finding that led, in turn, to measures curtailing unions' activities by the Thatcher government, under the Employment Acts of 1980 and 1982 (Dunn & Gennard, 1984).

Those on the radical left saw these moves as a reflection of Thatcher's microeconomic strategy (labor market deregulation) within a wider, laissez faire macroeconomic strategy (Barlow, 2008 [1997], 84–86). Alternatively, Eric Hammond, leader of the Electrical, Electronic, Telecommunications and Plumbing Union, summed up the situation in an appeal to history: "At the turn of the century I suppose the blacksmith could accuse the motor mechanic of poaching his job, because he was dealing with transport then which hitherto had been dealt with by horse and trap. But the blacksmith couldn't deal with the motor car."[23]

When in 1986 the print unions took industrial action following the insertion of a no-strike clause in contract proposals, Murdoch simply shifted production of all of his newspapers to Wapping, in East London. Technologically, where Murdoch had led, all of Britain's national newspapers followed. The new technology made it much cheaper for Murdoch to run his newspapers (he summarily dismissed thousands of his employees at the outbreak of the strike). But it offered other possibilities too, in terms of developing new magazines, sections, and other product initiatives. The new system incorporated templates that could be used quickly and effectively in breaking news, an increasingly important component in the then slowly emerging battle with twenty-four-hour broadcast news. New newspapers were launched and a (short-lived, temporary) boom in sales ensued (Seymour-Ure, 1996).

Becoming a member of the National Union of Journalists had been mandatory for infographic artist John Grimwade when he started work at the *Sunday Times* in the 1970s. He moved to *The Times* at the same time as Harold Evans, but found less editorial freedom there.[24] An ambivalent approach to the fraught industrial relations of this era was not uncommon among Britain's infographic artists (or visual journalists). The reproduction of art work (part of the culture of "re-keying" or "double key-stroking"), and the closed shop enforced by the print unions generated professional frustration. Difficult, collaborative work (and important news stories) were often buried due to, what seemed at times, little more than opportunistic protectionism. However, the thought of siding with Murdoch in the wider diminution of working conditions across industry, and not least in the mass sacking of colleagues seemed unconscionable to many.[25] Nevertheless, at Wapping, the visual journalist had new freedoms; the technology was in their control. For the first time the new workspace allowed visual journalists a sense of autonomy, unencumbered by officious, and arbitrary workplace rules.[26]

The Independent

The Independent, launched in 1986, was a product of the Wapping era. Its journalists and editors benefited from the new systems that had been used to kill off the print unions; however, its ownership (at least until 1994, when the *Mirror Group* acquired a controlling interest) spoke to a wider, growing concern about what appeared to be a second wave of increasingly powerful and unaccountable newspaper proprietors, and the (often secretive) relationships they benefited from within the corridors of government. *The Independent* was intended to appeal to a wide audience, and in particular to young readers. Its journalists would be emboldened; the old hierarchies imposed by hot metal would be consigned to history (Crozier, 1988). The newspaper adhered to broadly libertarian ideals; it rejected the old, protected trade, but also the new era of editorial manipulation that Rupert Murdoch seemed to represent (Ibid.). The paper's journalists relied on Atex systems (Ibid.); everyone received the information they needed directly at their desktops. Journalists input copy directly onto this system, and made up pages, an approach that led to a much quicker turnaround, involving a fraction of the staff required to undertake the same amount of work using the old, hot metal methods (Ibid.). The newspaper was informed by sophisticated market research from the outset; its founders were aware of the demands of their audience before dummy copies of the homepage had been created. Their market research found that 35 percent of the reading public felt underserved by broad-based newspapers and that some 20 percent were "very interested in reading a national newspaper aimed directly at 'people of my own age group doing my sort of job'" (Ibid., 15).

Although infographic artists had emerged from the Wapping dispute with increased power and autonomy, they had not yet won over the "word people" within Britain's wider newspaper culture. The early evolution of *The Independent's* front page design serves to illustrate this point. The earliest design templates for the newspaper, from January 1986 (produced by Stephen Hitchins), included infographics in different styles. A subsequent template, created by Ray Hawkey and Tony Mullins in June 1986, described by Crozier as "bold and vivid and not at all in keeping with the other quality newspapers" (1988, 72), also included a graphic and employed large color photographs, presented magazine-style. This style was, Crozier says, initially received warmly, but, following an editorial meeting in July, a number of substantive criticisms were raised, including the "appropriateness of graphics [being] questioned" (Ibid.) by some senior journalists.

Throughout the 1980s there is no real consistency in the look, feel, or substance of infographics in *The Independent*. Early graphs appear mostly in the paper's finance section, within articles written by Gavyn Davies. During the 2000s, infographics in grey scale and in color start appearing, the newspaper having gone full color in 2008. Bylined infographic artists star to appear (such as Michael Agar); and bold, stylish circular-based data charts begin to accompany a range of news stories. During this period, an increasingly sophisticated color house style is emerging. The shift from black and white to full color in wider news infographic design had occurred for many artists twenty years earlier, during the late era of computerization in the 1980s, though some infographic artists had been creating full-color infographics as far back as the 1970s and 1960s, for Sunday color supplements.[27] Two significant themes emerge among *Independent* infographics (and within the wider news industry) during the 2000s. First, a new kind of synoptic chart becomes increasingly prominent during this time: the social network diagram, which serves well for expressing the findings of complex news stories about companies in late-modern capitalism. Second, interactive news infographics emerge on newspaper websites. This is a consequence of the increasing maturation of the Internet as a source of news; of rising bandwidths, of new, dynamic programming languages (and software); and of changing patterns of consumption and behavior among online news audiences.

Eyes on the News in the Networked Newsroom

The late 1980s and early 1990s were an era of technological innovation in graphic design. Version 1.7 of Adobe Illustrator, *Illustrator 88*, included a range of new features and tools that would become essential to the emergence of computerized news infographics. Meanwhile, satellite technology was making possible new forms of news work. From the 1960s onward, satellite technologies, later combined with computer publishing technologies, led the newspaper industry from being labor intensive to capital intensive (Ward, 1989). By the 1980s these effects were felt in the newsroom. Indirectly, the potential to send pages in near real-time around the United States led to the launch of *USA Today*, which in turn would influence the wider American news market, in its adoption of graphics and other visual material directly (Martin & Copeland, 2003). The ability to send graphics electronically, when combined with the use of private bulletin boards, allowed designers to work in teams, further streamlining the process and workflows involved in the production of infographics.[28]

The Poynter Institute undertook a series of eye-tracking studies during the 1970s and 1980s that would later have a wide-reaching effect on British newspaper publishers. The study *Eyes on the News* (1991) was concerned with the use of color in newspapers, and only included a single use of infographics in a wider study of the use of images (both color and black and white). Nonetheless, the response rate was high: 73 percent of users engaged with the graphic, whether an accompanying picture was in color, or in black and white (Garcia, Stark, & Miller, 1991). Despite these relatively limited findings, this book was highly influential in UK news,[29] contributing, in time, to the rising profile of the infographic designer in the converging newsroom, and to the increasing presence of infographics (and in particular interactive infographics) in news culture. This new environment made possible a new business model, the infographics news agency, which began to appear in the early 1990s.

Graphic News

Having previously worked with Peter Sullivan at the *Sunday Times* in 1971, Duncan Mil moved to the *Daily Mail* to establish a graphics department, before becoming a freelancer in 1976. He was involved in the development, with Sullivan, of the *Reuters News Graphics Service*, which launched in May 1990. This was a subscription service that allowed news companies to select from a menu of what were initially mouse-generated graphics, hosted on a mainframe in Toronto (Long, 1990). In 1991, Mil launched a competitor, the *Graphic News Service* (Graphic News, n.d.).

Some of the earliest *Graphic News* designs are process diagrams, but by May 1991, experimental numerical infographics are being designed, incorporating some contentious methods, such as three-dimensional charts, and the use of shadow. By 1992, these infographics are beginning to incorporate bright colors with a good deal of accompanying visual content. A clear and consistent sense of visual style is at play; psephological charts, in particular, involve a marriage of bright colors and pictorial illustration—a highly impactful, photorealistic graphical hybrid. The subject matter explored in these infographics is wide ranging, from features issues, such as incidences of AIDS or child mortality in sanctions-era Iraq, to typical financial stories, such as the value of the Nikkei Index. By the 2000s, the color palate used is becoming noticeably subtler and some of the earlier, contentious methods are less prevalent.

The Converging Newsroom

During the early 2000s, as newspapers started to develop their presence online, a revolution in news infographics took place, made possible by the confluence of technical, social, and cultural factors, including increasing bandwidth, new interactive media and software, changing habits of news audiences, and new professional dynamics in the newsroom. *The Guardian*'s interactive team was created in 2001; the BBC News Specials team was launched in 2003; the FT Interactives team was formed in 2005; and Channel 4 News developed its interactive specialty in 2010 (Dick, 2014).

A new generation of interactive infographics have emerged in the era of Big Data; this is a concept still relatively elastic in terms of popular use, which technically speaking refers to data sets that are too big to be processed by conventional systems (Lewis & Westlund, 2015). Databases are by no means a new phenomenon in newsrooms, but the volumes of data now available in the newsroom—as much as the speed and capacity of systems that can be used to process and analyze it, and not least new consumer technologies that news audiences can use to interact with it—are all contributing to change, even, it is argued, contributing to new popular mythologies (Ibid.). In practice, there is now a more visible role for computational methods in the newsroom, from the programming of algorithms to the development of probability models (Diakopoulos, 2014).

In this new environment, today's visual journalists have acquired more autonomy than their offline predecessors had; albeit full artistic creativity is kept in check by budgetary constraints, and by the use of templates, designed to involve "word" journalists in *interactives* work to ease workflow and to improve style. Infographic designers find it easier to convey the value of what they do in today's networked newsroom, and easier too to negotiate with more senior word journalists. This new generation of interactive visual journalists often work in multidisciplinary teams; they are broadly involved in editorial decision-making from the start of commissions and projects (Dick, 2014).

The move online has fundamentally altered one of Sullivan's defining laws of news infographics: there is now endless white space within which to work. This in turn means that infographic work is less subject to being "spiked." More infographics are published, and the profile (and prestige) of the artist within the organization, is increased. A number of new professional awards (and new categories in existing awards) has emerged in the current decade that speaks to the growing recognition and self-confidence of the visual journalist. Interactives take many forms in online news: Big Data stories, where the audience is encouraged to interrogate data sets; nonstatistical visualizations (such as social network diagrams); and personalizable games such as niche calculators. The modern interactives designer is highly attuned to audience emotions, undertaking background research in their development of new initiatives and ideas. Audiences' emotions are an essential consideration of their work; conventional serious graphical forms are sometimes avoided because they are found to "turn off" or alienate certain audiences (Ibid.).

A new generation of interactive data visualizations are beginning to appear in elite media, such as the *New York Times*, *BBC News online*, and *The Guardian*, which incorporate innovations from the field of information visualization and present data and information to news audiences in increasingly sophisticated forms—a process that speaks to a wider cultural-historical shift from objectivity to trained judgement (Daston & Gallison, 2007). Some within industry have suggested that we are now past the peak of news interactives (Baur, 2017). News audiences seem to have taken a passive turn; the relatively meagre proportions of online news audiences that now regularly engage with interactive graphics cannot, it is argued, justify the time and expense involved in producing them. However, there can be no doubt that infographics, whether "hot" or "cool," according to McLuhan's typology of media interactivity (1964), will continue to be a significant part of our news and media.

Word People vs. Picture People in the Networked Newsroom

Wilson Lowrey (2002) has shown how the decision-making that takes place in newsrooms is subject to competing occupational subcultures, a situation that may in turn lead to decisions being made by those who are more committed to their professional group than to the organization for which they work. This in turn has consequences for news values in the newsroom; and indeed, may go some way toward explaining the relatively slow take up of infographics in British newsrooms. Picture people working in news gained autonomy after the Wapping dispute, but on the other hand, word people continued to limit this autonomy. In a separate study, Lowrey found what he described as a "service-department" mindset among US visual journalists, such as may be found in advertising agencies (2003, 138). As we have already seen, before Lowrey, scholars had been aware of this newsroom dynamic, sometimes framing it as being between "print people" and "type people" (Monmonier, 1986, 60). This was not uniformly the case in British newsrooms, as the *Sunday Times* of the late 1960s to 1970s demonstrates.[30] Nevertheless, the professional tensions between word people and picture people can be said to have shaped the emergence of news infographics in the UK, too.

Another way to think about these relations is offered by Chalaby (1998), who uses Bourdieu's (1993) notions of *cultural, social, and economic capital* to make sense of the exercise of power structures, or "structuration" within the newsroom. Chalaby argues that the struggle for hegemony in the field of journalism exists at three discrete levels: between positions within the same institution (at a professional level); in competition between like-for-like producers (industry-wide competition); and in competition among different types of producers (multimedia competition). The second and third of these typologies are, in this rationale, the chief (economic) drivers of press discourse, but also, importantly: "What differentiates journalism from the earlier forms of discourse produced by the press ['publicity']...is that the texts which form journalism are the products of conflictual relations of production" (Ibid., 33–34). In Chalaby's reading then, the emergence (or discursive formation) of the news infographic may be seen to have happened in a two-step process: first, the rise of "process journalists" to dominant positions in UK newsrooms during the 1930s; and second, the emergence of the professional graphic designer as "visual journalist," particularly the generation that emerged during the early 1960s. To conclude, the visual journalist as "picture person" would not gain full autonomy until the rise of the converged newsroom in the 2000s.

Conclusion

Isotype emerged in the modern *communication age* in the visual contexts of cinema, illustration, and mass advertising—first as state propaganda, then as consumer print culture. These forms were designed for eyes that scan rather than read visual communications media, an approach that would seep into news culture during the 1940s. These infographics were designed for mass audiences, in order to encourage and facilitate political engagement. Like the classical forms (and like the written word), Isotype extends reasoning and cognition. However, unlike modern social scientific data visualizations, Isotype was exclusively materialist and concerned with argumentation. The propagandistic Expressograph emerged during the mid-1950s, and by the 1960s, those responsible for its strong visual brand spread their influence across Fleet Street. The professional infographic artist arose from the shifting landscape of Britain's 1960s education system—albeit without strict training in statistics or numeracy—into an industry transformed by visionaries such as Randall, Hawkey, and Rand and given voice by the innovative upmarket designs of Peter Sullivan, at Harold Evans's the *Sunday Times*. This generation became professionally organized and unionized; but Margaret Thatcher's interference in industrial relations made possible creative and professional space in which the form flourished. Industrial relations reconfigured by the Wapping dispute had set infographic artists free, but further professional challenges loomed. During the 1990s, empirical evidence was mobilized toward raising awareness about the importance of visual journalism in news culture. New technologies and shifting cultures in news made possible a new wholesale market in infographics. In the newsroom, word people often continued to dominate picture people, until the emergence of the converged newsroom, during the 2000s, and the rise of the interactives journalist, who came of age as a fully autonomous visual journalist in the present decade.

It may be tempting to view the ideological phase of news infographics as a period during which practice and aesthetics were discursively subservient to ideology, but this would be misleading. Criticisms leveled at Isotype, in particular on account of its tendency to lack full numerical accuracy, are entirely valid in the contexts of scientific or social scientific professional communications. However, journalism has its own distinctive epistemology. It must engage with heterodox audiences who have variable understandings of and familiarities with graphical methods. News infographics have to communicate often complex news events effectively, and memorably. These pressures necessarily involve a tradeoff between numerical accuracy and audience impact in the creation of data visualizations in the news room. Isotype's legacy is the pragmatic approach to data visualization.

However, the Expressograph reminds us that post-truth politics has its roots further back than the present day. Of course, we should not assume that the audience for these infographics was necessarily duped or passively in thrall to them; popular newspapers are as much a form of entertainment as they are a source of news. We should be wary of assuming a strict transmission model of communication, and we should always remember that people engage critically with the world around them. The Expressograph's aesthetic influence is all too apparent among its immediate contemporaries; however its methodological shortcomings serve as a valuable, cautionary corrective.

It may also be tempting to view the professional phase of news infographics as representing a high point in newspaper infographics, and an era in which data visualization as well as information literacy are together progressively improving. But this too would be overly simplistic. While infographics designers in the news have become increasingly careful in their methods in recent decades, and while methodological rigor plays an increasingly important role in training and maintenance of standards in professional infographics design, news media are no less demanding of their staff in terms of schedules and enforcing commercial (institutional) pressures. Selective though they may be, the vast literature of examples in our news concerning how *not* to create infographics demonstrates that information literacy remains a continuing challenge in the newsroom as it does across society more broadly. Worse still, the rise of hyperpartisan news represents a new arena in which post-truth infographics may circulate and mislead online audiences that are increasingly fragmented, and diffuse.

The concluding chapter in this book comprises three sections. First, I will set out a detailed overview of the history of the news infographic. Second, I will address the issue of standards, best practice, and ethics in news infographics, exploring the reputation of news infographics and suggesting a way of understanding them that helps to contextualize their increasing value to society (irrespective of their early legacy). Third, and last, I will set out my own philosophical-theoretical justification for the visualization of data against its detractors, situated within wider debates in communications and cultural and journalism studies literatures.

6   Conclusion

A new life begins when a man once sees with his own eyes all that before he has
but partially heard or read of.

J. W. Goethe, *Travels in Italy* (1978), trans. A. J. W. Morrison

A Summary History of Infographics in British News

Infographics first appeared at the height of Britain's late-Enlightenment and
bourgeois public sphere. They were inspired and produced by two members of that loose network of individuals associated with the Lunar Society:
Joseph Priestley and William Playfair. Within this sphere, ideas were often
shared and engaged with in an environment that privileged the ear rather
than the eye, in communal spaces. However, while Playfair's infographics
were present during the long, slow emergence of what we today recognize
as public opinion, they only became a regular feature in the formation of
public opinion (in our news), much later, in the second half of the twentieth century. How might we account for this delay, given their purported
universality? And why didn't they take off, for example with the emergence
of Linotype printing?

Many reasons have been put forth to explain the delay in the adoption
of infographics in the social sciences over this period, some technological, some structural, some cultural (Wainer & Spence, 2005; Wainer, 2006).
Anderson (2018) has suggested that "both technological affordances and
production routines" (48) contributed to the failure of infographics to take
off in early twentieth-century journalism. But as I showed in chapter 5 with
regard to turn-of-the-century Dundee's newspapers, technique and routine

seem to represent a less compelling immediate explanation for the relative absence of infographics from British newspapers, than does the pervasive spirit of conservatism, and elitism that informed the struggle for control of the modern twentieth-century newsroom. There were other reasons too: for example, the usage (or lack of usage) of infographics in contingent professions, the degree to which journalists valorized the objective standard, and not least the matter of "manipulative" publicity. The principles of associationism, so important to the potential in infographics as a communicative form, also made infographics vulnerable to critique, after the rise of post-Freudian fears about sensory (particularly visual) manipulation techniques (Marcuse, 1955). All of these factors help, by degrees, to account for the comparative time lag in infographics becoming popularized in the UK.

The news infographic is distinct from its graphical precedents. It is, after Hollis's critique of popular news media (1970), a species informed by two distinct visual discourses, both of which evolved across earlier phases of data visualization: the proto-infographic, the classical, and the improving. The news infographic first appeared during what I call the commercial phase, during the nineteenth-century fin de siècle. One of the visual discourses it drew upon was contemporaneous social-scientific graphical forms that were in turn inspired by the much earlier works of Playfair and Priestley. But rather than being based on a visual rhetoric of "truth to nature," as these early graphical forms had been, the new social scientific charts were excised of impactful visual rhetoric and presented according to the scientific, objective standard of the time (Daston & Galison, 2007). These forms emerge in the work of Jevons and Bowles; they are plain, methodical, useful, structured, serious, and thoroughly utilitarian; they are visually Gradgrindian (inflexibly utilitarian). In the serious and financial press they were applied to *useful* or *serious,* abstract matters such as the weather or commodity prices. These were, in keeping with the discursive practices of nineteenth-century news, reproductions and representations of information, encouraging the reader's interpretation and analysis (Matheson, 2000). They were a "vehicle for public debate" (Ibid., 568); it is this status that constitutes their authority. There was no attempt in these early infographics to discursively convey a representation of reality; and as such, they do not represent a discourse of news.

Around the time that these neo-classical graphical forms start to emerge in British newspapers, an entirely separate, highly impactful infographic form emerges. These pictograms are employed either persuasively (such as may be found in Mulhall's work) or in the form of propaganda (later published in official almanacs of the Habsburg Empire). They provide a global-comparative perspective on the individual's place within society, and in turn, the rank of that society within the wider elite nations. They are a trivial, ephemeral, and miscellaneous consumer commodity. They represent general knowledge that may serve a purpose in certain social occasions; the earliest examples were concerned with the dominant political idea of the late nineteenth-century: nationalism.

The New Journalism embodied "a medley of various public styles, voices and types of text" (Matheson, 2000, 563), which was used to speak to a mass audience in terms they might understand, and enjoy. Illustrated weeklies and periodicals (and by degrees the early dailies, including the rapidly consolidating regional press) employed graphical forms both serious, and fun, arranged discursively in such a way as to speak to the wider public(s) they sought to reach. They started to appear in illustrated weeklies (including reproductions from third-party sources such as almanacs and year books) from the 1890s. They were occasionally bylined, but sources were rarely attributed. By the turn of the century, they were beginning to appear in the popular dailies too.

During the 1930s, around a decade after a unified discourse of written journalism first emerged (Matheson, 2000), the first, tentative news infographics discursively presented as "news" were published. Some are pictograms; others are "serious" chart forms with pictorial or illustrated accompaniment. They are discursively distanced from the minimalist model of the early social scientific graphs of the 1880s. They emerge in popular dailies like the *Daily Mirror* and the *Daily Mail*, and they are (sometimes) used to accompany relatively new types of news stories, including human interest features. They are discursively employed in broadening the scope of what contemporaneous audiences conceived news to be. The visual formula of the interwar tabloid newspaper, and the rise of the production or process journalists to key editorial positions during this period are important catalysts in this shift. The rise of the visual in advertising and in cinema were two important contingent influences. The social-scientific chart continues to appear in the serious local and financial presses, for readers who are increasingly coming into contact with infographics in formal education, from the turn of the century, until the outbreak of World War II.

Between the wars, the commercial phase gave way to an ideological phase. Animated Isotype pictograms gained a significant viewing in cinemas in the form of public information (propaganda) newsreels, and could occasionally be found in the newspaper press (particularly of the left). After the war, the Expressograph was the first example of a graphically composed, consistent brand of news infographic in British journalism—created by the first in-house graphic design department in Fleet Street. The style was bold—thick white trend-lines contrasted with black backgrounds. The style is highly impactful, and owes an obvious debt to professional graphic design. Despite a general and consistent use of misleading methods, the style and feel of these infographics began to influence the aesthetic of news infographics in the serious press, and in particular at the *Sunday Times*, throughout the 1960s, a byproduct of intensifying commercial pressure within wider industry. The Expressograph bridges the shift from the ideological phase to the modern professional phase.

The upmarket *Sunday Times* of the late 1960s and 1970s brought the news infographic into the serious business of reporting the news. Peter Sullivan's synoptic diagrams, and his journalistic-graphic method, were both essential ingredients in Harold Evans's progressive journalistic legacy. The increasing sophistication of the graphs published in the *Sunday Times* during this era speaks to a visual turn in newspapers. A further differentiation of graphical forms shows that some readers have an increasingly sophisticated grasp of infographics, a consequence of improvements in secondary education and of a new generation of white-collar roles in the postindustrial landscape.

In the early 1980s, infographic artists emerged from the chaos of Wapping with increased autonomy. New, computerized printing technologies (such as Atex and *Adobe Illustrator 88*) began to affect their working practices and the aesthetics of news infographics. During the 1990s, new communications technologies, or rather new commercial uses of these technologies (satellite technologies and the Internet) provided grounds for a new wholesale market in international news infographics. The following decade, the 2000s, brought increased Internet bandwidth, new tablet media, increasingly sophisticated software (including Flash), and changing audience behaviors, all of which contributed to the emergence of the autonomous and self-confident visual journalist. With the rise of the first newsrooms that prioritized the Internet in their distribution during the

2010s, the visual journalist was now involved in interaction design and in producing viral interactives that help audiences better understand the news in fun and engaging ways.

What Makes a Good News Infographic?

News infographics have, over the years, been routinely scorned in the mathematical-statistical literature. Misuse of graphical forms whether through ignorance or deliberate misuse (as with the Expressograph of the late 1950s) have been rightly pilloried. On the one hand, it may be true that too few journalists are grounded in statistical methods (and standards in visualizing data) in some British newsrooms, but on the other hand, legitimate critiques of news infographics are sometimes conflated with disputed standards (such as Huff's "gee whizz" graph, or the use of circles in charts). Where do we start, then, in making sense of what constitutes a "good" news infographic?

Drawing upon William Playfair's works, Costigan-Eaves and Macdonald-Ross (1990, 320–324) suggest five early-modern principles of "the graphical method" that seem to inform his designs, which I paraphrase here:

1. It is a way of making difficult or boring material more comprehensible.
2. Busy people require visual cues in their reading matter.
3. Data are more interpretable in charts than in tables.
4. It is attractive to the eye (is easy to interpret).
5. It makes data more memorable.

Too vague to represent standards in any practical sense, these principles nevertheless provide an insight into Playfair's contribution to the field—what might be called infographic *proto-ethics*. Ward (2004) traces the origins of modern journalism back to a messy collection of proto-ethics that first emerged during the seventeenth century among the Civil War propaganda of the period: "[a]…mix of puffery, opportunism, toadying to authority, and concern for truth. The editors could be both insincere and committed; their publications both biased and surprisingly factual. For ill or good, here is where journalism ethics starts" (Ibid., 102). Although published much later, as we have seen, Playfair's *Tomahawk! Or Censor general* perfectly embodies some of these qualities, not least in its title. But puffery, according to Ward, was gradually abandoned with the rise of *factual techniques* during the nineteenth century, such as: "unbiased news, eyewitnesses' accounts, reliable sources, and judicious editing" (Ibid., 107). A number of key factual techniques were either already present, or were emerging during Playfair's lifetime, including:

- Independent news gathering, which Defoe undertook during his reporting of the Great Lisbon earthquake (1755).
- Shorthand, early versions of which had existed as far back as Gurney (1750).
- Semaphore telegraphy that would (much later, in the 1870s, after semaphore lines had been replaced by the electric telegraph system) lead to the routinization of double-checking as a form of verification in news culture (Conboy, 2004). Playfair infamously is said to have sent a working model of the first French semaphore telegraph system to the Duke of York, during his time in France (Berkowitz, 2018).

These techniques were beginning to present a means of challenging the era of political subsidy (and bribery) that defined eighteenth-century journalism, serving (in principle, if not always in practice) to shape and to respond to public opinion while dis-intermediating prying church officials, corrupt politicians, and social worthies. Playfair's graphical innovations can therefore be said to represent a little discussed, modern journalistic factual technique. Thinking of infographics in this way, as one factual technique among many within the ethical purview of the journalist, represents a helpful way of distinguishing news infographics from the scientific ideal, and crucially, from the scientistic discourse of methodologically objective standards in infographic design.

The History of the Search for Standards in Infographics

A perceived need for standards governing graphical methods in diagrams and maps first arose in the sciences during the second half of the nineteenth century. With the emergence of international congresses, statisticians and scientists sought a universalizing language in order to challenge the babelization that seemed to be emerging due to inconsistencies in scientific practices across national boundaries (Palsky, 1999). The first coherent attempt to set out standards in infographic design were developed by Willard Brinton, who chaired the American Society of Mechanical Engineers committee on standards for graphical presentation, from 1914 (Funkhouser, 1937, 323); this document would inform more detailed, subsequent standards (The American Society of Mechanical Engineers, 1938). These early standards were tentative rather than rigid, and they were predicated on general, universalizing assumptions. For example, as published by Joint Committee on Standards for Graphic Presentation, the first "generally applicable principles of elementary graphic presentation" states: "The general arrangement of a diagram should proceed from left to right" (Brinton, 1915, 791). However, experiments in the field of cognitive psychology show that representations of temporal concepts are influenced by directionality of written language (Tversky, Kugelmass, & Winter, 1991). In other words, this is a culturally relative standard, rather than being a truly universal one.

The contemporary, mathematical-statistical approach to standards in graphic design are most clearly expressed in the works of Edward Tufte, though others including Huff (1954) and Paulos (1996) make contributions from a similar perspective. Tufte's Principles of Graphical Excellence are worth returning to here, for a more detailed critique:

1. Graphical excellence is the well-designed presentation of interesting data—a matter of substance, of statistics, and of design.
2. Graphical excellence consists of complex ideas communicated with clarity, precision, and efficiency.
3. Graphical excellence is that which gives to the viewer the greatest number of ideas in the shortest time with the least ink in the smallest space.
4. Graphical excellence is nearly always multivariate.
5. And graphical excellence requires telling the truth about the data. (1983, 51)

The first of these principles is predicated on an unexamined universalism concerning what may be found "interesting." The second (and arguably the fourth) concerns complexity—good infographics express complex (i.e., multivariate) ideas (even if news does not). The third principle seems to blend elements of associationism and utilitarianism. The antithesis of Tufte's principles are *chartjunk*; visual embellishment is considered patronizing and infantilizing. Tufte is particularly scathing about the work of Tim Holmes, designer at *Time* magazine through the late 1970s and 1980s, for producing work he considers both misleading and unsavory (Tufte, 1997).

Tufte blames the skills, attitudes, and organizational structures in which designers and editors work for shortcomings in news infographics. At the time he was writing, it seems that some of these claims were justified. John

Grimwade, not atypically for a newspaper graphic designer of his era, studied a foundation course at Canterbury College of Art, in 1969, before specializing in graphic design. On the nature of the syllabus of this course, he said:

> I did not learn a thing about statistics at college. Back then, data visualization training was basically zero. And it's still a common problem today. Charts are often being made by people who have no idea about the basic principles of statistics. I'm hoping this will change as chart-literacy gradually becomes part of the educational system. Anything that I know about handling data, I've gradually picked up along the way. The good news is that there's a lot of excellent online resources available today to help with good data-plotting practices.[1]

Tuft's principles, along with the works of visual journalists, have contributed to the raising of standards in the modern newsroom, where today, bespoke style guides and tip-sheets provide guidance for generalist journalists.[2] But this does not mean that Tufte's principles are necessarily the most appropriate fit for best practice in news infographics. They singularly fail to take account of the professional and organizational imperatives (and pressures) of the newsroom, and more broadly the culture of news. Unsurprisingly then, infographics practitioners working in the news, including Peter Sullivan (1987), Nigel Holmes (1984), Dona Wong (2010), and Alberto Cairo (2012), have sought to establish a discrete form of best practice in news infographics. Their approach broadly involves conceiving infographics as synonymous with "visual journalism"; therefore best practice in this field is drawn both from traditional, liberal journalistic ethics and values as well as from the positivist canon that informs infographic standards in the scientific community.

Infographics in this view are a tool or a technology (Cairo, 2012), rather than a methodology per se. They are made in the context of tensions arising from applied theory in the newsroom, in dichotomies such as professional and organizational values and the need to maintain graphical integrity while reaching out to a mass, undifferentiated audience, with a wide range of experiences, knowledge, and affective dispositions. Sullivan's (1987) approach is neither as structured nor as dogmatic as Tufte's, accommodating as it does the practical realities of audience need, publication schedule and space constraints, and the strictures that these process and protocols enforce on the design of newspaper infographics. For Sullivan, the "fundamental argument in favour of graphics is that, in many situations, they can give more or different information in a given space than words alone" (Ibid., 20). Sullivan's news values were defined by space, but they run counter to Tufte's principles in so far as space is an invitation to experiment and move beyond mere statistical charts, into the realms of imaginative visual representations: "When more space is available and the amount of information needing presentation is limited or an idea or option predominates, the possibilities grow almost in direct relation to size" (Ibid., 41). Sullivan's approach is pragmatic, opportunistic rather than idealist, embodying as it does the hegemony of organizational norms over professional ones. It deals with perceived audience need, and he acknowledges that news values are constrained by space, something an earlier generation of sociologists of the newsroom articulated in their findings (Fishman, 1980; Schudson, 1989). Best practice in news infographics is better understood as an ongoing debate, rather than as a fixed normative set list of representational methods.[3] News media have to weigh best practice against audience expectation.

Infographic standards as they emerged in the sciences and social sciences tended to be guided by a universal, guiding principle of objectivity; however, as I mentioned in chapter 1, in relation to history, the concept of objectivity has been under sustained assault in recent times, and moreover, objectivity has not always been a central concern within modern British newspaper journalism.[4] Even where the principle of objectivity (howsoever defined) is prized, in broadcasting, in news agencies, and in other news cultures, the pressure created by professional and institutional tensions within the newsroom often require that news work (including infographics) conforms to a form of best practice that incorporates, but is not led by, an adherence to objectivism. *Good* news infographics should therefore be defined as *factual techniques* that strike a pragmatic balance between wider standards in data visualization and journalistic ethics. They are created with a duty of care for the news audience, and they contribute to the discursive authority of news.

In Defense of Infographics: A Philosophical Critique

A range of criticism of infographics exists in cultural and communications literatures that are epistemic, rather than normative, in nature. In the remaining section of this chapter, I will set out a defense of infographics and data visualization against several of these criticisms. In turn I will, by contrast with those "critical" approaches that dominate in the field, present an optimistic theorization of the infographic as *synopticon*, a data visualization tool that nurtures and extends critical thought that is essential in modern, postindustrial democracy.

Some of the most trenchant criticisms of infographic forms have emerged from the left. These are relatively common even today. A typical contemporary example from this school of thought is provided by Davies, who decries the selective choice of numbers that in infographic form are often used to "ram home" (2018, 75–76) political arguments. This approach represents a continuation of post-Freudian pessimism about sensory (particularly visual) manipulation techniques that are employed in the mass media. But the origins of leftist critique in this field go further back still. Indeed, one of the earliest critiques of infographics may be inferred from Karl Marx's *Das Kapital* (*Capital*) (2004 [1867]), according to which abstract graphical forms that express abstract (rather than "real," that is *social*) relationships may be said to represent a form of *commodity fetishism*. That said, this fetishism may in turn say more about the human capacity for anthropomorphism than it does about any particular mode of thought in capitalist society (Cowen, 1998).

Later, Marxist critical theorists Horkheimer and Adorno offered a critique of numerical equivalence (and so by definition, the visual representation of numbers) in the context of what they perceived to be the failings of the Enlightenment: "Bourgeois society is ruled by equivalence. It makes dissimilar things comparable by reducing them to abstract quantities. For the Enlightenment, anything which cannot be resolved into numbers, and ultimately into one, is illusion; modern positivism consigns it to poetry. Unity remains the watchword from Parmenides to Russell. All gods and qualities must be destroyed" (Horkheimer & Adorno, 2002 [1987], 4–5). But the Enlightenment desire to destroy gods or "qualified belief" identified here was certainly not one shared by Priestley, whose utilitarianism was underwritten by a profound, indeed a radical sense of faith. In fact, Priestley used scientific method to challenge those myths that complicate and cloak democratic processes in order to challenge the hegemonic structures of his day. While no radical, he can hardly be portrayed as a reactionary either. Playfair, as we have seen, was a common-sense pragmatist. Clearly then, the figures most closely associated with the emergence of infographics do not conform to this dogmatic characterization; and neither can they fairly be held accountable for later interpretations and applications of their innovations.

Later still, in the preface to *On Television* (1998), Pierre Bourdieu set out a defense of his choice of format for the lecture he presented. Though these words concern the genre of television news generally, more specifically a critique of the infographic may be discerned, from a French poststructural-ist perspective. I present a relatively long quotation here in order to develop a sustained critique of Bourdieu's muddled position.

> To maintain the focus on the crucial element—the lecture itself—and contrary to what usually happens on television I chose, in agreement with the producer, to eliminate effects such as changes in the format or camera angles. I also left out illustrations (selections from broadcasts, reproductions of documents, statistics, and so on). Besides taking up precious time, all of these things undoubtedly would have made it harder to follow my argument. The contrast with regular television—the object of analysis—was, by design, a way of affirming the inde-pendence of analytical and critical discourse, even in the cumbersome, didactic and dogmatic guise of a large public lecture. Television has gradually done away with this kind of discourse (political debates in the United States are said to allow no one to speak for more than seven seconds). But intellectual discourse remains one of the most authentic forms of resistance to manipulation and a vital affirma-tion of the freedom of thought. (Bourdieu, 1998, 11)

First, the notion that infographics "take up precious time" may seem odd to anyone familiar with the eye-tracking studies of newspapers in the 1980s; with the marketing literature of the 1920s and 1930s; or with the psycho-logical prescience Playfair alighted upon in the justifications that accom-panied his inventions in the late eighteenth century. On the contrary, the evidence suggests that infographics are in fact a highly efficient commu-nicative medium; indeed, their rise in modern society is due to this very quality. It is their efficiency that makes infographics an ideal means of chal-lenging information overload (Toffler, 1970) in postindustrial societies that, as Daniel Bell (1999 [1973]) observed, necessarily rely on "the codification of knowledge into abstract systems of symbols" (20).

Second, Pictorial Superiority Effect (PSE) shows us that information con-veyed using a combination of text and images is more likely to be retained than the same information conveyed in text alone. Yet Bourdieu seems to prefer the public lecture as medium, despite its association with the dogma-tism of twentieth-century dictators, because, on his terms, the spoken word represents "the independence of analytical and critical discourse." There is in this criticism a sense of the idea that information conveyed using infographics (a medium designed for the eye) tends to drive out information conveyed using spoken discourse (the ear's medium). Infographics are, according to this reasoning, a form of visual manipulation that tends to thwart the authenticity of critical thought and that must be resisted. But conversation is not the soul of democracy (Schudson, 1997). And as we have seen, Priestley's charts were intended to be pedagogically supportive of rather than substitutive of critical thought.

Third, the notion that infographics make arguments harder to follow, excepting one or two types in certain circumstances, is little more than a myth. Certainly, the use of a scatter plot to support a news story may well make following an argument more difficult for a portion of the audience that struggles to interpret this particular graphical format (Kehaulani Goo, 2015). However, news media have developed a range of infographic styles and formats in order to appeal to mass audiences comprising diverse sub-groupings, with a range of capacities for (and familiarities with) graphical forms (Dick, 2014). Some of these forms are relatively self-explanatory; others (particularly new, interactive forms of data visualization) may require some detailed explanation. From elsewhere on the political spectrum, classicists may criticize infographics on the grounds that that they do not traditionally belong within the bounds of "intellectual discourse." Barn-hurst and Nerone identify this argument in Marshall McLuhan's famous aphorism "the medium is the message" whereby all that is good in "high" fields of knowledge, that contributes to our intellectual enlightenment, is bound up with formal characteristics, and so, vice versa, the visual characteristics associated with popular news media, such as *USA Today*, must therefore make us stupid (Barnhurst & Nerone, 2002, 8). The denigration of the visual in news (whether manifest in the patronizing or the feminization of these forms) is a long-running theme in newsrooms as it is among the wider reading public. It is something that may be traced back to the thinking of that high priest of Victorian classicism, Matthew Arnold. Are news infographics too simplistic, too patronizing? British school children have been taught in the use of graphs since at least the turn of the twentieth century, albeit in the early decades this was in a limited and haphazard way. It was only into the interwar period that infographics started being routinely taught (among a majority of students) in schools. In the 1960s, with the rise of misleading infographics in news, *data literacy* started being taught in secondary school syllabuses. Today British children are examined on their understanding of graphic forms from the ages of seven and eight.[5] Clearly, we are learning how to interpret graphs increasingly early in life, and in increasingly sophisticated ways; and we are becoming increasingly dependent on them, with the rise of postindustrial, information-based jobs and roles across society. This situation can hardly be said to represent a process that is making us more stupid, however "stupid" may be defined.

The Bourgeois Public Sphere and the Discursive Formation of Infographics

Jurgen Habermas's (1989) concept of the *bourgeois public sphere* is situated in the seventeenth and eighteenth centuries. It arose during the unraveling of feudalism, and with the emergence of privileged opinion groups, whose members used their ideas to competitively pursue what they considered to be in the public interest. In this hypothetical forum, ideas had to be discursively framed in order to be convincing; they had to be essentially (in Habermas's terms) rational. This sphere replaced the mere representation of feudal, monarchical power before the people; and it was only made possible by what Habermas calls institutional criteria that included discursive spaces, such as coffee houses, which provided sanctuary for a collective critical appraisal of authorities' activities.

Early infographics that seem to speak a "universal" language that allows anyone to speak to everyone would, in Habermas's analysis, have been the ideal communicative form for this public sphere. However, this critique risks being ahistorical, for although the early pioneers of graphical forms thought of their handiwork as universally comprehensible, as we have seen, until the final quarter of the nineteenth century infographics were more or less especially designed to communicate exclusively with the middle and upper classes in society. Synoptic graphical formats from their conception were inherently ideological; they expressed Nightingale's reforming zeal; Playfair's Pittite free-market ideology; and Priestley's radical millenarianism. But these early works were by no means discursively monolithic. The text that accompanies Priestley's charts is avowedly transparent and objective; he is very clear about his influences (and the limitations of his findings, in terms of his intended audiences). The purpose of his synoptic charts was to encourage the reader to critically engage with the subject matter at hand. His works dissect the deeds of the powerful, in such a way that they empower the audience. It is easy to see why they became popular as a pedagogic tool and how their basic idea was adopted and applied to teaching environments far removed from the dissenting academy.

By contrast, the texts that accompany Playfair's early infographic works were more didactic than enabling. Playfair's discourse was compromised by the lack of consistency in transparency, in later editions, and not least by his implicit "willing" of England to win its trade wars. These texts were part of an (overt) ideological campaign rather than bound up with the discursive format of other reference works of the late Scottish Enlightenment. This may in turn help to explain why Playfair's innovations failed to become popular in the idealistic sphere of the day, associated as they were with closed-minded rather than critical discourse. It may also go some way to explaining why the impact of Playfair's innovations, the visual rhetoric and embellishments of these forms, were excised from the modern utilitarian, social-scientific graphs of Jevons, Bowles, and others; these elements were perhaps too closely associated with Playfair's reactionary agenda.

A Poetics of Infographics

Modern cognitive psychology helps, as we have seen, explain the appeal of infographics in terms of understanding; but what of their aesthetic appeal? Pierre Bourdieu seems to suggest that infographics are somehow inauthentic, in the context of independent critical thought, a critique that echoes Walter Benjamin's (Benjamin & Underwood, 2008 [1935]) denigration of mechanical reproduction. Against these criticisms we may profitably borrow from the (admittedly, overly pessimistic) literary criticism of Roland Barthes—who in *New Critical Essays* (Barthes, 1980) set out a considered critique of Diderot's *Encyclopédie*'s illustrative and diagrammatic plates that may help to explain, by degrees, the aesthetic appeal of infographics. First, Barthes suggests that the *Encyclopédie*'s plates are representative of a discourse of transparency and of an absence of secrecy; he is naturally skeptical about these claims for to him they reveal nothing more than the rise of modern ocularcentrism. Jay (1993) traces the centrality of the eye and the enduring hegemony of the visual in contemporary life, back to the privileging of sight over the other faculties in ancient Greek thought and culture, and in particularly to Platonism. In terms of helping to understand Barthes' position, Ezrahi traces suspicion of the eye in French modern intellectual thought more specifically to "a long tradition identifying the gaze with social domination and control of the individual, a threat to his or her personal freedom and autonomy" (Ezrahi 1999, 331–332). Monarchs throughout history, from Louis XVI, to Victoria and Albert, to Franz Joseph I of Austria, have, as we have seen, recognized (or have been said to have recognized) the potential and the appeal of data visualization. However, while it is clear that the association with Hapsburg-era pictographic propaganda stands opposed to the principle of free, critical thought, it should not be forgotten that infographic forms, particularly those of the reforming progressives of the nineteenth century, represent a visual-material discourse of persuasion that served to mediate the diffusion of democratic power. Persuasion, Jowett and O'Donnell remind us, is categorically distinct from propaganda, in so far as it is transactional; it assumes an active, not a passive audience, and it assumes either "interactive or trans-active dependency" (2014 [1986], 32) between persuader and persuadee that in turn involves the resolving of mutual needs. In pragmatic (if not in poststructuralist) terms then, this quality of persuasion (as distinct from propaganda) is clearly a positive boon, at least in so far as regulating the state, and other powerful bodies in society, is concerned.

Second, as a series of vignettes that materially break up the continuity of lived experience, the *Encyclopédie's* plates, Barthes argues, seem to serve to drive out fear of the material world. More recent radical theorists, drawing upon the writing of Gilles Deleuze, have criticized synoptic chronologies in similar terms on the grounds that they seek to "dominate complexity through linearity" (Arienzo, 2016, 96), and that they authorize a mode of certainty that is out of step with the indeterminacy, continuity, and relativism of the modern world. On the other hand, it may be countered that infographics, after the field of statistics more generally, seek to drive out uncertainty and risk and that, in terms of how modern life is actually lived, this approach serves an important social function that contributes toward the improvement of our lives.

The Panopticon/Synopticon Dualism

Bentham built both his ideas for education and democratic accountability on the rationale of *The Panopticon* (1791). The essential difference between these concepts concerns what criminologist Thomas Mathiesen (1997) calls the "arithmetic of power optics." In Bentham's approach the many are observed by the few, whereas in a representative democracy, the opposite holds true. Mathiesen explores this dichotomy in terms of a panoptic/synoptic dualism, and in so doing, he challenges a central tenet in Foucault's *Discipline and Punish* (1975)—namely, that at some point between the mid-1700s and the mid-1800s, the process of criminal punishment in France shifted from a system defined as *synopticon* (the many observing the few) to one defined as *panopticon* (the few observing the many). Mathiesen argues instead that the two coexisted and continue to coexist; they are in fact related. This assumption that the synoptic and the panoptic are mutually assuring is, however, overly pessimistic; it ignores (or at least unduly de-emphasizes) the role of personal agency in the contemporary context of new information and communication technologies. Instead, if we assume Dewey's pragmatic approach, which holds that our faculties are active, constantly engaging with, and probing reality, rather than passively quiescent in it, a new perspective on the synopticon is possible. It is one in which, as Hier rightly observes: "media narratives embedded in complex discursive formations operate in fluid and, often, contradictory ways" (2002, 405).

From Synoptic Gaze to Synopticon

Synopticism is essential to the discursive power of both timelines and infographics. Here I would like to return to the topic of what makes a "good" data visualization in news, but this time specifically in the context of public discourse. Central to what I propose is a tension in the meanings of the word "synoptic." The term bridges the general and the comprehensive:

1. The first definition, with respect to charts and tables (that is constitutive), represents "furnishing a general (summary) view of some subject" (Lexico, 2019b).

2. The second, with respect to a mental act (that is performative) represents "taking a combined or comprehensive mental view of something" (Ibid.).

All numeric infographics are synoptic in the first of these senses, offering a trend line (or an implied trend line) or a simple, visual comparative account on certain broadly (if not universally) agreed, normative terms. Some data visualizations, particularly those that are multivariate (such as may be found in Playfair's later works; in Nightingale's trilogy of diagrams; in the Isotype social exhibits of the Museum for Social and Economic Affairs in Vienna; or in any collection or combination of thematically consistent charts across a wall chart, a page, or a screen), make possible and sustain synoptic thinking, too. Playfair observed that the superiority of his innovations over tables resided in their capacity to present proportion, progression, and quantity all within a single field of vision, in an appeal to what De Bruyn calls *visual acuity* (2004). Correspondingly, data visualizations often present a range of variables across a single viewing, allowing viewers to spot correlations between variables, to make inferences, and to test propositions. These infographics require (in keeping with Dewey's wider pragmatism) active, critical engagement on the audiences' part. Such charts, as Berkowitz observes, incorporate covariation and correlation—which is helpful, because "it helps answer 'if/then/when' questions—if we do this, then we should expect that to happen, perhaps when other conditions hold" (2018, 328).

A data visualization is what I call a *synopticon* when, in addition to satisfying the two preceding criteria, the data communicated also allows the many (in a mass society) in some way to critically engage with or appraise the actions of the few. This is true whether that data is generated by governmental body, private enterprise, or nonprofit; and whether the data generated is a consequence of activities undertaken on our behalf, or as a consequence of activities that have some bearing on our lives. The synopticon, where it has been designed in accordance with good standards in infographic (and journalistic) best practice, is an essential tool in the formation of public opinion; it allows the public to hold the powerful to account, before the attestive gaze of an increasingly information-literate, postindustrial society. The synopticon has, on McLuhan's terms, extensible qualities; it extends the body as it extends the body politic, retaining the power to shape and to transform both.

The Epistemological Basis of the Synopticon

The will to somehow contain, or to limit our sense of connectedness with the universe seems to be an essential component in what it means to be human. This is an idea that, as Iris Murdoch observed, is in turn predicated on an assumption of continuity in space and in time (1994). So it is that infographics perform an important purpose in our lives, representing those numbers that may help us to account for the blind spots in our empirical engagement with the world around us (Blastland & Dilnot, 2008). However, as Jay (1994) observes, the mapmaker cannot avoid the biases (in terms of both perspective and culture) that are constitutive of their *point of view*; there can be no detachment, no view from nowhere. The same is true of the author of the synopticon. Data are always created from (and viewed from) a particular point of view. Nevertheless, Jay observes that a process of synoptic analysis is essential to the historic exploration of ideas, expressing as it does (albeit with caveats) "a certain cautious optimism" (Ibid., 18) about communication. The same, I will argue, may be true of journalism and its function in modern life.

For some, not least Henri Bergson, the simplicity of the synoptic timeline (and its implicit reductionism) seems to represent its central shortcoming (Rosenberg, 2004). But we should not confuse form with function. The synopticon is an ideological narrative that may be presented to a wider audience for deliberation, just as Priestley intended his charts to be used. Priestley's *A Chart of Biography* offered a staged display (in keeping with his Whiggish reading of history and his qualified optimism in progress), intended to develop the critical faculties of his students as part of a wider educational philosophy that eschewed paternalism, and encouraged debate and critical reasoning. These charts "expressed the potential of the graphic image and amplified the virtues of historical study itself" (Rosenberg & Grafton, 2010, 122). Priestley was open and honest about this ideology, and about its purpose. Rather than being unduly reductive, his synopticons were, on the contrary, intended to stimulate critical thought, among groups comprising a heterodox range of perspectives.

Like an epic poem, the synopticon incorporates both mimetic and diegetic senses; it offers a grand narrative, but it also accommodates a detailed, atomized reading of variables (be they biographical timelines or data points) in selective isolation. The synopticon challenges the pessimism of modern critical thought; it enables what Michael Power (1999) calls an *Evaluation Society*. At its origins, the synopticon represented the symbolic form of the rising middle classes in the late eighteenth century. It took its place among the various elements of the new visual reality that reflected the shifting power structures of that society, moving from court to town. Priestley foresaw (and helped to create) this new visual order, and his charts played no small role in this process. The synopticon then, is a powerful, reforming source of knowledge that challenges head-on conservative transcendentalism, and the old "mysteries" of political power.

The Synopticon: Accountability, Transparency, Publicity

Because the synopticon both shapes and is shaped by public opinion, it is therefore necessary to consider it in the wider context of theories of publicity. Bentham conceived of publicity as "the fittest law for securing the public confidence" (quoted in Splichal, 2002, 45). He broadly viewed public authorities with distrust. For Bentham, society was comprised of individuals, each seeking out personal interests, and the primary purpose of legislation was to secure this state of affairs (Ibid.). Public opinion was not simply disciplinary and censorious; in Bentham's *public opinion tribunal*, it served a number of important functions too, chief among them being "statistic" or "evidence-furnishing," providing the public with a means of securing information about the running of the state (quoted in Cutler, 1999, 328).

In Bentham's approach, however, Habermas observes a central problem, which he expresses in the context of television coverage of the German parliament: "Before the expanded public sphere the transactions themselves are stylized into a show. Publicity loses its critical function in favor of a staged display; even arguments are *transmuted into symbols* to which again one cannot respond by arguing but only by identifying with them" (Habermas, 1989, 206; emphasis mine). Infographics (if we interpret them here as being words or arguments *transmuted into symbols*) are, again, seen to drive out critical discourse. Habermas locates the rise of manipulative publicity within approximately the same era that pictograms emerge: the late nineteenth century. During this time, Habermas argues, the unity of public opinion came under pressure following the expansion of the market economy and the increased franchise, leading to, on his terms, a re-feudalization of the public sphere; this is seen in the private resolution of private interests in private, rather than in public, and a new (old) public discourse comprising successive displays of (manipulative) publicity that drown out any attempt toward transactive, mutually engaged critical publicity (Ibid.). However, the synopticon, as we have seen, originated in the late Enlightenment, long before this period, and some of its most ardent proponents (not least Priestley) sought to use timelines to inform, not to thwart critical discourse. We should be wary, therefore, of attributing to the synopticon a guiding determinism over its essential communicative potential.

Priestley's timelines and Playfair's charts may be understood within what Ezrahi (1992) calls the wider "civil epistemologies" of the late Enlightenment era. Like the "noble roads" he called for and his revolutionary scientific paraphernalia, Priestley's synopticons offer an alternative to the idle pageantry of the court; they made government action and ideas visible to the public (whether in terms of the rise, spread, or decline of empires, or the comparative life spans of historical figures). This process required a shift in its subjects' line of vision from the celebratory gaze of a critically unengaged public, to the attestive gaze of an informed citizen-witness; and one that became increasingly familiar with graphical forms from a relatively early age. On these terms, the synopticon represents "a strategy of legitimating the exercise of political power by externalizing or objectifying the actions of individual agents and rendering them public" (Ibid., 366–367), which may in turn be interpreted by a public that is increasingly equipped with the critical faculties to meaningfully do so.

Ezrahi suggests that the "technicalization of action and the objectification of sight" (1992, 368) have broadly been interpreted in one of two ways: the first positive, viewed as part of the move away from mythology and religion, toward scientific, political modernity; the second, more skeptical and relativistic, viewing "progress" as a literalization of history, manifest in a range of new, modern myths. Viewed from the first of these approaches, it is possible to understand the power infographics hold over modern society, not because of their association with progress, but rather, because they represent certain truths that we tend to prefer over other truths that may mislead—and that we must continue to discard.

Conclusion

Infographics are a democratizing technology conceived of in the same spirit of naive empiricism that saw facts as speaking universally interpretable truths for themselves; inspired by the progressive amateur and bureaucrat improvers of the nineteenth century. In the mid-twentieth-century they emerged as routine in the UK mass media, often in highly misleading forms, pushing overzealous and disingenuous propaganda and disinformation. Given this legacy, what hope is there, anyone reading this book might reasonably ask, that visual journalism can contribute something meaningful in the current post-truth era, when modern democracy, with its reliance on rationality and expertise, is under seemingly unrelenting threat from a rising tide of populism? Best practice in data visualization has taken a relatively long time to catch up with our news; and maintaining these standards remains an ongoing challenge. But best practice is clearly more than a mere checklist of agreed conventions. Both good and bad infographics are laden with other meanings that audiences interpret and that are in turn affected by the symbolic, the metaphorical, and the contextual. This includes affective disposition; there are forms that some news audiences just do not like.

It is therefore necessary to challenge some shibboleths that are seen (by some) as organizing principles in the design of infographics and data visualization. In particular I am concerned here with the supposed bad practice of patronizing audiences with certain down-market infographic forms. In the current climate, this matter must be weighted as a much less pressing concern than is the risk of vast swathes of the public switching off and disengaging from reliable news media completely, because their media do not reflect their ideas and their knowledge of the world around them, in the forms (including visual-discursive forms) and approaches that they recognize and enjoy. It is essential to acknowledge the role that audience affect and emotion play in public engagement in news; and that necessarily means that visually alluring data visualizations have a crucial role to play in the formation of our modern news and media, regardless of their tendency to reduce numerical fidelity or accuracy (or indeed, as they may challenge standards in taste and decency). An exclusive focus on what audiences understand in data, information, and facts represents a limited means of determining excellence in the field. Excellence in data visualization must also take into consideration what audiences identify with (in form and content), what they like and enjoy, and what, ultimately they will make practical use of. In conceptual terms, this requires that we revisit a relatively old anthropological idea, namely that news audiences (as people) should be considered less as comprising *rational animals*, and more as comprising *symbolic animals* (Cassirer, 1944).

Modern journalism, if it is to serve any meaningful purpose, must recognize and acknowledge its roles in both reflecting and shaping its audiences' experiences and views of the world. We need a modern journalism that reflects, cultivates, and reproduces those qualities that speak to the values of democracy. We need a news media that speaks truth to power, valorizing free speech in the public interest, and risking sanction and approbation in so doing. Good journalism is all around us, if we care to look for it—but it is neither easy, nor accidental, nor inevitable.

Today's visual journalists cannot undo the effects of long-buried memories of boredom in our school systems. Nor can they realistically combat on their own, the range of wild conspiracy theories that are embraced by a worryingly large proportion of the population in modern democracies. Nonetheless, visual journalists can continue to serve democracy well by communicating data with rigor, transparency, and fairness—if not with objective certainty—in forms that their audiences enjoy, and that accommodate and express their thoughts, their ideals, and how they want modern democracy and communication to be represented.

Notes

Chapter 1

1. Park's reasoning is set out in a thorough-going way by Rasmus Kleis Nielsen (2017) and has previously been applied in this field by Chris Anderson (2018).

2. An earlier iteration of these ideas was published in Dick (2017).

3. These categories were developed initially using empirical data and open coding during previous research (Dick, 2014, 2015a, b); my findings were tested iteratively, and improved, in the process of establishing a wider reach and scale of data collection, within the present project.

4. Dick (2015b), 5–36.

Chapter 2

1. The Corporation (1661) and Test (1673) Acts required an oath, and the reception of Anglican communion. This led the more orthodox believers (especially Baptists) toward commerce, and away from traditional, civic life. Dissenters were tolerated (unlike Catholics), but anyone who failed to uphold the Trinity (Church, King, and Parliament) was excluded (Braithwaite, 2003, 2–3).

2. For example, according to Watts, Anna Barbauld (Aitken), in her *Early Lessons* (1778) and *Hymns in / Prose for Children* (1781) pioneered educational texts written in a conversational discursive mode for young children (Watts, 1998, 6–7).

3. "Had I drawn the chart to be published in any other part of the world," he observes, "I should naturally, with the same ideas of relative fame, have made a different choice of names" (Priestley, 1764, 18).

4. "Now it is plain that when any person applies the terms long and short to the idea of time without apprehending any figure, or sensibly perceiving any harshness in the application, to him the properties of real length and shortness are the natural properties of time; and consequently the idea of something which hath length or

shortness is actually suggested by the terms. And what can this be but the idea of a line, or at least something lineal?" (Priestley, 1765b, 6).

5. "Time is continually suggested to us, by the view of this chart, under the idea of a river, flowing uniformly on, without beginning or end....If we compare the lives of men with that portion of it which this chart represents, they are little more than so many small straws swimming on the surface of this immense river" (Priestley, 1765b, 26).

6. The time after 1765 Priestley left blank in order "to be filled up by those who purchase the chart, as the changes shall take place, without being obliged to erase any thing" (Priestley, 1765b, 10).

7. "Even then, a wish (I mind its power), / A wish that to my latest hour / Shall strongly heave my breast—/ That I for puir auld Scotland's sake / Some usefu' plan or beuk could make, Or sing a sang at least" (Burns, "To the Guidwife of Wauchop House," *The Poetical Works of Robert Burns* (1870), 198).

8. Playfair argued that common sense was "the great charter of the human mind, and cannot be infringed upon or violated by the most splendid show of reason, or any argument, however it may be dressed out in all the trappings of the most refined art and ingenuity." From *The Tomahawk, or, Censor general*, December 1, 1795, 121.

9. For example, De Bruyn (2004) detects an element of associationism in Playfair's works, which he traces back to the Lockean idea of the mind as processor of sense impressions (122). Playfair's own reasoning about the chief advantages of his new method betrays a clear affinity with this ideal: "Whatever presents itself clearly...to the / mind, sets it to work, to reason, and think" (Playfair, 1801a [1786], 6–7). Playfair perceived his graphs as helping to speed the cognitive processes—and as an aid to memory (Wainer & Spence, 2005, 29).

10. *The Scots Magazine* republished Playfair's "Ballance of payments in England" line graph, January 1, 1787, 55.

11. The uncoupling of this concept from the word would not emerge until after the Great Reform Act of 1832.

12. In a (largely) positive critique of a previous version of *The Commercial and Political Atlas*, Dr. Gilbert Stuart, writing in *The Political Herald*, had urged Playfair "to do whatever he can, in any future editions, to make his leading ideas as familiar as possible to every imagination, by additional illustrations and directions; for these in some instances seem to be wanting" (Playfair, 1801a [1786], vii–viii).

13. *The Tomahawk, or, Censor general*, October 27, 1875, 1.

14. Ibid., January 13, 1796.

15. *Anticipation*, March 12, 1808, 16. During the 1790s there appears to have been some growth in print culture aimed at the lower classes in society (Harris, 2008), including *The Tomahawk, or, Censor general*.

16. "As knowledge increases among mankind, and transactions multiply, it becomes more and more desirable to abbreviate and facilitate the modes of conveying information from one person to another, and from one individual to the many" (Playfair, 1801a [1786], vii).

17. "Suppose the money received by a man in trade were all in guineas, and that every evening he made a single pile of all the guineas received during the day, each pile would represent a day, and its height would be proportioned to the receipts of that day; so that by this plain operation, time, proportion, and amount, would all be physically combined" (Playfair, 1801a [1786], xi).

18. "There might be some difference of opinion as to modes and rates" Playfair suggests, "but there was none as to the general principle" (1805a, 243). A few years earlier, Pitt, at war with the French and fearing the spectre of Jacobinism, had sought to repress his opponents, creating a febrile atmosphere that broached dangerous ground in 1795, with the stoning of King George III's carriage and the subsequent passage of legislative "Gagging Acts." In setting out a justification for paying for his war with the French, Pitt appealed to collective self-interest and to patriotism, both of which are clearly embodied in Playfair's work.

19. Those mathematical graphs that predate Playfair (with one or two examples excepted) emerged from a similar approach to science as may be found in Cartesian rationalism; this was a very different way of thinking about data, as Wainer observes, than the a posteriori, atheoretical plotting (and exploration) of data that arose in the mid-eighteenth century (2006, 10). The extent to which it may be said that these earlier mathematical examples influenced Playfair is the subject of some dispute within the scientific literature. Some argue, on the one hand, that the dominant Cartesian-rationalist-deductive philosophy of the seventeenth and early eighteenth centuries was an essential stepping stone in the history of the graphical display of data (Funkhouser, 1937; Beniger & Robyn, 1978). On the other hand, it is argued that this rationalist mindset actually helped to suppress the emergence of infographics in the sciences (Wainer & Velleman, 2001) and that it was only with the emergence of the inductive approach, and of realist empiricism, during the mid-eighteenth century, (via Dugald Stewart, and others) (Wainer & Spence, 2005) that information graphics, as a paradigmatic shift in scientific thinking, became possible. The fact that both the chief stated inspiration behind Playfair's innovations, and the innovator himself, were authors working firmly within the Newtonian worldview would suggest that a rationale for data visualization did not exist within the Cartesian paradigm; and so for this reason, Wainer and Velleman's argument would seem to be the more compelling.

20. For example, Playfair, like Priestley, provided space in his charts for readers to annotate and create their own knowledge this way (Berkowitz, 2018, 36).

21. "Chart of the National Debt of Britain" from *The Commercial and Political Atlas* (Ibid., 37).

Chapter 3

1. Writing to Sydney Herbert in 1857, she said: "I have written to Dr Farr for the diagram *which is to affect thro' the Eyes what we may fail to convey to the brains of the public through their word-proof ears*" (quoted in Diamond & Stone, 1981, 69; emphasis mine).

2. While Brasseur's critique is highly engaging, some care is required in extrapolating the rhetorical message (and logic) in these diagrams. These same three diagrams (albeit with slightly altered titles) appeared in the reverse order in Nightingale's earlier *Notes on Matters Affecting the Health and Hospital Administration of the British Army* (1858). In this official report to government, over one thousand pages in length, these three diagrams were scattered throughout the text, hundreds of pages apart from each other. Clearly then, the combined visual rhetoric of these three diagrams that Brasseur outlines do not carry from one publication to the other.

3. That said, his outlook was intellectually aligned with many of the ideas and ways of thinking that we have already encountered. For example, he wrote a treatise on associationism, *What to Teach and How to Teach It So That the Child May Become a Wise and Good Man* (1842). Though an outsider, Mayhew shared many of the assumptions and ideas of the middle-class reformers with whom he shared the surveying instinct, including the importance of self-control and of the family and wider environmentalism, and a belief in the dignity of work (Englander & O'Day, 1995).

4. Mayhew combined an anthropologist's concern for the dignity of the individual with a modern, "objective" journalistic reportorial technique, seeing himself as an intermediary between the classes, albeit one tied to the "old" modes of narration rather than the "new" mode of data analysis (Maxwell, 1978, 89).

5. *Liverpool Mercury*, May 9, 1820, 1.

6. *The Black Dwarf 6 (2)*, January 10, 1821.

7. *Poor Man's Guardian* 1832 (89), Saturday, February 16, 1.

8. *The Athenæum: A Journal of Literature, Science, the Fine Arts*, Jan. 13, 1844, 30.

9. The *Illustrated Police News*, June 1, 1867.

10. Dupin's *Forces productives et commerciales de la France* (1827); Guerry's *Essai sur la Statistique Morale de la France* (1833); Scrope's *Principles of Political Economy* (1833); Quetelet's *L'homme et le développement de ses facultés; ou Essai de physique sociale* (1835); Fletcher's *Summary of the Moral Statistics of England and Wales* (1849?); Snow's *On the Mode of Transmission of Cholera* (1849); Nightingale's *Notes on Matters Affecting the Health and Hospital Administration of the British Army* (1858); and *A Contribution to the Sanitary History of the British Army* (1859); Martineau's *England and Her Soldiers* (1859); Mayhew's *London Labour and the London Poor* (Volume 4, 1862); and Booth's *Life and Labour of the People in London* (1892–1897) (various volumes).

11. An entry on "Cheap Maps" in an 1846 edition of Knight's *Penny Magazine* credits the publication of the Society's maps with their perceived increasing use in schools, and among the common reader more generally (221–223). Given John Snow used commercial maps to construct his statistical diagrams (Koch, 2005, 130), perhaps this claim is not quite as self-serving as it may at first seem.

12. The *Cyclopedia* became a cause célèbre in the campaign to repeal the taxes on knowledge, in which Knight took a conspicuous part (Altick, 1957, 282).

13. *Proceedings of the Statistical Society of London*, 1(8), 1836–37, 190.

14. According to Goldsworthy, an emphasis on the plain served to delay the rise of the picture in British newspapers (2006, 391).

Chapter 4

1. *St James's Gazette*, September 23, 1887.

2. *Pall Mall Gazette*, September 23, 1884.

3. *The Graphic*, December 29, 1883; *The Globe*, April 19, 1887.

4. As may be found, for example, in the contribution of the *Daily Telegraph* artists' impression of "railway murderer" Percy Lefroy Mapleton, toward his timely arrest, in 1881.

5. Some examples include: A synoptic view of the ships lost at sea for the year 1904–1905 (*Illustrated London News*, November 24, 1906); a choropleth map used to show the extent to which regions were increasing or decreasing in numbers, according to the 1911 census (with London inset) (*Illustrated London News*, June 3, 1911); a map showing the numbers of deaths by earthquake (*Illustrated London News*, January 8, 1921).

6. *Illustrated London News*, March 5, 1921, 6.

7. *Illustrated London News*, February 18, 1922, 15.

8. *Illustrated London News*, October 18, 1924, 11.

9. *The Sphere*, March 16, 1901, 19.

10. *The Sphere*, February 2, 1907, 22.

11. *The Sphere*, January 27, 1912, 16.

12. *The Sphere*, July 7, 1917, 3.

13. *The Sphere*, September 7, 1918, 8.

14. *The Sphere*, November 24, 1917, 10.

15. *The Sphere*, June 9, 1923, 42.

16. *Daily Mail*, December 6, 1900, 7.

17. *Daily Mail*, May 1, 1901, 7.

18. *Daily Mail*, December 6, 1900, 7.

19. *Daily Mail*, June 11, 1926, 6; January 25, 1934, 9; July 13, 1935, 10.

20. *Daily Mail*, June 27, 1905, 9.

21. *Daily Mail*, June 7, 1930, 7.

22. *Daily Mail*, March 11, 1937, 2.

23. *Daily Mirror*, August 3, 1914, 5.

24. *Daily Mirror*, April 1, 1914, 6.

25. *Daily Mirror*, April 21, 1921, 4.

26. *Daily Mirror*, October 18, 1921, 8.

27. *Daily Mirror*, November 4, 1921, 11.

28. *Daily Mirror*, July 6, 1926, 19.

29. *Daily Mirror*, January 21, 1937, 8; February 9, 1937, 8; March 11, 1938, 10.

30. Dale Carnegie, in *Public Speaking: A Practical Course for Business Men* (1926), wrote of the superior qualities of visual symbolism over auditory: "Visual impressions…come with a terrific impact. They embed themselves. They stick. They tend to drive out all opposing suggestion as Bonaparte drove away the Austrians" (283). Earlier, in *Influencing Men in Business* (2005 [1911]), Walter Dill Scott had argued: "Pictures, especially if coloured, were like the actual visual perceptions of the object. Hence pictures were more dynamic than verbal descriptions. A diagram or a chart also partakes of the nature of direct perception and frequently secures action in a most astonishing way" (158).

31. *Daily Mirror*, November 1, 1934, 10; May 30, 1935, 12; September 13, 1935, 12.

32. "It is feather-brained. It throws out assertions at a venture because it wishes them true; does not correct either them or itself, if they were false; and to get at the state of things as they truly were seems to feel no concern whatever" (Arnold, 1887, 638–639).

33. See *The Times*, January 25, 1894, 11; January 21, 1895, 13.

34. *Financial Times*, July 3, 1903, 5.

35. *Financial Times*, June 30, 1924, 3.

36. *Financial Times*, September 12, 1937, 18.

37. *Financial Times*, May 2, 1958, 1.

38. *Financial Times*, August 2, 1967, 1.

39. The *Dundee Advertiser*, January 3, 1889, 2.

40. The *Dundee Advertiser*, January 5, 1895, 3; January 3, 1896, 2.

41. Other examples appear in the *Dundee Courier & Argus*, October 30, 1900, 7; May 21, 1900, 7; December 7, 1900, 7; and December 28, 1900, 7.

42. The *Dundee Courier & Argus*, May 24, 1900, 7.

43. The *Dundee Courier & Argus*, November 21, 1903, 7.

44. The *Dundee Courier & Argus*, October 20, 1905, 7.

45. The *Dundee Courier & Advertiser*, December 27, 1926, 3.

46. These include: Daniel Fish's *The Complete Arithmetic: Oral and Written* (1874), and George A. Walton's *Written Arithmetic* (1876).

47. This textbook is only concerned with linear graphical forms and there is no discussion of best practice or the dangers of misleading use.

48. Such as: R. S. Tarr & F. M. McMurry, *Tarr and McMurry Geographies* (1901); and R. E. Dodge, *Dodge's Advanced Geography* (1904).

49. Such as: J. G. Bartholomew, *The Survey Gazetteer of the British Isles* (1914) and *The Citizen's Atlas of the World* (1912).

50. Such as: C. V. Durell & A. W. Siddons, *Graph Book* (1929). This text makes direct reference to Circular 884 and covers a broader range of issues on graph design including column graphs, locus graphs, a section on axes and scales, as well as line graphs.

51. In the United States, pictorial statistics acquired a degree of traction in the publications of Progressive Era government agencies; they were used essentially to democratize knowledge and a number of them can be found, republished, in Brinton's work (1939). Some of Dewey's intellectual heirs and followers had applied Isotype principles in their social-scientific publications too, including Paul Kellogg, Lewis Hine, Rexford Tugwell, and Roy Stryker. These efforts were preceded by sociologist W. E. B. DuBois, who developed a range of infographic forms in his pioneering anti-racist writings, and exhibitions. But by the 1930s, the connection between pictograms and the social sciences began unraveling, due in part to changes in the professional boundary work of American sociology (Anderson, 2018), and in part to the popularization of the Vienna Method that in turn generated fears about the potential for manipulation. Isotype was seen to be used more broadly in society, as a means of propaganda, rather than as a means of democratizing information (Loic & Giraud, 2013).

52. The most influential educational texts in Britain from the turn of the century to the 1920s were Sir John Adams's *The Evolution of Educational Theory* (1912) and *The New Teaching* (1918). From the 1920s to the 1950s, the key text was Sir Percy Nunn's *Education: Its Data and First Principles* (Darling & Nisbet, 2000). In this work, Nunn deals with graph drawing ("frequency diagrams") by using a similar metaphorical example to Playfair's: "Imagine all the pennies collected from the street telephones of a city during a certain period to be arranged in piles, each containing only the pennies of a particular date" (quoted in Darling & Nisbet, 2000). Nunn's work in particular represents, in some senses, a mode of thinking that is oppositional to Dewey; for example, he eschewed the social context of education (Darling & Nisbet, 2000).

53. Within this report (*Plowden Report*, 1967), it is suggested that primary school children pass through three phases of formal education in geography; the third stage involves "the analysis and comparison of phenomena.... A sequence of events in human activity is recorded; temperatures were measured, clouds were classified and the directions of their movements described by points of the compass, traffic is counted and classified. Tables, graphs and written descriptions were commonly used as well as models and pictures ..." (231–232).

54. For example, *The School Certificate Examination in Algebra* set by the Welsh Joint Education Committee in 1950 contains a barometric line graph.

Chapter 5

1. *The Daily Worker* (1930–1966) published Isotype-style charts in 1935, in a cut-out-and-fold pamphlet concerning rising childhood malnutrition among the poor, unemployment, and wage cuts under the national government (*Daily Worker*, June 8, 1935, 1). Elsewhere, advertisements using Isotype-like pictograms appeared occasionally in the serious press, used to promote "the Izal system of industrial hygiene" as an antidote to sickness absenteeism (*The Times*, January 26, 1943, 2). Isotype-like charts were produced in the *Illustrated London News*, in an effort to enliven the conventional statistical graphs produced in the government report *Statistics Relating to the War Effort of the United Kingdom 1944* (*Illustrated London News*, December 9, 1944). This represents an early example of newspaper illustrators reworking official statistical diagrams with a view to their own news values and audience expectations.

2. Walker's career included working for the BBC's European Service (1940–1944) and chairing the British Film Institute (1946–1947) and would eventually involve high political office, first as Secretary of State for Foreign Affairs (1964–1965), then as Secretary of State for Education and Science (1967–1968).

3. *The Independent*, January 11, 2013, 1.

4. Infographics are conspicuously absent from the *Daily Mirror*'s coverage during the 1960s. So for example, in an election year, 1964, between the dissolution of

Parliament (September 15) and the day of the announcement of the general election result (October 16) no infographics were published. On the rare occasion that they do appear, they accompany features, such as concern for rising unemployment (*Daily Mirror*, February 22, 1963, 9), the numbers of school leavers, in the context of a skills shortage (*Daily Mirror*, September 3, 1970, 7), and the effect of rising inflation on purchasing power (*Daily Mirror*, September 8, 1976, 5). They also appear in lighter features, such as one concerning an increase in wine consumption (*Daily Mirror*, January 3, 1962, 4), and even a parody of opinion polling, based on the color of toilet paper (*Daily Mirror*, March 30, 1966, 15). Sports statistics were occasionally covered, particularly football (*Daily Mirror*, November 5, 1971, 30; November 15, 1971, 26), suggesting perhaps a gendered approach to the form. "Charts" in the *Daily Mirror* of this period largely refer to data in tabular form, accompanying stories concerning numbers of nuclear warheads (*Daily Mirror*, May 18, 1973, 16–17); MPs' expenses (*Daily Mirror*, February 14, 1969, 13) and a range of statistics relating to the Vietnam War (*Daily Mirror*, November 6, 1968, 17).

5. *The Observer*, March 30, 1958, 7.

6. *The Observer*, August 31, 1958, 4.

7. For example, a range of graphs relating to tourism appear at the foot of a column containing "news in brief" about the subject midway down that contains no reference to the chart (*The Observer*, July 13, 1958, 7).

8. These employ, for example thick white trend lines on a black background (*The Observer*, November 13, 1960, 2; *August* 5, 1962, 24); or heavy black bordering (*The Observer*, June 24, 1962, 32).

9. White trend lines on a black background are used more frequently (*The Observer*, April 2, 1961, 4; May 21, 1961, 3; February 23, 1964, 9; July 4, 1965, 6).

10. *The Observer*, November 6, 1966, 6.

11. Before this time, art education had conformed to a classical, technical training; after, the focus shifted to the individual, to creativity, and to a broader, more theoretical, liberal education (Candlin, 2001).

12. Interview with Fiona Robertson, May 22, 2018.

13. There is evidence of *Daily Express*-influenced "fun" infographics in the city/business section, accompanying the columns of the paper's City Correspondent, Richard Kellett (*Sunday Times*, April 6, 1958; 2; August 9, 1959, 3); albeit these alternate with more "serious," conventional chart styles (*Sunday Times*, April 5, 1959, 3; August 23, 1964, 9) and synoptic displays (*Sunday Times*, January 21, 1962, 9). Infographics also appear, occasionally, in the sports pages (*Sunday Times*, March 5, 1961, 21). Between 1964 and 1965, some consistency in the appearance of financial charts begins to emerge such as those concerning industrial outputs (*Sunday Times*, November 22,

1964, 28); short-term debt (*Sunday Times*, October 4, 1964, 28); an "investment gap" (*Sunday Times*, May 16, 1965, 30); and the tax burden (*Sunday Times*, October 16, 1966, 22). Polling charts begin to appear during this period too, although sporadically. The most visually impactful graphs of this era appear in display advertising such as for United Steel (*Sunday Times*, January 8, 1961, 9). In 1963, Michael Rand was recruited by the *Sunday Times* (Greenslade, 2004); he was at the *Sunday Times Magazine* when Evans took editorial control.

14. *Sunday Times*, May 9, 1971, 9.

15. *Sunday Times*, February 18, 1968, 2.

16. *Sunday Times*, February 23, 1969, 10.

17. *Sunday Times*, November 5, 1967, 34.

18. *Sunday Times*, September 21, 1969, 13.

19. *Sunday Times*, March 1, 1970, 10.

20. *Sunday Times*, January 25, 1970, 2; June 27, 1971, 2.

21. *Sunday Times*, May 14, 1967, 4.

22. *Sunday Times*, September 5, 1976, 13.

23. Eric Hammond, *The Reunion*, BBC Radio 4, London, August 20, 2017.

24. Interview with John Grimwade, May 30, 2018.

25. Ibid.

26. Ibid.

27. Ibid.

28. Interview with Fiona Robertson, May 22, 2018.

29. Ibid.

30. Interview with John Grimwade, May 30, 2018.

Chapter 6

1. Post-interview communication with John Grimwade, May 31, 2018.

2. Some style guides offer very prescriptive guidance on appropriate use of certain chart types, suggesting that journalists across the organization may be expected to develop them (Klein, 2017).

3. One of the most intractable of these debates concerns the use of circles and circular data presentations and proportional circle graphics (Christiansen, 2011), a debate

that has some pedigree; Brinton (1914) observed that "circle charts" (what we now call pie charts) were more widely found during the first wave of popular infographics, but were nonetheless undesirable. He preferred instead the flexibility offered by horizontal bar graphs. At the heart of this debate lies the central tension in this communicative form: the balance between maintaining the fundamental integrity of visual display, and the need to engage the audience in the data, by using appealing shapes.

4. Hampton (2008) shows that the importance of "objectivity," often assumed to be a shared Anglo-American tradition, and central to the authority and legitimacy of UK journalism (certainly among its broadcasters and news wholesalers) was of less concern to British newspaper journalists than ideals such as independence, fair play, and state nonintervention.

5. Since 2014 the UK's national curriculum has specified that Year 3 primary school pupils (typically those aged seven to eight), studying at Key Stage 2 "should be taught to interpret and present data using bar charts, pictograms and tables...[and should be taught how to use]...information presented in scaled bar charts and pictograms and tables" (Department for Education, 2014).

References

Abrams, P. (1968). *The Origins of British Sociology, 1834–1914: An Essay with Selected Papers*. Chicago: University of Chicago Press.

ACRL (Association of College & Research Libraries). (2011). ACRL Visual Literacy Competency Standards for Higher Education. http://www.ala.org/acrl/standards /visualliteracy [accessed May 7, 2019].

Albers, P. (2013). Visual discourse analysis. In *New Methods of Literacy Research*, ed. Penny Albers, Teri Holbrook, & Amy Seely Flint, 101–114. Abingdon-on-Thames: Routledge.

Altick, R. D. (1957). *The English Common Reader: A Social History of the Mass Reading Public, 1800–1900*. London: Chicago University Press.

American Society of Mechanical Engineers. (1938). *Time Series Charts: A Manual of Design and Construction. Prepared by the Committee on Standards for Graphic Presentation. Approved by American Standards Association*, 1–68. November. ASA Z15.2. New York.

Anderson, C. W. (2018). *Apostles of Certainty: Data Journalism and the Politics of Doubt*. Oxford: Oxford University Press.

Anderson, R.G.W. (1987). Priestley displayed. In *Medicine and Dissent: Joseph Priestley (1733–1804), Papers Celebrating the 250th Anniversary of the Birth of Joseph Priestley Together with a Catalogue of an Exhibition Held at the Royal Society and the Wellcome Institute for the History of Medicine*, ed. R. G. W. Anderson and C. Lawrence, 91–96. London: Wellcome Trust and the Science Museum.

Anonymous. (1823). Mr. William Playfair. *The Gentleman's Magazine: And Historical Chronicle*, Jan. 1736–Dec. 1833; June 564–566.

Anonymous. (1897). Newspaper illustration. *Penrose Annual*, 3, 17–33.

Anonymous. (1903). The monetary position in New York. *Financial Times*, July 3, 5.

Arienzo, A. (2016). Time out of joint: Gilles Deleuze and Felix Guattari on time and capitalism. In *The Concept of Time in Early Twentieth-Century Philosophy*, ed. Flavia Santoianni, 95–102. Heidelberg: Springer.

Armytage, W. H. G. (1965). *Four Hundred Years of English Education*. London: Cambridge University Press.

Arnold, M. (1887). Up to Easter. *Nineteenth Century* XXI (May), 638–639.

Aspinall, A. (1945). The social status of journalists at the beginning of the nineteenth century. *Review of English Studies*, 21(83), 216–232.

Asquith, I. (1978). The structure, ownership and control of the press, 1780–1855. In *Newspaper History from the Seventeenth Century to the Present Day*, ed. George Boyce, James Curran, & Pauline Wingate, 98–116. London: Constable & Company Limited.

Bailey, P. (1977). "Mingled mass of perfectly legitimate pleasures": The Victorian middle class and the problem of leisure. *Victorian Studies*, 21(1), 7–28.

Baly, M. E., & Matthew, H. C. G. (2004). Nightingale, Florence (1820–1910). In *Oxford Dictionary of National Biography*, 904–912. Oxford: Oxford University Press.

Baker, W. M., & Bourne, A. A. (1903). *Elementary Graphs*. London.

Baker, W. M., & Bourne, A. A. (1902). *Elementary Geometry, by W. M. Baker and A. A. Bourne*. London: G. Bell & Sons.

Barker, H. (2000). *Newspapers, Politics and English Society, 1695–1855*. New York: Longman.

Barlow, K. (2008 [1997]). *The Labour Movement in Britain from Thatcher to Blair*. Berlin: Peter Lang.

Barnhurst, K. G., & Nerone, J. (2002). *The Form of News: A History*. New York: Guilford Press.

Barthes, R. (1980). The plates of the encyclopedia. In *New Critical Essays*. Trans. R. Howard, 23–40. New York: Hill and Wang.

Bartholomew, J. (1912). *The Citizen's Atlas of the World: Containing 156 Pages of Maps and Plans, with an Index, a Gazetteer, and Geographical Statistics*. Edinburgh: John Bartholomew & Co.

Bartholomew, J. (1914). *The Survey Gazetteer of the British Isles, Topographical, Statistical and commercial, comp. from the 1911 census and the Latest Official Returns... with Appendices and Atlas*. Edinburgh: John Bartholomew & Co.

Baur, D. (2017). The death of interactive infographics? *Medium*. https://medium.com/@dominikus/the-end-of-interactive-visualizations-52c585dcafcb [accessed May 7, 2019].

Baynes, K. (1971). *Scoop, Scandal, and Strife: A Study of Photography in Newspapers*. New York: Hastings House.

Bell, D. (1999 [1973]). *The Coming of Post-Industrial Society: A Venture in Social Forecasting*. New York: Basic Books.

Bell, D. (2011). Empire and imperialism. In *The Cambridge History of Nineteenth-Century Political Thought*, ed. G. Stedman Jones and G. Claeys, 864–892. Cambridge, UK: Cambridge University Press.

Beniger, J. R., & Robyn, D. L. (1978). Quantitative graphics in statistics: A brief history. *The American Statistician*, 32(1), 1–11.

Benjamin, W., & Underwood, J. A. (2008 [1935]). *The Work of Art in the Age of Mechanical Reproduction*. Vol. 10. London: Penguin.

Bentham, J. (2017 [1777–1780]). *Correspondence of Jeremy Bentham, Volume 2*. London: University College London Press.

Bentham, J. (1791). *Panopticon: or, The inspection-house. Containing the idea of a new principle of construction applicable to any sort of establishment, in which persons of any description are to be kept under inspection, etc.* London: Thomas Byrne.

Bentham, J. (1843). *The Works of Jeremy Bentham, vol. 8 (Chrestomathia, Essays on Logic and Grammar, Tracts on Poor Laws, Tracts on Spanish Affairs)*. Edinburgh: W. Tait.

Berridge, V. (1978). Popular Sunday papers and mid-Victorian society. In *Newspaper History from the Seventeenth Century to the Present Day*, ed. G. Boyce , J. Curran, & P. Wingate, 247–264. London: Constable & Company Limited.

Bertin, J. (1983 [1965]). *Semiology of Graphics: Diagrams, Networks, Maps*. Trans. W. J. Berg. Madison: University of Wisconsin Press.

Beirne, P. (Ed.). (1994). *The Origins and Growth of Criminology: Essays on Intellectual History, 1760–1945*. Altershot, UK: Dartmouth.

Berkowitz, B. (2018). *Playfair: The True Story of the British Secret Agent Who Changed How We See the World*. Fairfax, VA: George Mason University Press.

Bingham, A. (2004). *Gender, Modernity, and the Popular Press in Inter-War Britain*. Oxford: Oxford University Press.

Bingham, A. (2010). The digitization of newspaper archives: Opportunities and challenges for historians. *Twentieth Century British History*, 21(2), 225–231.

Bingham, A., & Conboy, M. (2015). *Tabloid Century: The Popular Press in Britain, 1896 to the Present*. Oxford: Peter Lang.

Black, J. (1987). *The English Press in the Eighteenth-Century*. Philadelphia: University of Pennsylvania Press.

Blasio, A. J., & Bisantz, A. M. (2002). A comparison of the effects of data–ink ratio on performance with dynamic displays in a monitoring task. *International Journal of Industrial Ergonomics*, 30(2), 89–101.

Blastland, M., & Dilnot, Andrew. (2008). *The Tiger That Isn't: Seeing Through a World of Numbers*. London: Profile Books.

Blom, P. (2008). *The Vertigo Years: Change and Culture in the West, 1900–1914*. New York: Basic Books.

Board of Education. (1914). *Circular 884 (The Place and Use of Graphs in Mathematical Teaching)*. London: HMSO.

Board of Education. (1925). *Circular 884 (The Place and Use of Graphs in Mathematical Teaching—Revised)*. London: HMSO.

Board of Education. (1931). *Report of the Consultative Committee on the Primary School*. London: HMSO.

Bogost, I, Ferrari, S., & Schweizer, B. (2010). *Newsgames: Journalism at Play*. Cambridge, MA: MIT Press.

Booth, C. (1902). *Life and Labour of the People in London. Final volume, Notes on Social Influence and Conclusion*. London: Macmillan & Co.

Bourdieu, P. (1993). *The Field of Cultural Production: Essays on Art and Literature*. Cambridge, UK: Polity.

Bourdieu, P. (1998). *On Television and Journalism*. Trans. Priscilla Parkhurst Ferguson. London: Pluto.

Braithwaite, H. (2003). *Romanticism, Publishing and Dissent: Joseph Johnson and the Cause of Liberty*. Basingstoke: Palgrave.

Brake, L., & Demoor, M. (Eds.). (2009). *Dictionary of Nineteenth-Century Journalism in Great Britain and Ireland*. Cambridge, MA: Academia Press.

Brasseur, L. (2005). Florence Nightingale's visual rhetoric in the Rose Diagrams. *Technical Communication Quarterly*, 14(2), 161–182.

Breakell, J. (2002). The teaching of mathematics in schools in England and Wales during the early years of the Schools Council 1964 to 1975. Doctoral dissertation, Institute of Education, University of London.

Brewer, J. (1997). *The Pleasures of the Imagination: English Culture in the Eighteenth-Century*. London: HarperCollins.

Breuilly, J. (2011). On the principle of nationality. In *The Cambridge History of Nineteenth-Century Political Thought*, ed. G. Stedman Jones and G. Claeys, 77–109. Cambridge, UK: Cambridge University Press.

Brinton, W. (1914). *Graphic Methods for Presenting Facts*. New York: The Engineering Magazine Company.

Brinton, W. (1915). Joint Committee on Standards for Graphic Presentation. *Publications of the American Statistical Association*, 14(112), 790–797.

Brinton, W. (1939). *Graphic Presentation*. New York: Brinton Associates.

Bromley, M. (1997). The end of journalism? Changes in workplace practices in the press and broadcasting in the 1990s. In *A Journalism Reader*, ed. M. Bromley & T. O'Malley, 330–350. London: Psychology Press.

Brown, L. (1985). *Victorian News and Newspapers*. Oxford: Oxford University Press, USA.

BSI (British Standards Institution). (1992). *British Standard 7581:1992 A Guide to the Presentation of Tables & Graphs*. London: BSI.

Burke, C. (2011). The linguistic status of Isotype. In *Image and Imaging in Philosophy, Science and the Arts, Volume 2*, ed. Richard Heinrich, Elisabeth Nemeth, Wolfram Pichler, & David Wagner, 31–57. Frankfurt: Verlag.

Burke, C. (2013a). Introduction. In *Isotype: Design and Contexts 1925–1971*, ed. C. Burke, E. Kindel, & S. Walker, 9–20. London: Hyphen Press.

Burke, C. (2013b). The Gesellschafts- und Wirtschaftsmuseum in Wien (Social and economic museum of Vienna), 1925–34. In *Isotype: Design and Contexts 1925–1971*, ed. C. Burke, E. Kindel, & S. Walker, 21–102. London: Hyphen Press.

Burke, C. (2013c). The atlas Gesellschaft und Wirtschaft. In *Isotype: Design and Contexts 1925–1971*, ed. C. Burke, E. Kindel, & S. Walker, 186–215. London: Hyphen Press.

Burke, C., Kindel, E., & Walker, S. (Eds.). (2013). *Isotype: Design and Contexts 1925–1971*. London: Hyphen Press.

Burns, J. (1986). From "polite learning" to "useful knowledge." *History Today*. https://www.historytoday.com/james-burns/polite-learning-useful-knowledge [accessed May 7, 2019].

Burns, R. (1870). *The Poetical Works of Robert Burns. Re-edited from the best editions. With explanatory glossarial notes, memoir, etc. etc.* London: Frederick Warne & Co.

Butterfield, H. (1931). *The Whig Interpretation of History*. London: W. W. Norton & Company.

Bygrave, S. (2012). I Predict a Riot: Joseph Priestley and languages of Enlightenment in Birmingham in 1791. *Romanticism*, 18(1), 70–88.

Cain, M. T. (1994). The maps of the society for the diffusion of useful knowledge: A publishing history. *Imago Mundi*, 46(1), 151–167. DOI: 10.1080/03085699408592794.

Cairo, A. (2012). *The Functional Art: An Introduction to Information Graphics and Visualization*. San Francisco: New Riders.

Campbell, K. (2003). W. E. Gladstone, W. T. Stead, Matthew Arnold and a new journalism: Cultural politics in the 1880s. *Victorian Periodicals Review*, 36(1), 20–40.

Candlin, F. (2001). A dual inheritance: The politics of educational reform and PhDs in art and design. *International Journal of Art and Design Education*, 20(3), 302–310.

Carey, J. W. (1974). The problem of journalism history. *Journalism History* 1(1), (Spring), 3–5.

Carey, J. W. (1986). Walter Benjamin, Marshall McLuhan, and the emergence of visual society. *Prospects*, 11, 29–38. doi:10.1017/S036123330000524X.

Carey, J. W. (2007). A short history of journalism for journalists: A proposal and essay. *The Harvard International Journal of Press/Politics*, 12(1), 3–16.

Carey, J. W. (2008). *Communication as Culture, Revised Edition: Essays on Media and Society*. Abingdon-on-Thames: Routledge.

Carlyle, T. (1972 [1830]). On history. In *The Varieties of History: From Voltaire to the Present*, ed. F. Stern. New York: Vintage Books.

Carnegie, D. (1926). *Public Speaking: A Practical Course for Business Men*. New York: Association Press.

Cassirer, E. (1944). The concept of group and the theory of perception. *Philosophy and Phenomenological Research*, 5(1), 1–36.

Cat, J. (2004). Otto Neurath, visual education. *Stanford Encyclopedia of Philosophy*. https://plato.stanford.edu/entries/neurath/visual-education.html [accessed May 7, 2019].

Central Advisory Council for Education. (1967). *Children and Their Primary Schools*. London: HMSO.

Chalaby, J. (1998). *The Invention of Journalism*. Basingstoke: Macmillan.

Chandler, D., & Munday, R. (2011). *A Dictionary of Media and Communication*. Oxford: Oxford University Press.

Christiansen, J. (2011). Infographics: The great circle debate. *Scientific American*. https://blogs.scientificamerican.com/observations/infographics-the-great-circle-debate/ [accessed May 7, 2019].

Clery, E. J. (2017). *Eighteen Hundred and Eleven: Poetry, Protest and Economic Crisis*. London: Cambridge University Press.

Cockett, R. (1991). *David Astor and "The Observer."* London: André Deutsch Limited.

Collins, J. (1975). Journalism and design: A marriage can be arranged. *Penrose Annual*, 68, 37–49.

Conboy, M. (2002). *The Press and Popular Culture*. Thousand Oaks, CA: Sage.

Conboy, M. (2004). *Journalism: A Critical History*. Thousand Oaks, CA: Sage.

Cook, E. T. (1913). *The Life of Florence Nightingale*. London: MacMillan and Co.

Cook, R., & Wainer, H. (2016). Joseph Fletcher, thematic maps, slavery, and the worst place to live in the UK and the US. In *Visible Numbers: Essays on the History of Statistical Graphics*, ed. Charles Kostenick, 83–106. Burlington, VT: Routledge.

Cordery, S. (1988). Joshua Hobson and the business of radicalism. *Biography*, 11(2), 108–123.

Costigan-Eaves, P., & Macdonald-Ross, M. (1990). William Playfair (1759–1823). *Statistical Science*, 5(3), (August), 318–326.

Cowen, T. (1998). *In Praise of Commercial Culture*. Cambridge, MA: Harvard University Press.

Crimmins, J. E. (2017). Jeremy Bentham. *Stanford Encyclopaedia of Philosophy*. https://plato.stanford.edu/entries/bentham/ [accessed May 7, 2019].

Crosland, M. (1987). The image of science as a threat: Burke versus Priestley and the "Philosophic Revolution." *The British Journal for the History of Science*, 20(3), 277–307.

Crowley, D., & Heyer, P. (2013). Media. In *The Handbook of Communication History*, ed. P. Simonson, J. Peck, R. T. Craig, & J. Jackson, 58–75. Abingdon-on-Thames: Routledge.

Crozier, M. (1988). *The Making of the Independent*. London: G. Fraser.

Cullen, M. J. (1975). *The Statistical Movement in Early Victorian Britain: The Foundations of Empirical Social Research*. Brighton: Harvester Press.

Cutler, F. (1999). Jeremy Bentham and the public opinion tribunal. *The Public Opinion Quarterly*, 63(3), (Autumn), 321–346.

Dalbello, M. (2002). Franz Josef's time machine: Images of modernity in the era of mechanical photoreproduction. *Book History*, 5(1), 67–103.

Dalbello, M., & Spoerri, A. (2006). Statistical representations from popular texts for the ordinary citizen, 1889–1914. *Library & Information Science Research*, 28(1), 83–109.

Darling, J, & Nisbet, J. (2000). Dewey in Britain. In *Dewey and European Education: General Problems and Case Studies*, ed. Heinz Rhyn & Jurgen Oelkers, 39–52. Dordrecht: Springer.

Daston, L., & Galison, P. (2007). *Objectivity*. Brooklyn, NY: Zone Books.

Davie, G. E. (1981). *The Scottish Enlightenment*. London: Historical Association.

Davies, W. (2018). *Nervous States: How Feelings Took Over the World*. New York: Random House.

De Berg, K. C. (2011). Joseph Priestley across theology, education, and chemistry: An interdisciplinary case study in epistemology with a focus on the science education context. *Science & Education*, 20(7–8), 805–830.

De Bruyn, F. (2004). From Georgic Poetry to statistics and graphs: Eighteenth-century representations and the "state" of British society. *The Yale Journal of Criticism*, 17(1), 107–139.

De Foville, M. (1887). The abuse of statistics. *Journal of the Royal Statistical Society*, 50(4), (December), 703–708.

Department for Education. (2014). National curriculum in England: Mathematics programmes of study. UK Government. https://www.gov.uk/government/publications /national-curriculum-in-england-mathematics-programmes-of-study/national -curriculum-in-england-mathematics-programmes-of-study#year-1-programme-of -study [accessed May 7, 2019].

Desrosières, A. (2002). *The Politics of Large Numbers: A History of Statistical Reasoning*. Cambridge, MA: Harvard University Press.

Dewey, J. (1916). *Democracy and Education: An Introduction to Philosophy of Education*. New York and London: MacMillan.

Dewey, J. (1997 [1938]). *Experience and Education*. New York: Kappa Delta Pi (Touchstone).

Dewey, J., & Skilbeck, M. (1970). *John Dewey*. Ed., with introduction by, M. Skilbeck. London: Collier-Macmillan.

Diakopoulos, N. (2015). Algorithmic-accountability: The investigation of black boxes. *Digital Journalism*, 3(3), 398–415.

Diamond, M., & Stone, M. (1981). Nightingale on Quetelet. *Journal of the Royal Statistical Society*. Series A (General), 144, 66–79.

Dick, M. (2014). Interactive infographics and news values. *Digital Journalism*, 2(4), 490–506.

Dick, M. (2015a). Just fancy that: An analysis of infographic propaganda in The Daily Express, 1956–1959. *Journalism Studies*, 16(2), 152–174.

Dick, M. (2015b). News values in online and visual data journalism. Doctoral dissertation. Brunel University London.

Dick, M. (2017). Developments in infographics. In *The Routledge Companion to Digital Journalism Studies*, ed. Bob Franklin & Stephen Eldridge, 498–508. London: Routledge.

Dickinson, H. T. (Ed.) (2008). Popular politics and radical ideas. In *A Companion to Eighteenth-Century Britain*, ed. H. T. Dickinson, 97–111. Hoboken, NJ: John Wiley & Sons.

Dikovitskaya, M. (2012). Major theoretical frameworks in visual culture. In *The Handbook of Visual Culture*, ed. Ian Heywood & Barry Sandywell. New York: Berg. doi: 10.1207/s15427625tcq1402_3.

Dodge, R. E. (1904). *Dodge's Advanced Geography*. Chicago: Rand, McNally & Co.

Donnachie, I. (2014). People, places and spaces: Education in Robert Owen's New Society. In *Informal Education, Childhood and Youth*, ed. Sarah Mills & Peter Kraftl, 81–96. New York: Springer.

Donnachie, I., & Hewitt, G. (1993). *Historic New Lanark: The Dale and Owen Industrial Community since 1785*. Edinburgh: Edinburgh University Press.

Dorling, D. (2012). *The Visualisation of Spatial Social Structure*. Hoboken, NJ: John Wiley & Sons.

Dunn, S., & Gennard, J. (1984). *The Closed Shop in British Industry*. London: Macmillan.

Dunyach, J. (2014). William Playfair (1759–1823) Scottish Enlightenment from below? In *Jacobitism, Enlightenment and Empire, 1680–1820*, ed. Allan I. Macinnes & J. Douglas, 159–172. Hamilton. London: Pickering & Chatto.

Dunyach, J., & Thomson, A. (Eds.). (2015). *The Enlightenment in Scotland: National and International Perspectives*. Oxford: Voltaire Foundation, University of Oxford.

Durell, C. V., & Siddons, A. W. (1929). *Graph Book, an Exercise Book and Text Book*. London: G. Bell & Sons, Ltd.

Eagleton, T. (2016). *Materialism*. New Haven, CT: Yale University Press.

Eco, U. (1976). *A Theory of Semiotics (Advances in Semiotics)*. London: Indiana University Press.

Edgeworth, M., & Edgeworth, R. L. (1798). *Practical Education*. London: J. Johnson, St. Paul's Church Yard.

Engel, M. (1996). *Tickle the Public: One Hundred Years of the Popular Press*. London: Gollancz.

Englander, D., & O'Day, R. (Eds). (1995). *Retrieved Riches: Social Investigation in Britain, 1840–1914*. Aldershot: Scolar Press.

Evans, H. & Taylor, E. (1978). *Editing and Design: A Five-Volume Manual of English, Typography and Layout*. London: Heinemann [for] the National Council for the Training of Journalists.

Evans, H., & Taylor, E. (1997 [1978]). *Pictures on a Page: Photojournalism and Picture Editing*. London: Wadsworth Publishing Company.

Evans, R. J. (1996). *Rituals of Retribution: Capital Punishment in Germany, 1600–1987*. Oxford: Oxford University Press.

Evans, R. J. (1997). *In Defence of History*. London: Granta Books.

Eyler, J. M. (1979). *Victorian Social Medicine: The Ideas and Methods of William Farr*. Baltimore: Johns Hopkins University Press.

Ezrahi, V. (1999). Dewey's critique of democratic visual culture and its political implications. In *Sites of Vision: The Discursive Construction of Sight in the History of Philosophy*, ed. David Michael Levin, 315–336. Cambridge, MA: MIT Press.

Ezrahi, Yaron. (1992). Technology and the civil epistemology of democracy. *Inquiry*, 35(3–4), 363–376, doi: 10.1080/00201749208602299.

Farr, W. (1843). *Annual Report of the Registrar-General of Births, Deaths, and Marriages in England and Wales*. Fifth report. London: HMSO.

Fienberg, S. E. (1979). Graphical methods in statistics. *The American Statistician*, 33(4), 165–178.

Fish, D. (1874). *The Complete Arithmetic: Oral and Written*. New York: Ivison, Blakeman, Taylor & Co.

Fishman, M. (1980). *Manufacturing the News*. Austin: University of Texas Press.

Fletcher, J. (1849). Moral and educational statistics of England and Wales. *Journal of the Statistical Society of London*, 12, 151–176.

Fletcher, J. (1849?). *Summary of the Moral Statistics of England and Wales*. London: Privately printed.

Flood, R, Rice, A., & Wilson, R. (Eds). (2011). *Mathematics in Victorian Britain*. Oxford: Oxford University Press.

Fox, C. (1977). The development of social reportage in English periodical illustration during the 1840s and early 1850s. *Past & Present*, 74, 90–111.

Franklin, B. (1997). *Newszak and News Media*. London: Arnold.

Friendly, M. (2008a). The golden age of statistical graphics. *Statistical Science*, 23(4), (November), 502–535.

Friendly, M. (2008b). A brief history of data visualization. In *Handbook of Data Visualization*, ed. C. Chen, W. K. Härdle, & M. Friendly, 15–56. Berlin: Springer.

Funkhouser, H. G. (1937). Historical development of the graphical representation of statistical data. *Osiris*, 3, 269–404.

Garcia, M. R., Stark, M. M., & Miller, E. (1991). *Eyes on the News*. St. Petersburg, FL: Poynter Institute.

Garfinkel, H. (1967). *Studies in Ethnomethodology*. Englewood Cliffs, NJ: Prentice-Hall.

Garrett, C. (1973). Joseph Priestley, the millennium, and the French Revolution. *Journal of the History of Ideas*, 34(1), 51–66.

Gatto, M. A. C. (2015). *Making Research Useful: Current Challenges and Good Practices in Data Visualisation*. Oxford Internet Institute. Oxford: OUP.

Gill, C., & Gill, G. (2005). Nightingale in Scutari: Her legacy re-examined. *Clinical Infectious Diseases* 40(12), (June 15), 1799–1805.

Goldsworthy, S. (2006). English nonconformity and the pioneering of the modern newspaper campaign. *Journalism Studies*, 7(3), 387–402.

Graphic News. (n.d.) Graphic News history. *Graphic News.* http://www.graphicnews .com/base/info.php?q=179&s=GN [accessed May 7, 2019].

Greenslade, R. (2004). *Press Gang: How Newspapers Make Profits from Propaganda.* London: Macmillan.

Gripsrud, J. (2000). Tabloidization, popular journalism and democracy. In *Tabloid Tales: Global Debates over Media Standards,* ed. Colin Sparks & John Tulloch, 285–300. London: Rowman & Littlefield Publishers.

Habermas, J. (1989). *The Structural Transformation of the Public Sphere.* Cambridge, UK: Polity.

Hampshire-Monk, I. (2006). British radicalism and the anti-Jacobins. In *The Cambridge History of Eighteenth-Century Political Thought (Vol. 1),* ed. M. Goldie & R. Wokler. London: Cambridge University Press.

Hampton, M. (2004). *Visions of the Press in Britain, 1850–1950.* Champaign: University of Illinois Press.

Hampton, M. (2005). Defining journalists in late-nineteenth-century Britain. *Critical Studies in Media Communication* 22(2), 138–155.

Hampton, M. (2008). The "objectivity" ideal and its limitations in 20th-century British journalism. *Journalism Studies,* 9(4), 477–493.

Hankin, G. T. (1948). Review: Material for visual education. Daily Mail School Aid Series, *History,* 33(117/118), 188.

Harris, B. (2008). Print culture. In *A Companion to Eighteenth-Century Britain,* ed. H. T. Dickinson, 283–293. Hoboken, NJ: John Wiley & Sons.

Harris, R. (1999). *Information Graphics: A Comprehensive Illustrated Reference.* New York: Oxford University Press.

Harrison, J. F. C. (1971). *The Early Victorians, 1832–1851.* London: Weidenfeld and Nicolson.

Hartmann, F. (2006). After Neurath: The quest for an "inclusive form of the icon." *Analogue to Digital Visualisation. Symposium Lecture at Stroom Den Haag,* Oct. 31. http://09 .022.017.new.medienphilosophie.net/wp-content/uploads/2017/04/Hartmann_After _Neurath_The_Quest_for_an_Inclusive_Form_of_the_Icon.pdf [accessed May 7, 2019].

Hartmann, F. (2008). Visualizing social facts: Otto Neurath's ISOTYPE project. In *European Modernism and the Information Society: Informing the Present, Understanding the Past,* ed. R. W. Boyd, 223–240. Aldershot, UK: Ashgate.

Hartog, F. (2015 [2003]). *Regimes of Historicity: Presentism and Experiences of Time.* New York: Columbia University Press.

Hawkey, R. (1975). Graphic design in newspapers. *Penrose Annual,* 68, 116–125.

Hedley, A. (2018). Data visualization and population politics in *Pearson's Magazine*, 1896–1902. *Journal of Victorian Culture*, 23(3), 421–441.

Henry, M. A. (2008). The making of elite culture. In *A Companion to Eighteenth-Century Britain*, ed. H. T. Dickinson, 311–328. Hoboken, NJ: John Wiley & Sons.

Hewitt, M. (2014). *The Dawn of the Cheap Press in Victorian Britain: The End of the "Taxes on Knowledge" 1849–1869*. London: Bloomsbury Academic.

Hickman, L. A. (1990). *John Dewey's Pragmatic Technology*. Bloomington: Indiana University Press.

Hier, S. P. (2002). Probing the surveillant assemblage: On the dialectics of surveillance practices as processes of social control. *Surveillance & Society*, 1(3), 399–411.

Hilton, M., & Shefrin, J. (Eds.). (2009). *Educating the Child in Enlightenment Britain: Beliefs, Cultures, Practices*. Farnham: Ashgate.

Hitchcock, T. (2013). Confronting the digital: Or how academic history writing lost the plot. *Cultural and Social History*, 10(1), 9–23.

Hollis, P. (1970). *The Pauper Press: A Study in Working-Class Radicalism of the 1830s*. Oxford: Oxford University Press.

Holmes, N. (1984). *Designer's Guide to Creating Charts and Diagrams*. New York: Watson-Guptill Publications Inc.

Horkheimer, M., & Adorno, T. W. (2002 [1987]). *Dialectic of Enlightenment*. Ed. G. S. Noerr. Trans. E. Jephcott. Redwood City, CA: Stanford University Press.

Huff, D. (1954). *How to Lie With Statistics*. New York: W. W. Norton & Company.

Hughes, C. (1986). Imperialism, illustration and the Daily Mail, 1896–1904. In *The Press in English Society from the Seventeenth to Nineteenth Centuries*, ed. Michael Harris & Alan Lee, 187–200. Rutherford, NJ: Fairleigh Dickinson University Press.

Hume, D. (1878 [1738–1740]). *Hume's A Treatise of Human Nature*, ed. Lewis Amherst Selby-Bigge. Second edition. Oxford: Clarendon Press.

Hunt, M. R. (1996). *The Middling Sort: Commerce, Gender, and the Family in England, 1680–1780*. Oakland, CA: University of California Press.

Hutt, A. (1973). *The Changing Newspaper: Typographic Trends in Britain and America 1622–1972*. London: Gordon Fraser Gallery.

Huxley, E. (1975). *Florence Nightingale*. London: Weidenfeld and Nicolson.

Inbar, O., Tractinsky, N., & Meyer, J. (2007). Minimalism in information visualization—Attitudes towards maximizing the data-ink ratio. In *Proceedings of the 14th European Conference on Cognitive Ergonomics*, ed. W. Brinkman, D. Ham, & B. L. William Wong, 185–188. London: ACM Press.

Innis, H. A. (2007 [1950]). *Empire and Communications*. Second edition. London: Rowman & Littlefield.

Irving, H. (2016). Paper salvage in Britain during the Second World War. *Historical Research* 89(244), 373–393.

Israel, J. (2011). *Democratic Enlightenment: Philosophy, Revolution, and Human Rights 1750–1790*. Oxford: Oxford University Press.

Itzkin, E. S. (1978). Bentham's *Chrestomathia*: Utilitarian legacy to English education. *Journal of the History of Ideas*, 39(2), (Apr.–Jun.), 303–316.

Jansen, A. (1996). Isotype and infographics. In *Encyclopedia and Utopia: The Life and Work of Otto Neurath (1882–1945)*, ed. Elisabeth Nemeth & Friedrich Stadler, 143–156. Dordrecht: Kluwer.

Jansen, W. (2009). Neurath, Arntz and ISOTYPE: The legacy in art, design and statistics. *Journal of Design History*, 22(3), 227–242.

Jay, M. (1993). *Downcast Eyes: The Denigration of Vision in Twentieth-Century French Thought*. Oakland: University of California Press.

Jeffery, T., & McClelland, K. (1987). A world fit to live in: The *Daily Mail* and the middle classes 1918–1939. In *Impacts and Influences*, ed. J. Curran, A. Smith, & P. Wingate, 27–52. London: Routledge.

Jowett, G. S., & O'Donnell, V. (2014 [1986]). *Propaganda & Persuasion*. Sixth edition. London: Sage.

Julien, N. (2012). *The Mammoth Book of Lost Symbols: A Dictionary of the Hidden Language of Symbolism*. London: Hachette UK.

Jung, C. G. (Ed.) (1964). *Man and His Symbols*. London: Aldus Books in association with W. H. Allen.

Jung, C. G. (1977). *The Symbolic Life: Miscellaneous Writings*. Abingdon-on-Thames: Routledge.

Katz, E. (1957). The two-step flow of communication: An up-to-date report on an hypothesis. *Public Opinion Quarterly*, 21(1), 61–78.

Kehaulani Goo, Sara. (2015). The art and science of a scatter plot. *Pew Research*. http://www.pewresearch.org/fact-tank/2015/09/16/the-art-and-science-of-the-scatterplot/ [accessed May 7, 2019].

Kimball, C. (2016). Mountains of wealth, rivers of commerce: Michael G. Mulhall's graphics and the imperial gaze. In *Visible Numbers: Essays on the History of Statistical Graphics*, ed. C. Kostenick, 127–152. Burlington, VT: Routledge.

Kittler, F. A. (1999). *Gramophone, Film, Typewriter*. Redwood City, CA: Stanford University Press.

Klein, S. (2017). ProPublica data style guide. *Git Hub*. https://github.com/propublica /guides/blob/master/news-apps.md [accessed May 7, 2019].

Kneale, J. (2001). The place of drink: temperance and the public, 1856–1914. *Social & Cultural Geography*, 2(1), 43–59.

Koch, T. (2005). *Cartographies of Disease: Maps, Mapping, and Medicine*. Redlands, CA: Esri Press.

Koss, S. (1983). *The Rise and Fall of the Political Press in Britain: The Nineteenth Century*. Chapel Hill: University of North Carolina Press.

Kramnick, I. (1986). Eighteenth-century science and radical social theory: The case of Joseph Priestley's scientific liberalism. *Journal of British Studies*, 25(1), 1–30.

Kuhn, T. (1956). *The Structure of Scientific Revolutions*. Chicago: University of Chicago Press.

Lakoff, G. (2002). *Moral Politics: How Conservatives and Liberals Think*. Chicago: University of Chicago Press.

Lakoff, G. J., & Johnson, M. M. (1985 [1980]). *Metaphors We Live By*. Second edition. London: University of Chicago Press.

Lang, J., Didkins, G., & Benn, T. (2011). *Bad News: The Wapping Dispute*. Nottingham: Spokesman Books.

Lawrence, C. (1987). Priestley in Tahiti: The medical interests of a dissenting chemist. In *Medicine and Dissent: Joseph Priestley (1733–1804), Papers Celebrating the 250th Anniversary of the Birth of Joseph Priestley Together with a Catalogue of an Exhibition Held at the Royal Society and the Wellcome Institute for the History of Medicine*, ed. R.G.W. Anderson and C. Lawrence, 1–10. London: Wellcome Trust and the Science Museum.

Leapman, M. (1999). Obituary: Mike Randall. *The Independent*, December 14, 58.

Lee, A. J. (1976). *The Origins of the Popular Press in England, 1855–1914*. Lanham, MD: Rowman & Littlefield Inc.

Leggatt Report (1979). *'Report of Inquiry into certain Trade Union Recruitment Activities.'* Cmnd 7706. London: HMSO.

LeMahieu, D. L. (1988). *A Culture for Democracy: Mass Communication and the Cultivated Mind in Britain Between the Wars*. Oxford: Oxford University Press.

Leonard, R. J. (1999). Seeing is believing: Otto Neurath, graphic art and the social order. *History of Political Economy*, 31(5), 452–478.

Lewis, S. C., & Westlund, O. (2015). Big data and journalism: Epistemology, expertise, economics, and ethics. *Digital Journalism*, 3(3), 447–466.

Lexico. (2019a). Infographic. http://www.oxforddictionaries.com/definition/english /infographic [accessed May 7, 2019].

Lexico. (2019b). Synoptic. http://www.oxforddictionaries.com/definition/english /synoptic [accessed May 7, 2019].

Li, H., & Moacdieh, N. (2014). Is "chart junk" useful? An extended examination of visual embellishment. In *Proceedings of the Human Factors and Ergonomics Society Annual Meeting*, 58(1), 1516–1520. Sage, CA: Los Angeles.

Lima, M. (2011). *Visual Complexity: Mapping Patterns of Information*. New York: Princeton Architectural Press; Reprint edition.

Liversedge, A. J. (1921). Twenty-one years of coal in the United Kingdom, the United States and Germany Shown at a Glance in Eight Graphs. *Financial Times*, August 10, 3.

Loic, C., & Giraud, Y. (2013). Economics for the masses: The visual display of economic knowledge in the United States (1910–45). *History of Political Economy*, 45(4), 567–612.

London, E. (1930). *Printing in the Twentieth Century: A Survey; Reprinted from the Special Number of the Times, October 29, 1929*. London: The Times Publishing Company Ltd.

Long, A. (1990). Illustrations put Reuters in news. The *Sunday Times*, May 13 (un-numbered).

Lowe, R. (2008). Education, 1900–1939. In *A Companion to Early Twentieth-Century Britain*, ed. Chris Wrigley, 425–437. Hoboken, NJ: John Wiley & Sons.

Lowrey, W. (2002). Word people vs. picture people: Normative differences and strategies for control over work among newsroom subgroups. *Mass Communication & Society*, 5(4), 411–432.

Lowrey, W. (2003). Normative conflict in the newsroom: The case of digital photo manipulation. *Journal of Mass Media Ethics*, 18(2), 123–142.

Mainardi, P. (2017). *Another World: Nineteenth-Century Illustrated Print Culture*. New Haven, CT: Yale University Press.

Makkreel, R. A. (2012). The emergence of the human sciences from the moral sciences. In *The Cambridge History of Philosophy in the Nineteenth-Century (1790–1870)*, ed. A. W. Wood & S. S. Hahn, 293–322. London: Cambridge University Press.

Marcuse, H. (1955). *Eros and Civilization. A Philosophical Inquiry into Freud*. London: Routledge & Kegan Paul.

Marey, M. (1876). Lectures on the Graphic Method in the Experimental Sciences, and on Its Special Application to Medicine. *British Medical Journal*, 1, 1–3.

Martin, S. E., & Copeland, D. A. (2003). *The Function of Newspapers in Society: A Global Perspective*. London: Praeger.

Marx, K. (2004 [1867]). *Capital: A Critique of Political Economy*. Trans. Ben Fowkes. London: Penguin Classics.

Matheson, D. (2000). The birth of news discourse: Changes in news language in British newspapers, 1880–1930. *Media, Culture & Society*, 22(5), 557–573.

Mathiesen, T. (1997). The viewer society: Michel Foucault's Panopticon revisited. *Theoretical Criminology*, 1(2), 215–234.

Maxwell, R. (1978). Henry Mayhew and the life of the streets. *Journal of British Studies*, 17(2), 87–105.

Mayer-Schönberger, V., & Cukier, K. (2013). *Big Data: A Revolution That Will Transform How We Live, Work, and Think*. New York: Houghton Mifflin Harcourt.

Mayhew, H. (1862). *London Labour and the London Poor*. Vol. 4. London: Woodfall.

McCandless, D. (n.d.) About. *Information Is Beautiful*. http://www.informationisbeautiful .net/about/ [accessed May 7, 2019].

McCandless, D. (2012). *Information Is Beautiful*. London: Collins.

McCandless, D. (2014). *Knowledge Is Beautiful*. London: Collins.

McChesney, R. (2000). *Rich Media Poor Democracy: Communications Politics in Dubious Times*. New York: The New Press.

McChesney, R. (2007). *Communication Revolution: Critical Junctures and the Future of Media*. New York: The New Press.

McDonald, L. (2014). Florence Nightingale, statistics and the Crimean War. *Journal of the Royal Statistical Society: Series A (Statistics in Society)*, 177(3), 569–586.

McEvoy, J. G., & McGuire, J. E. (1974). God and nature: Priestley's way of rational dissent. *Historical Studies in the Physical Sciences*, 6, 325–404.

McKendrick, N., Brewer, J., & Plumb, J. H. (1982). *The Birth of a Consumer Society: The Commercialization of Eighteenth-Century England*. Bloomington: Indiana University Press.

McLachlan, H. (1923). *The Methodist Unitarian Movement*. Manchester: The Manchester University Press.

McLuhan, M. (1964). *Understanding Media: The Extensions of Man*. London: Routledge & Kegan Paul.

McLuhan, M. (1968). *Through the Vanishing Point: Space in Poetry and Painting*. New York: Harper & Row.

Meredith, G. P. (1946). *Visual Education and the New Teacher: A Study of Children and Machines of Organization and Men*. Exeter: Visual education Centre.

Mill, J. S. (1836). Civilization. *The London and Westminster Review*, 25–26, 1–16.

Milward-Oliver, E. (2010). Edward Raymond Hawkey—a personal note from Edward Milward-Oliver. *Deighton Dossier*. http://deightondossier.blogspot.com/2010/08/ray mond-hawkey-personal-note-from.html [accessed May 7, 2019].

Mirzoeff, N. (1999). *An Introduction to Visual Culture*. London: Psychology Press.

Modley, R. (1938). Pictographs today and tomorrow. *The Public Opinion Quarterly*, 2(4), 659–664.

Monmonier, M. (1986). The rise of map use by elite newspapers in England, Canada, and the United States. *Imago Mundi*, 38(1), 46–60, DOI: 10.1080/03085698608592604.

Monmonier, M. (2018 [1991]). *How to Lie with Maps*. Third edition. Chicago: The University of Chicago Press Ltd.

Mulhall, M. G. (1892 [1886]). *Mulhall's Dictionary of Statistics*. Third edition. London: G. Routledge and Sons.

Murdoch, Iris. (1994). *Metaphysics as a Guide to Morals*. London: Penguin.

Nerone, J., & Barnhurst, K. G. (2003). News form and the media environment: A network of represented relationships. *Media, Culture & Society*, 25(1), 111–124.

Nielsen, R. K. (2017). Digital news as forms of knowledge: A new chapter in the sociology of knowledge. In *Remaking the News: Essays on the Future of Journalism Scholarship in the Digital Age*, ed. Pablo Boczkowski & Chris Anderson, 91–109. Cambridge, MA: MIT Press.

Nightingale, F. (1858). *Notes on Matters Affecting the Health, Efficiency, and Hospital Administration of the British Army: Founded Chiefly on the Experience of the Late War*. London: Harrison and Sons.

O'Brien, P. K. (2008). Finance and Taxation. In *A Companion to Eighteenth-Century Britain*, ed. H. T. Dickinson, 30–39. Hoboken, NJ: John Wiley & Sons.

O'Malley, T. (1997). Labour and the 1947–9 Royal Commission on the press. In *A Journalism Reader*, ed. M. Bromley & T. O'Malley, 126–158. London: Psychology Press.

Otis, L. (ed). (2002). *Literature and Science in the Nineteenth Century: An Anthology*. Oxford: Oxford University Press.

Palsky, G. (1999). The debate on the standardization of statistical maps and diagrams (1857–1901). Elements of the history of graphical semiotics. *Journals Open Edition*. http://journals.openedition.org/cybergeo/148 [accessed May 7, 2019].

Park, R. E. (1940). News as a form of knowledge: A chapter in the sociology of knowledge. *American Journal of Sociology*, 45(5), 669–686.

Parry, G. (2006). Education. In *The Cambridge History of Eighteenth-Century Philosophy (Vol. 1)*, ed. K. Haakonssen, 608–638. Cambridge, UK: Cambridge University Press.

Passmore, J. (1967). Logical Positivism. In *The Encyclopedia of Philosophy*, vol. 5, ed. Paul Edwards, 52–57. New York: Macmillan.

Paulos, J. A. (1996). *A Mathematician Reads the Newspaper: Making Sense of the Numbers in the Headlines*. New York: Doubleday.

Penrose, J. M. (2008). Annual report graphic use: A review of the literature. *Journal of Business Communication*, 45(2), 158–180.

Playfair, W. (1796). *The History of Jacobinism, Its Crimes, Cruelties and Perfidies*. Philadelphia: Printed for William Cobbett.

Playfair, W. (1801a [1786]). *The Commercial and Political Atlas; Representing By Means of Stained Copper-Plate Charts, the Exports, Imports, and General Trade of England,…with Observations…to Which Are Added, Charts of the Revenue and Debts of Ireland*. London: J. Corry.

Playfair, W. (1801b). *Statistical Breviary; Shewing, on a Principle Entirely New, the Resources of Every State and Kingdom in Europe*. London: Wallis.

Playfair, W. (1805a). *An Inquiry into the Permanent Causes of the Decline and Fall of Powerful and Wealthy Nations,…Designed to Shew How the Prosperity of the British Empire May Be Prolonged*. London: Greenland & Norris.

Playfair, W. (1805b). *Statistical Account of the United States of America*. Trans. D. F. Donnant. London: J. Whiting London.

Playfair, W. (1822). *A Letter on Our Agricultural Distresses, Their Causes and Remedies*. London: W. Sams.

Playfair, W. (1824). *Chronology of Public Events and Remarkable Occurrences within the Last Fifty Years*. London: G. and W. B. Whittaker.

Porter, R. (2002). Matrix of modernity? *Transactions of the Royal Historical Society*, 12 (December), 245–259.

Porter, T. M. (1986). *The Rise of Statistical Thinking, 1820–1900*. Princeton, NJ: Princeton University Press.

Power, M. (1999). *The Audit Society: Rituals of Verification*. Oxford: Oxford University Press.

Prabu, D. (1992). Accuracy of visual perception of quantitative graphics: An exploratory study. *Journalism Quarterly*, Summer, 273–292.

Priestley, J. (1765a). *A Chart of Biography*. Warrington: Warrington Academy.

Priestley, J. (1765b). *A Description of a Chart of Biography*. Warrington: Warrington Academy.

Priestley, J. (1769a). *A Description of a New Chart of History*. Warrington: Warrington Academy.

Priestley, J. (1769b). *A New Chart of History*. Warrington: Warrington Academy.

Priestley, J. (1778). *Miscellaneous Observations relating to Education. More especially, as it respects the conduct of the mind*. Bath, UK: R. Cruttwell.

Priestley, J. (1788). *Lectures on History, and General Policy*. Birmingham.

Priestley, J. (2005 [1817]). *History of the Present State of Electricity*. In *Theological and Miscellaneous Works of Joseph Priestley*, ed. J. T. Rutt. London: G. Smallfield.

Princeton University Library. (n.d.) Sociology and economics ("moral statistics"). http://libweb5.princeton.edu/visual_materials/maps/websites/thematic-maps/quantitative/sociology-economics/sociology-economics.html [accessed May 7, 2019].

Purdon, J. (2015). *Modernist Informatics: Literature, Information, and the State*. London: Oxford University Press.

Putnam, R. (2000). *Bowling Alone: The Collapse and Revival of American Community*. New York: Simon and Schuster.

Quetelet, A. (1835). *Sur l'homme et le développement de ses facultés, ou Essai de physique sociale*. Paris.

Reid, A. (2014). *Guardian* forms new editorial teams to enhance digital output. *Journalism.co.uk*. https://www.journalism.co.uk/news/guardian-forms-new-editorial-teams-to-enhance-digital-output/s2/a562755/ [accessed May 7, 2019].

Rendgen, S. (2018). *The Minard System: The Complete Statistical Graphics of Charles-Joseph Minard*. San Francisco: Chronicle Books.

Rendgen, S., Wiedemann, J., Ciuccarelli, P., Wurman, R. S., Rogers, S., & Holmes, N. (2012). *Information Graphics*. Cologne: Taschen.

Riasanovsky, N. (1984). *A History of Russia*. Fourth edition. New York: Oxford University Press.

Richards, T. (1991). *The Commodity Culture of Victorian England: Advertising and Spectacle, 1851–1914*. Redwood City, CA: Stanford University Press.

Rintoul, S. (2015). *Intimate Violence and Victorian Print Culture: Representational Tensions*. London: Palgrave Macmillan.

Robinson, A. H. (1982). *Early Thematic Mapping in the History of Cartography*. London: University of Chicago Press.

Rosenberg, C. E. (1992). *Explaining Epidemics*. London: Cambridge University Press.

Rosenberg, D. (2004). The trouble with timelines. In *Histories of the Future*, ed. Daniel Rosenburg & Susan Harding, 281–295. Durham, NC: Duke University Press.

Rosenberg, D. (2007). Joseph Priestley and the graphic invention of modern time. *Studies in Eighteenth-Century Culture*, 36(1), 55–103.

Rosenberg, D., & Grafton, A. (2010). *Cartographies of Time: A History of the Timeline*. Hudson, NY: Princeton Architectural Press.

Schmid, C. F. (1954). *Handbook of Graphic Presentation*. New York: Ronald Press Co.

Schofield, R. E. (1997). *The Enlightenment of Joseph Priestley: A Study of His Life and Work from 1733 to 1773*. University Park: Pennsylvania State University Press.

Schudson, M. (1978). *Discovering the News: A Social History of American Newspapers*. New York: Basic Books.

Schudson, M. (1989). The sociology of news production. *Media, Culture & Society*, 11(3), 263–282.

Schudson, M. (1997). Why conversation is not the soul of democracy. *Critical Studies in Media Communication*, 14(4), 297–309.

Schultz, M., & Hatch, M. J. (1996). Living with multiple paradigms: The case of paradigm interplay in organizational culture studies. *Academy of Management Review*, 21(2), 529–557.

Scott, S. (1987). Enlightenment and the spirit of the Vienna Circle. *Canadian Journal of Philosophy* 17(4), 695–709.

Scott, W. D. (2005 [1911]). *Influencing Men in Business: The Psychology of Argument and Suggestions*. Boston: Cosimo Inc.

Searle, G. R. (2008). The politics of national efficiency and of war, 1900–1918. In *A Companion to Early Twentieth-Century Britain*, ed. Chris Wrigley, 56–70. Hoboken, NJ: John Wiley & Son.

Seaton, J., & Curran, J. (2003 [1981]). *Power Without Responsibility: The Press, Broadcasting, and New Media in Britain*. Seventh edition. London: Routledge.

Seed, J. (1985). Gentlemen dissenters: The social and political meanings of Rational Dissent in the 1770s and 1780s. *The Historical Journal*, 28(2), 299–325.

Seymour-Ure, C. (1996). *The British Press and Broadcasting Since 1945*. Oxford: Blackwell.

Shefrin, J. (2009a). Adapted and used in infants' schools, nurseries, &c: Booksellers and the infant school market. In *Educating the Child in Enlightenment Britain: Beliefs, Cultures, Practices*, ed. Mary Hilton & Jill Shefrin, 173–190. Farnham: Ashgate.

Shefrin, J. (2009b). *The Dartons: Publishers of Educational Aids, Pastimes & Juvenile Ephemera, 1787–1876*. Altadena, CA: Cotsen Occasional Press.

Sherman, C. (1976). *Diderot and the Art of Dialogue*. Genéve: Librairie Droz.

Shields, M. C. (1937). The early history of graphs in physical literature. *American Journal of Physics*, 5(2), 68–71.

Simonson, P., Peck, J., Craig, R. T., & Jackson, J. (Eds). (2013). *The Handbook of Communication History*. Abingdon-on-Thames: Routledge.

Smith, A. C. H., Immirzi, E., & Blackwell, T. (1975). *Paper Voices: The Popular Press and Social Change, 1935–1965*. Lanham, MD: Rowman and Littlefield.

Snow, J. (1849). *On the Mode of Transmission of Cholera*. Churchill, London.

So, A. (2012). You suck at infographics. *Wired*. http://www.wired.com/2012/07/you-suck-at-infographics/ [accessed May 7, 2019].

Spence, I. (2005). No humble pie: The origins and usage of a statistical chart. *Journal of Educational and Behavioural Statistics*, 30(4), 353–368.

Spence, I. (2006). William Playfair and the psychology of graphs. In *Proceedings of the American Statistical Association, Section on Statistical Graphics*, 2426–2436. Alexandria, VA: American Statistical Association.

Spiegelhalter, D. (2004). Bastardy in the UK. *Significance*, 1(3), 134–135.

Splichal, S. (2002). *Principles of Publicity and Press Freedom*. London: Rowman and Littlefield.

Staley, D. J. (2003). *Computers, Visualization and History: How New Technology Will Transform Our Understanding of the Past*. London: M. E. Sharpe.

Sullivan, P. (1987). *Newspaper Graphics*. Darmstadt: IFRA.

Sutcliffe, A. (2008). Culture in the Sceptr'd Isle. In *A Companion to Early Twentieth-Century Britain*, ed. C. Wrigley, 485–501. Hoboken, NJ: John Wiley & Sons.

Tarr, R. S., & McMurry, F. M. (1901). *Tarr and McMurry Geographies*. New York: Macmillan Co.

Taylor, A. J. P. (1972). *Beaverbrook*. Harmondsworth: Penguin.

Taylor, B. (1982). A note in response to Itzkin's "Bentham's Chrestomathia: Utilitarian legacy to English education." *Journal of the History of Ideas*, 43(2) (Apr.–Jun.), 309–313.

Theibault, J. (2013). Visualizations and historical arguments. In *Writing History in the Digital Age*, ed. Jack Dougherty & Kristen Nawrotzki, 173–185. Ann Arbor: University of Michigan Press.

Thomas, D. O. (1987). Progress, liberty and utility: The political philosophy of Joseph Priestley. In *Medicine and Dissent: Joseph Priestley (1733–1804), Papers Celebrating the 250th Anniversary of the Birth of Joseph Priestley Together with a Catalogue of an Exhibition Held at the Royal Society and the Wellcome Institute for the History of Medicine*, ed. R. G. W. Anderson & C. Lawrence, 73–80. London: Wellcome Trust and the Science Museum.

Thompson, E. P. (1971). Mayhew and the *Morning Chronicle*. In *The Unknown Mayhew: Selections from the Morning Chronicle, 1849–50*, H. Mayhew. London: Merlin Press.

Tilling, L. (1975). Early experimental graphs. *The British Journal for the History of Science*, 8(03), 193–213.

Toffler, A. (1970). *Future Shock*. London: Pan Books.

Townsend, D. (1993). The aesthetics of Joseph Priestley. *The Journal of Aesthetics and Art Criticism*, 51(4), 561–571.

Tufte, E. (1983). *The Visual Display of Quantitative Information*. Cheshire, CT: Graphics Press.

Tufte, E. (1997). *Visual Explanations: Images and Quantities, Evidence and Narrative*. Cheshire, CT: Graphics Press.

Tukey, J. (1990). Data-based graphics: Visual display in the decades to come. *Statistical Science*, 5(3), 327–339.

Tukey, J. W. (1972). Some graphic and semi-graphic displays. In *Statistical Papers in Honor of George W. Snedecor*, ed. Theodore Alfonso Bancroft, 293–316. Iowa: Iowa State University Press.

Tulloch, J. (2000). The eternal recurrence of new journalism. In *Tabloid Tales: Global Debates over Media Standards*, ed. Colin Sparks & John Tulloch, 131–146. London: Rowman and Littlefield.

Turner, F. M. (2014). *European Intellectual History from Rousseau to Nietzsche*. Ed. R. A. Lofthouse. New Haven, CT: Yale University Press.

Turner, G. (1999). Tabloidization, journalism and the possibility of critique. *International Journal of Cultural Studies*, 2(1), 59–76.

Tversky, B., Kugelmass, S., & Winter, A. (1991). Cross-cultural and developmental trends in graphic productions. *Cognitive psychology*, 23(4), 515–557.

Vossoughian, N., & Neurath, O. (2011). *Otto Neurath: The Language of the Global Polis*. Rotterdam: NAi Publishers.

Wainer, H. (1984). How to display data badly. *The American Statistician*, 38(2), 137–147.

Wainer, H. (1990). Graphical visions from William Playfair to John Tukey. *Statistical Science*, 5(3), 340–346.

Wainer, H. (2006). *Graphic Discovery: A Trout in the Milk and Other Visual Adventures*. Princeton, NJ: Princeton University Press.

Wainer, H., & Spence, I. (2005). Introduction. In *Commercial and Political Atlas and Statistical Breviary*, W. Playfair, 1–35. Cambridge, UK: Cambridge University Press.

Wainer, H., & Velleman, P. F. (2001). Statistical graphs: Mapping the pathways of science. *The Annual Review of Psychology*, 52(1), 305–335.

Walton, G. A. (1876). *Written Arithmetic*. Boston: Brewer & Tileston.

Ward, K. (1989). *Mass Communication and the Modern World*. London: Palgrave.

Ward, S. J. A. (2004). *The Invention of Journalism Ethics: The Path to Objectivity and Beyond*. London: McGill-Queen's Press.

Waterhouse, R. (1974). News that's fit to draw. *Design Journal*. https://vads.ac.uk /diad/article.php?title=307&year=1974&article=d.307.32 [accessed May 7, 2019].

Watts, R. (1998). Some radical educational networks of the late eighteenth century and their influence. *History of Education*, 27(1), 1–14.

Welch, C. B. (2011). Social science from the French Revolution to positivism. In *The Cambridge History of Nineteenth-Century Political Thought*, ed. G. Stedman Jones & G. Claeys, 171–199. Cambridge, UK: Cambridge University Press.

Wiener, J. H. (Ed.). (1988). *Papers for the Millions: The New Journalism in Britain, 1850s to 1914*. New York: Greenwood.

Wilde, O. (1891). *The Picture of Dorian Gray*. London: Ward, Lock and Co.

Williams, K. (2009). *Read All About It! A History of the British Newspaper*. London: Routledge.

Williams, R. (1973). *The Country and the City*. London: Chatto and Windus.

Wong, D. (2010). *The Wall Street Journal Guide to Information Graphics: The Dos and Don'ts of Presenting Data, Facts, and Figures*. New York: W. W. Norton & Company.

Woodham-Smith, C. (1950). *Florence Nightingale 1820–1910*. London: Constable.

Yeo, E. (1971). Mayhew as a Social Investigator. In *The Unknown Mayhew: Selections from the Morning Chronicle, 1849–50*, H. Mayhew. London: Merlin Press.

Yeo, R. (2001). *Encyclopaedic Visions: Scientific Dictionaries and Enlightenment Culture*. London: Cambridge University Press.

Index

Adler, M., 144
Adobe Illustrator 88, 160, 170
Adorno, T., 176
Albert, Prince Consort, 66
American Society of Mechanical
    Engineers, 172
Anderson, B., 101
Anglican Church, 32, 57
Anti-classicism, 28
Anti-Jacobinism, 28, 32, 47, 59, 60, 89
Aristotelianism, 20
Arnold, Matthew, 98, 99, 121, 122, 178,
    194
    and New Journalism, 99, 122
Associationism, 28, 44, 85, 168, 173,
    190, 192
Atex, 158, 170
Athenaeum, The, 85
"Attractiveness of orchestrated variety,"
    18, 98, 130, 136, 146, 154. *See also*
    Conboy, Martin

Bacon, Francis, 59
    Baconian method, 61
Barbauld, A., 189n2 (chap. 2)
Barbeu-Dubourg, J., 40
    Carte Chronographique, 40
Bar chart. *See* Infographics
Barlow, E., 157
Barnhurst, Kevin, 27, 178
Barthes, Roland, 180–181

Bartholomew, Guy, 105, 119, 120, 122,
    139
Beaverbrook, Max, 145, 148, 149, 150,
    155
Bell, Andrew, 90
Bell, Daniel, 177
Benjamin, Walter, 103, 180
Bentham, Jeremy, 64, 70, 90, 122, 181,
    185
    Chrestomathia, 90–91
    Panopticon, 90, 181–182 (*see also* Pub-
        lic opinion)
Bergson, Henri, 184
Berkowitz, Bruce, 15, 47, 48, 49, 57,
    172, 183, 191n20
Bertin, Jacques, 18, 20
Booth, Charles, 63, 78, 80–81, 85, 88
    Life and Labour of the People in London,
        78, 80
Boundary work (of visual journalism),
    46, 195n50
Bourdieu, Pierre, 177, 180
    On Television, 177
Bourgeois public sphere, 57, 167,
    179
Bowley, A., 134–135
Brinton, Willard C., 6, 20, 141,
    172–173, 195n51, 199n3
British Standards Institute (BSI), 8
Burke, Edmund, 36
Butterfield, Herbert, 11–12